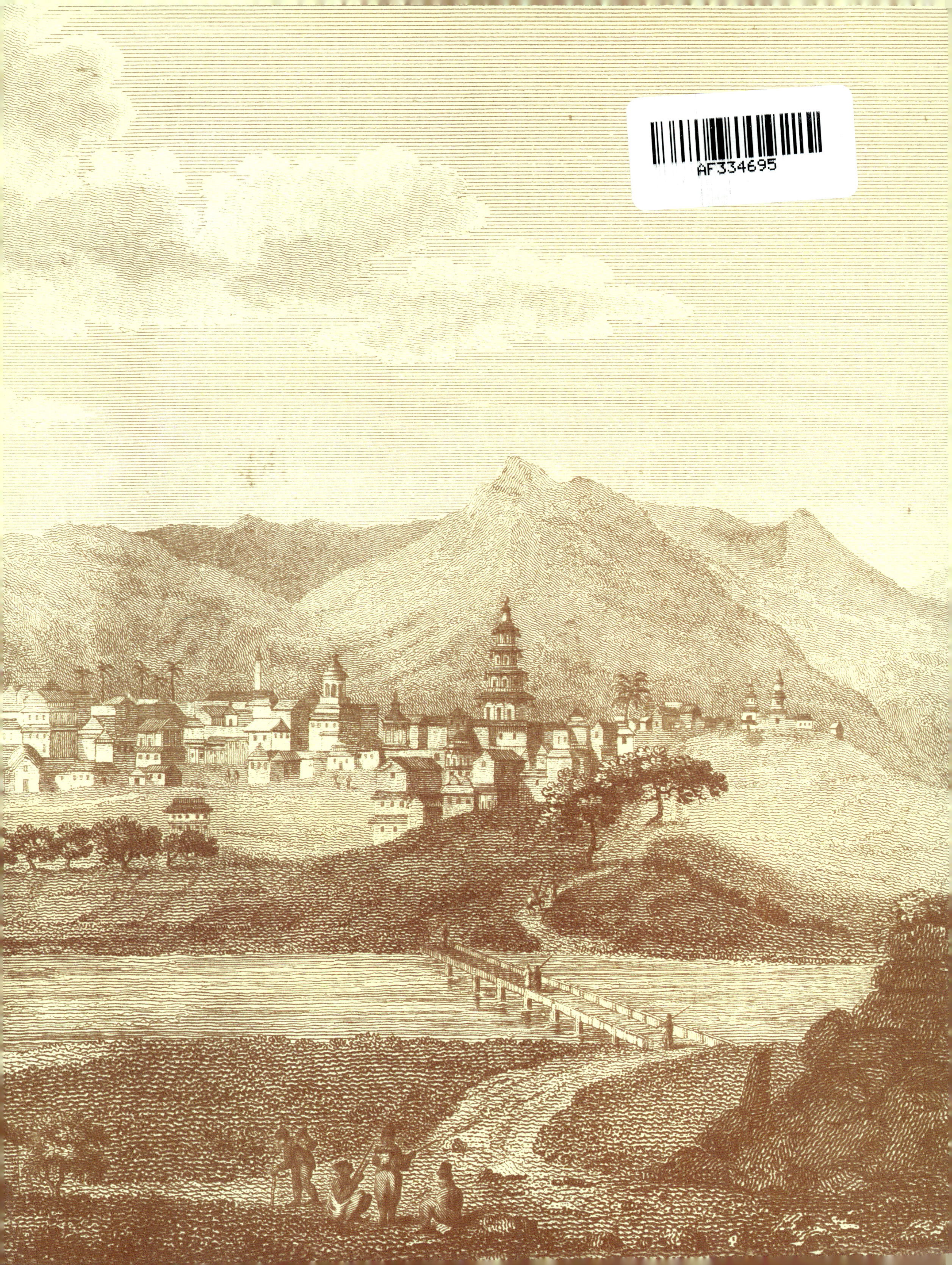

# THE SULIMA PAGODA

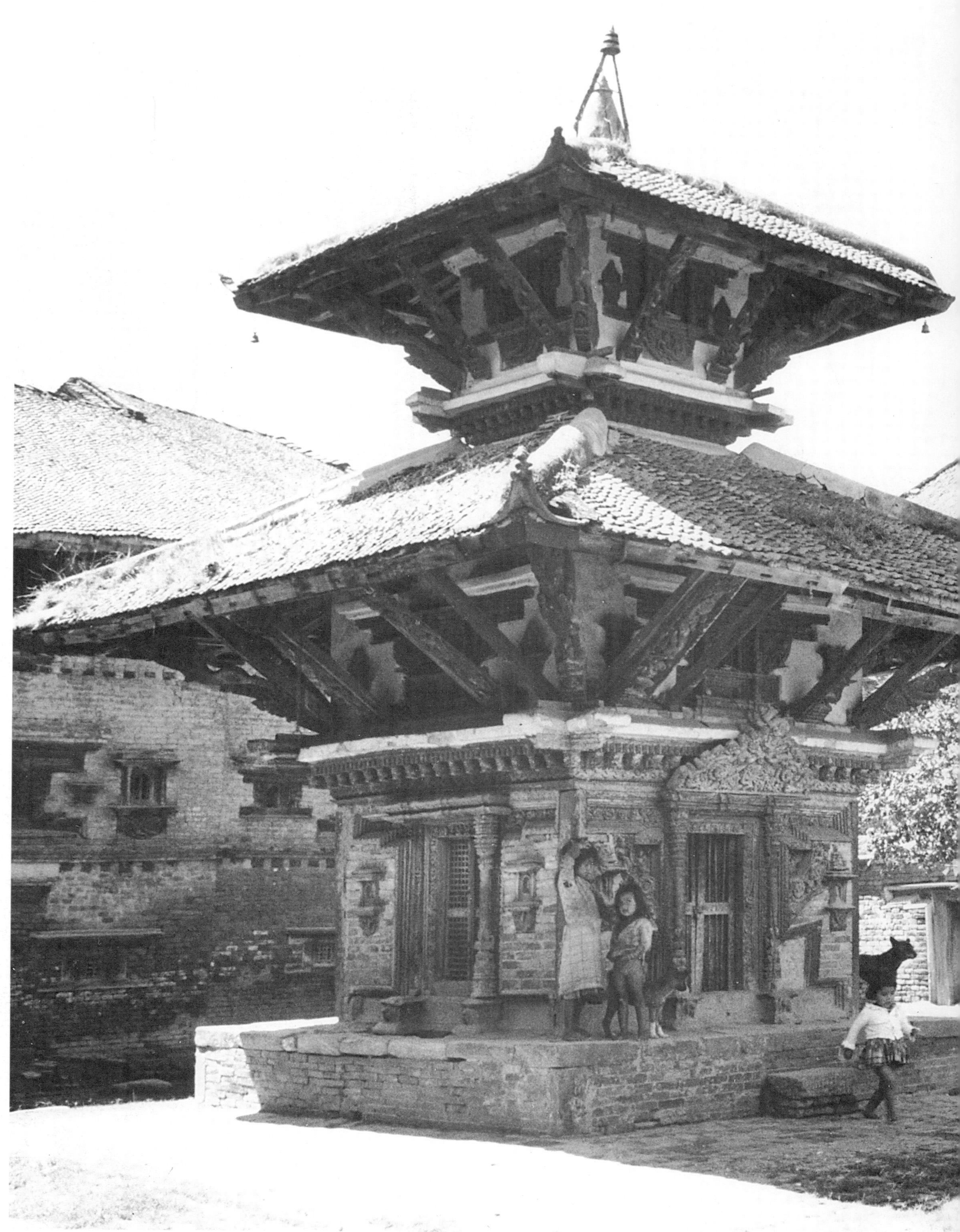

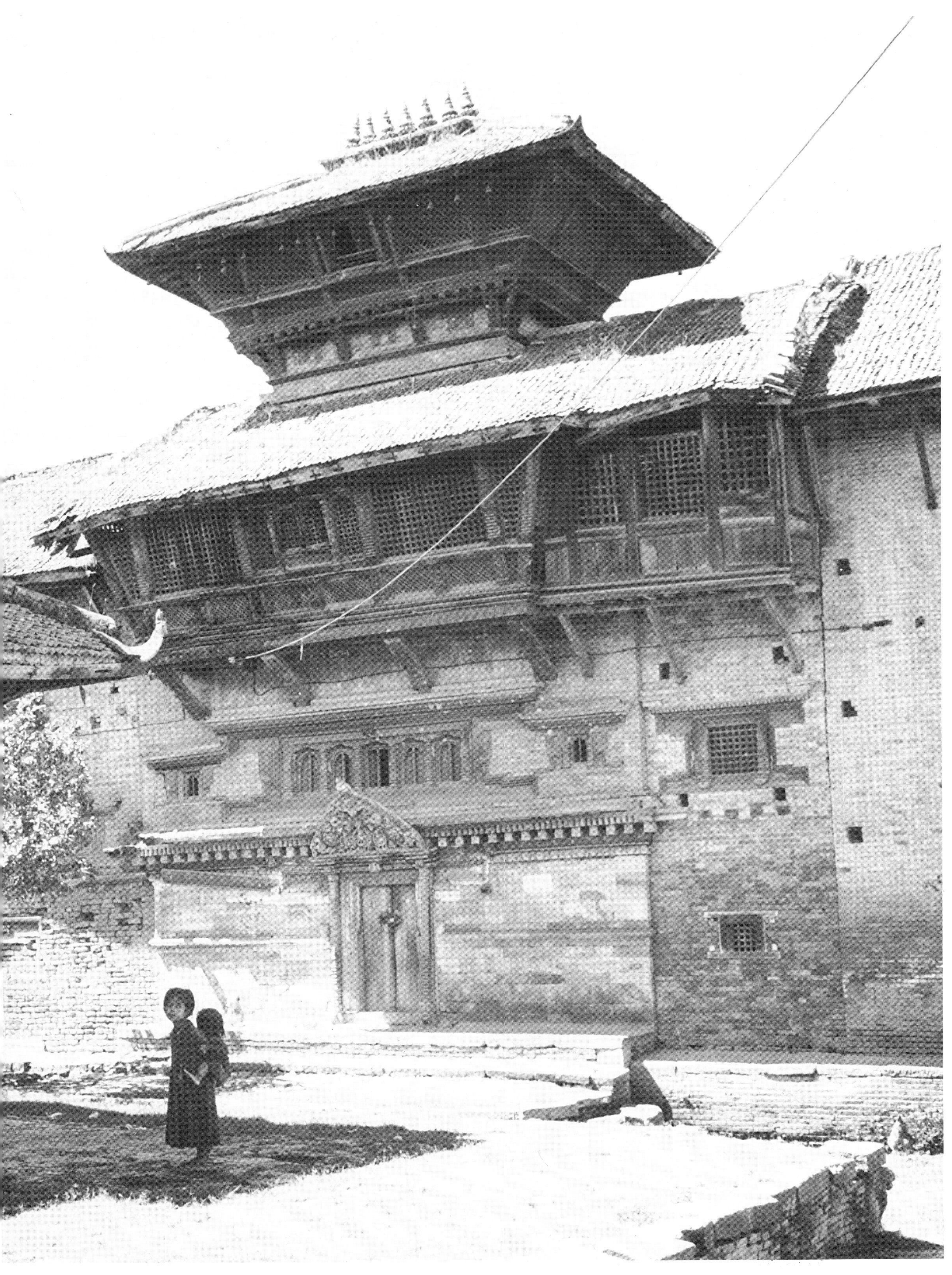

# THE SULIMA PAGODA

East meets West in the Restoration of a Nepalese Temple

editors
Erich Theophile and Niels Gutschow

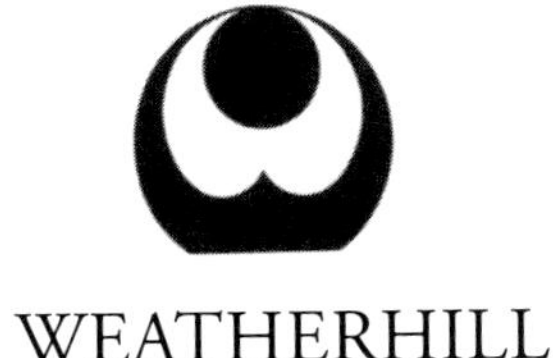

WEATHERHILL

# DEDICATION

This publication is dedicated to Mary Shepherd Slusser, whose photographs of the temple and the surviving woodcarvings served as the principal historical record for the restoration of the Sulima Temple. Her scholarship, insights, and wit continue to inspire all those who study the art and architecture of the Kathmandu Valley.

# CONTENTS

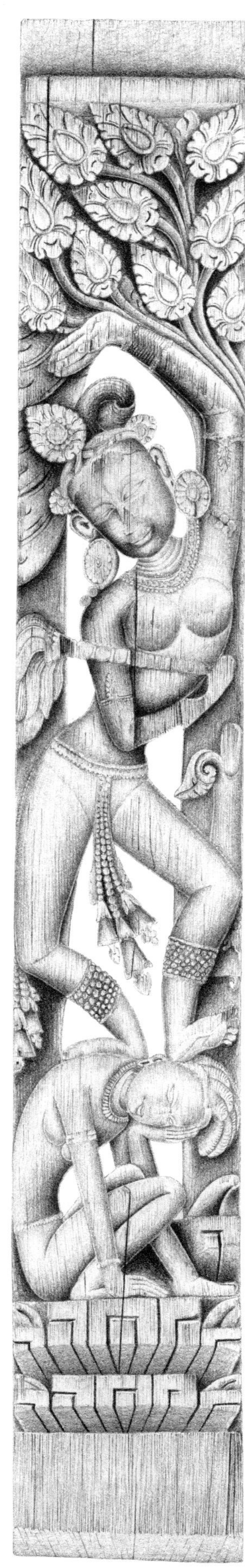

One of the surviving Sulima
roof struts depicting a *yaksini,*
or demi-goddess
Drawing by Bijay Basukala

# ACKNOWLEDGEMENTS

This publication grew out of a symposium organized by the Kathmandu Valley Preservation Trust in November 1999 and supported by the World Monuments Fund.

We extend our sincere appreciation to the following individuals and institutions who helped make this publication possible: Laurie Beckelman, Bonnie Burnham, Felicia Mayro and John H. Stubbs of the World Monuments Fund; Mary Daniels and Eduard F. Sekler of the Frances Loeb Library and the Graduate School of Design, Harvard University; Riddhi Pradhan and Shobha Shrestha of the Department of Archaeology, HMG Nepal; Dr. Saphalya Amatya of the Ministry of Culture, Tourism and Civil Aviation, HMG Nepal; Cathryn Collins, Michael F. Doyle, John Gilmore Ford, Nancy Mannes, and other members of the Board of the Kathmandu Valley Preservation Trust.

The Sulima Temple restoration project was generously supported by the Robert W. Wilson Challenge to Support Our Heritage (under the auspices of the World Monuments Fund), the Sulima Ratneshvara Guthi, the Patan Conservation Program (German Technical Cooperation), and the Lalitpur Municipality.

The initial pledge by Prithvi Pande of the Himalayan Bank Ltd. was the first pledge ever made by a Nepali corporation in the field of architectural preservation. It enabled the project to attract additional support from other businesses in Nepal. We also extend our sincere thanks to the individuals and companies who joined the corporate campaign: Ace Finance Company, Diwakar Golcha and the Golcha Group, employees of the Himalayan Bank, Ram Pratap Mohpal, Pratima Pande, Mohan Rajbhandari, Rajesh Man Sherchan, the SAARC Secretariat Women's Association, Manoj Shrestha, and Laxman Shrestha.

The commitment to preservation efforts shown by friends in Nepal and abroad continues to encourage us. We thank Mayor Buddhiraj Bajracharya of Lalitpur, Prafulla Man Pradhan, Dilendra Raj Shrestha, Prayag Raj Joshi, Bhuju Raj Sakya, Purna Man Shakya, Ambika Shrestha, Sangeeta Shrestha, Rajendra Pradhananga, Anil Chitrakar, Anne Hobbes, Junko Taniguchi, Minja Yang, Bijay Basukala, Raju Roka, Sushil Rajbhandari, Indrakaji Silpakar, Götz HagmØller, Ludmilla Hungerhuber, Imrana Rashid, Linda Kentro, John Sanday, Surya Bhakta Sangacche, Sudarshan Raj Tiwari, Kanak Dixit, Sallie Fischer Limbu, Thomas Schrom, Mani Lama, Stanislaw Klimek, Kiran Chitrakar, Nutandhar Sharma, their Excellencies Timothy George and Julia Chang Bloch, Regina Henry, Joe Bruno, Tej Ratna Tamrakar, and Himalaya B. Pande.

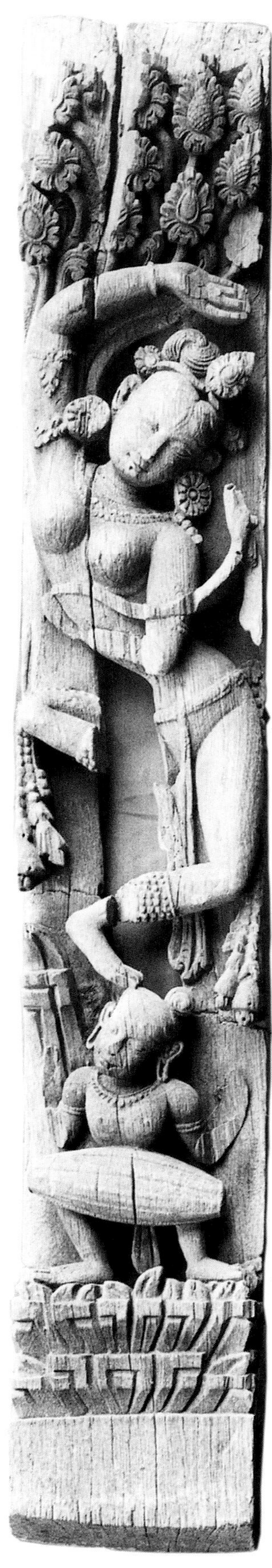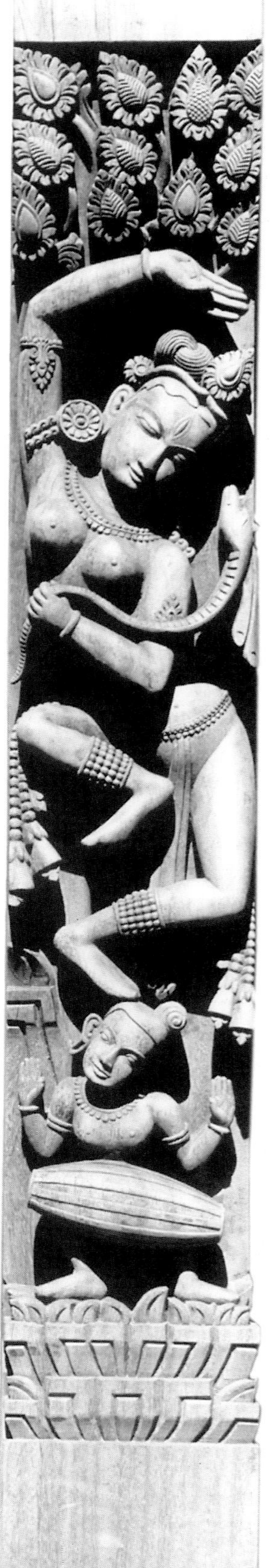

# INTRODUCTION

## The Missing Dialogue

Erich Theophile

Twenty-nine years of international participation in historic preservation in Nepal's Kathmandu Valley has revealed significant differences in restoration approaches to historical buildings, some even controversial. For example, since 1993 UNESCO has been on the verge of listing the Valley's seven World Heritage Sites as endangered sites. While local limitations of funding and political support account for a wide range of preservation standards, philosophical gaps exist that UNESCO's recommendations do not address.

The present study and publication have been undertaken to begin what might be termed "the missing dialogue," an overdue examination of the interactions between international (*i.e.* foreign-funded) and local projects in Nepal. The idea of diversity in the field has been acknowledged in recent years in the international arena by the 1994 Nara Charter of Authenticity, but there remains little documentation of the real, sometimes painful meetings of different schools of thought. The tiny, monument-studded Kathmandu Valley serves as an ideal laboratory for such investigations, not only for its historical riches, but also for its numerous collaborations of local and international actors in a Hindu kingdom, a place where the medieval confronts the modern on a daily basis.

With this in mind, in 1999 the Kathmandu Valley Preservation Trust organized a working mission of eight international experts to discuss the meeting of East and West in Nepali conservation practice, focusing on its recently completed restoration of the fourteenth-century Sulima Temple in Patan. The temple, possibly the oldest intact and surviving multi-tiered temple in the Kathmandu Valley, is the twelfth achievement in the U.S.-based Trust's campaign to save 15 historical structures around the Patan Darbar Square World Heritage Site. The two-tiered pagoda is also significant for its rare, original iconographic and decorative woodcarvings.

In particular, the question of recarving the temple's stolen roof struts served as a springboard for discussion. Should lost carvings be reproduced based on historical documentation? Should new replacements be left plain? Should they look contemporary or use reduced historical forms? Where the records were unclear, should design by local craftsmen, those traditionally responsible for the task, be encouraged? International or western practice advocates that "freezing" a building in time is possible, if not mandatory, whereas traditional societies—feeling no such distance from a building or its evolution—remain ever-ready to modify or even replace the building according to present needs or religious aspirations. The following documentation of the project and of the philosophical and design challenges, as well as reviews by our colleagues, address these issues, suggesting positive directions for a global dialogue.

**Sulima Struts**
**A fourteenth-century carved timber roof strut (opposite page) that supported the upper roof of the temple, and the copy by master carver Indrakaji Silpakar**

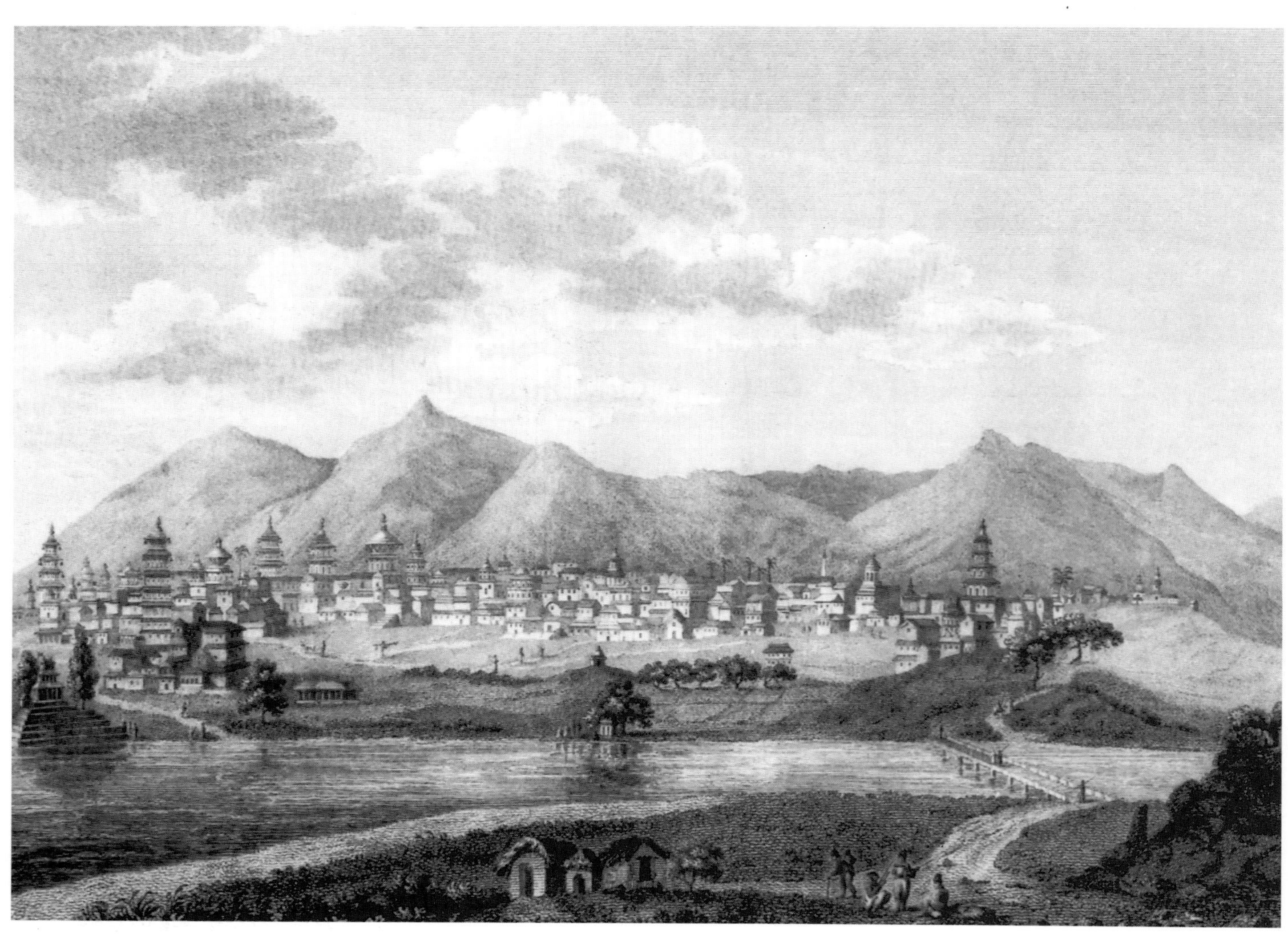

This fantastic view of Kathmandu, published by Colonel Kirkpatrick in 1811, reveals the colonial fascination with the building type and the predilection to romanticize it.

*opposite:* Current research in Japan tries to establish a line of evolution and links between second-century towers (such as the example above, reconstructed based on archeological evidence) and seventh-century "pagodas" (below). The early archetype was constructed to encase a stupa's most important element, its central tree. Illustrations from a poster for a seminar held at the National Museum of Japanese History in Sakura, October 12, 1999



**The Sulima Pagoda**

# What Is a Pagoda?

Niels Gutschow and Erich Theophile

The two authors of the Hobson-Jobson, a "glossary of colloquial Anglo-Indian words and phrases,"[1] could not agree in 1886 about the origin of the term *pagoda* or *pagode*, as it was used among Portuguese in the early sixteenth century to describe exotic towers. The etymology indeterminate, the authors relied on descriptions of usage for "an idol temple," "an idol," or "a coin," betraying a derogatory tone. By the end of the nineteenth century, the term *pagoda* was widely used to denote the towering temple structures across Asia, including those of India, Burma, China, and Japan. Essentially colonial, the term has outlived the Empire and entered many languages. Despite a diversity of religious conceptions and forms associated with it, even art historical publications use *pagoda* as if it constitutes a clear type.

In general, a pagoda is a towering edifice, usually square in plan and with tiered roofs. Initially the term was used for the towering *gopurams* in South India and in particular for the Sun Temple in Konark, Orissa, known until recently as the "Black Pagoda." In the twentieth century the term was applied to the multi-tiered roofed temples of Nepal, Burma, and Thailand, the multi-tiered roofed *stupas* of China and Japan, and to early East Asian examples such as the structures found at early Chinese burial sites. The type existed on Nepali soil from early on, as suggested in seventh century accounts by a Chinese pilgrim.[2]

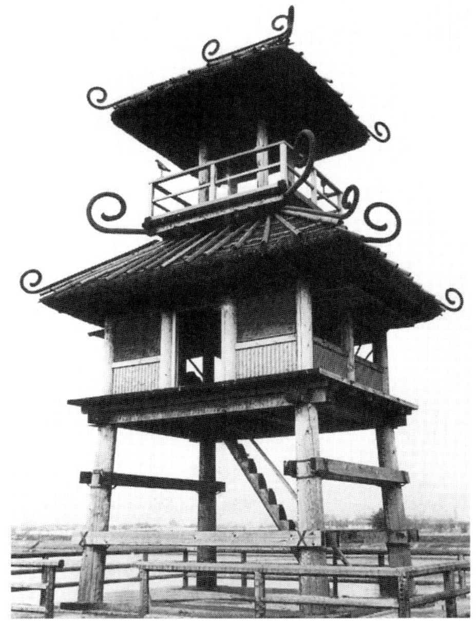

Until recently, art historians seeking to trace the origin of the building type have looked to the lost structures of Northern India and China, believing in a common source. New research and hypotheses in Japan establish a different focus, analyzing local developments and indigenous roots of such temple structures, as for example in the assessment of the seventh-century Heijo-kyo pagoda at Nara.[3] Recent restoration and research projects by the Kathmandu Valley Preservation Trust lay the groundwork for specific investigations about the evolution of the pagoda in Nepal's Kathmandu Valley. The Orientalists' claim of a common origin for a pan-Asian pagoda, although an intriguing myth, may only gain scientific credibility based on a number of such investigations.

## What is a Nepali pagoda?

In Nepal the term *pagoda* was relatively unknown until recently, when tourism needed a name for these memorable buildings which, despite their myriad variations, can be seen as a definite family of structures. In Nepali any temple of brick or stone of any shape, single or multi-storied, is called a *mandir*. In Newari, the language of the craftsmen and kings who built most of these structures, a similarly generic term, *degah*, is employed. Both of these blanket terms also apply to both Hindu and Buddhist religious buildings. Interestingly enough, there is no indigenous word in the many tongues of the Kathmandu Valley for what we know as *pagoda*. The three other basic temple types found in the Kathmandu Valley whose developments are independent of the pagoda type are the *stupa*, the *shikara*, and the later domed temples.

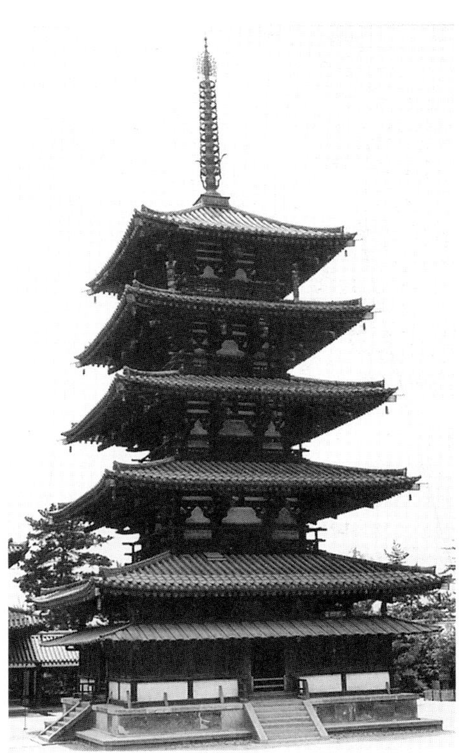

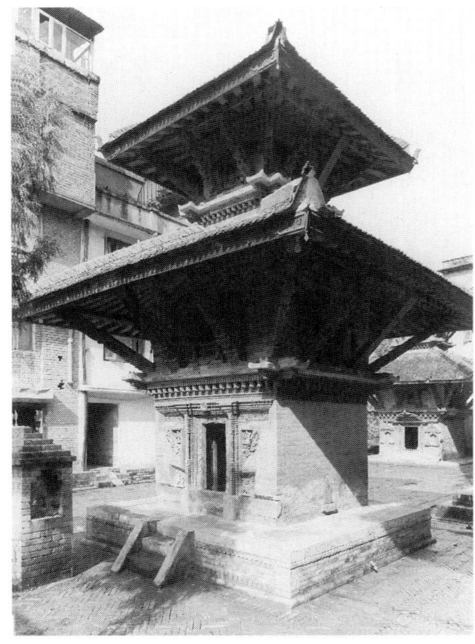

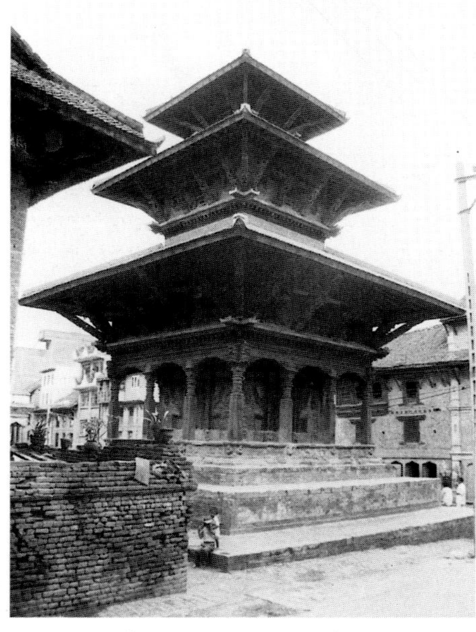

*above, top:* **Kulima Narayan Temple**
*above:* **Radha Krishna Temple**
**These two temples from the same period demonstrate the range of elaboration between local and royal constructions. The three-tiered Radha Krishna with its elevated plinth, arcaded ground floor, and virtuoso carvings stands in contrast to the simpler Kulima structure. Both temples were restored by the Kathmandu Valley Preservation Trust between 1992 and 1999.**

More often than not, the Nepali pagoda is a free-standing brick building, square in plan, with two to five roof tiers or stories, and timber roof framing. There is no central column or *axis mundi*, in contrast to Far Eastern examples. In a few but prominent cases, the pagoda plan is rectangular; in rarer cases, octagonal or circular. Usually only the ground floor provides interior space for the sanctuary, while upper levels remain empty, unused attic spaces. Hatches in the ceiling of the sanctuary are provided to allow access for repairs.

Sometimes the pagoda is conceived not as a free-standing building, but rather as a superstructure atop another structure, a rooftop elaboration to a residential shrine (*agamchen* in Newari, literally a "shrine house") or palace building. Sometimes the diminishing tiers above are reflected in a stepping plinth below, which raises the sanctuary many meters above the ground level.

Timber openings, stone and terracotta decorative details, and cornices punctuate tightly laid brick walls of the pagoda—the decorative carver is ever-generous and inventive in his artful elaboration of all. The struts include the most ambitious sculptural detail, supporting the temples' massive roof overhangs. Wall openings reflect iconographic and symbolic aspirations more than the need to ventilate or light interior space; most openings are very tiny in relation to the decorative and sculptural frames. The diminutive size of buildings in the Kathmandu Valley also deserves special mention: one can practically touch upper floor windows given the low heights of floor levels.

The characteristically stepped form of the Nepali pagoda results from diminishing and set-back roofs and wall planes. Levels diminish in a regular way such that the eavesboards of the roofs can always be connected by one line. A gilt metal pinnacle surmounts the layers of timber-framed roofs below.

The all-important stepped quality is achieved in the following ways. In the simplest two-tiered scheme, the walls of an inner shrine extend up *through* the lower roof to carry the upper roof, with the lower roof carried by an additional, outer wall layer. In a typical elaboration, a timber arcade replaces the outer wall to create a continuous ambulatory. In a variation to achieve more tiers, the upper-level walls, smaller in plan, perch on timber beams carried by the ground floor cella, as a kind of "inward cantilever." The lower floor and upper masonry walls are thus discontinuous.

These structural configurations contrast with pagodas of the Far East, which are generally post and beam structures (sometimes even hanging structures with a central column) or masonry structures whose walls are vertically continuous and diminish in section as they rise.

## Religious distinctions

The intermingling of Hindu and Buddhist deities and rituals is a remarkable and rich phenomenon in the Kathmandu Valley. The pagoda is similarly non-denominational and houses Hindu and Buddhist icons.

In the Kathmandu Valley one can distinguish between two fundamental types of shrines with pagoda structures, those "revealing" a *genius loci, i.e.* housing a deity "found" at a site, and those housing an "installed" deity. These differences have several implications for the conception of the pagoda. Those of the *genius loci* variety are never raised on plinths—the god emerges from the earth, and ground floors are



**The Sulima Pagoda**

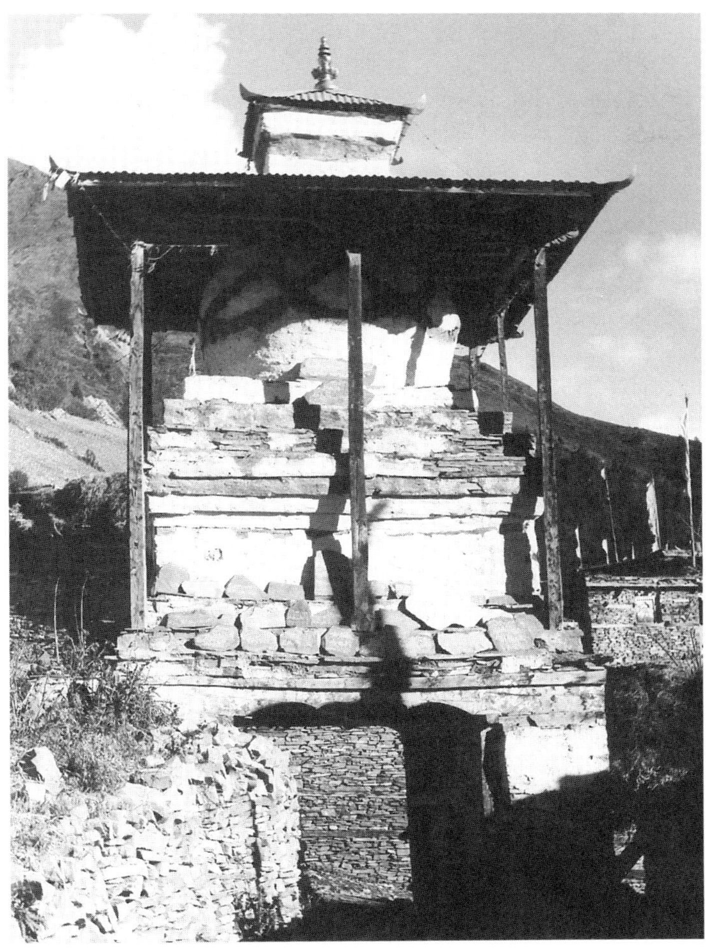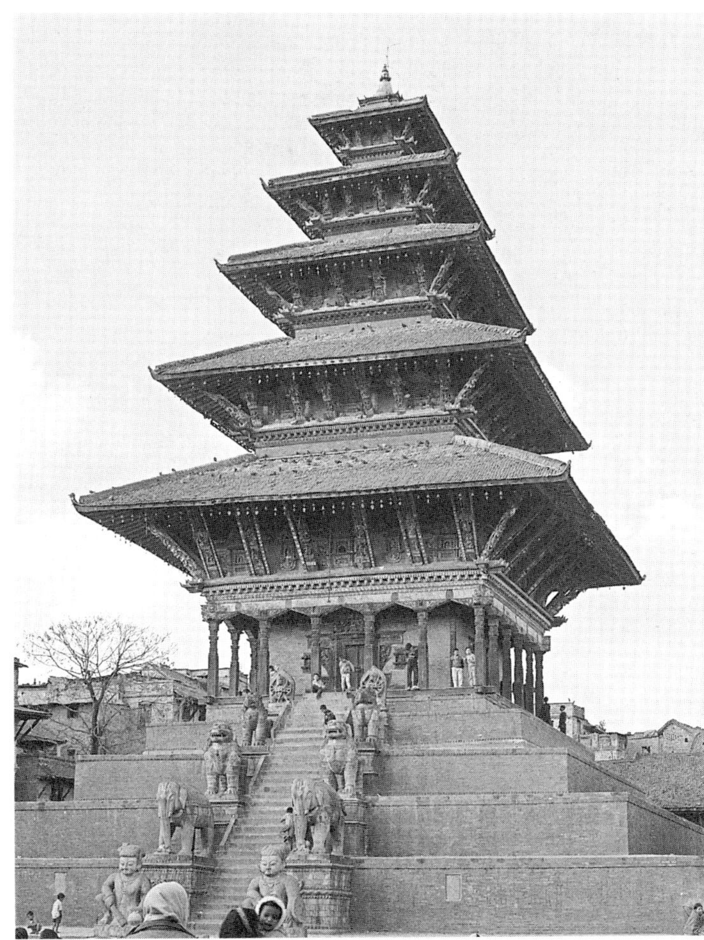

conceived as open arcades instead of masonry walls to let the site "breathe." They celebrate local deities such as the protective mother goddesses.

Installed deities, especially those of royal donation, incorporate the stepping plinth, an eloquent counterpoint to the stepping form of the roofs above. The latter is typified by royal donations, often in prominent urban sites, and dedicated to the Brahmanical trio.

Although the religious importance and symbolism behind the layered or stepping form is beyond the scope of the present work, some preliminary remarks can be made. Formal analysis of the buildings and their proportional systems confirms the role of regulating lines and cosmic diagrams as found in early Indian texts such as the *Vastu Sastra*. The multiplication of roofs nevertheless remains a daring formal leap consistent with, but not explained by, the Indian prescriptive manuals. Art historian Stella Kramrisch comes close to a metaphysical explanation of this will to multiply in

*above: Caitya* and pagoda
While some scholars have linked the formal evolutions of the pagoda and the Buddhist *caitya* or stupa in Southeast Asia, the historical development of the two building types in Nepal is independent.
A later roof structure enclosing a Buddhist *caitya* in West Nepal approximates the pagoda form.

*above right:* Nyatapvala Temple, Bhaktapur—The temple is one of two five-tiered pagodas surviving in the Kathmandu Valley, a royal donation of exquisite proportions and silhouette. It houses the early seventeenth-century personal deity of a past king and is no longer worshipped.
The temple was restored in 1998 by the Bhaktapur Municipality.

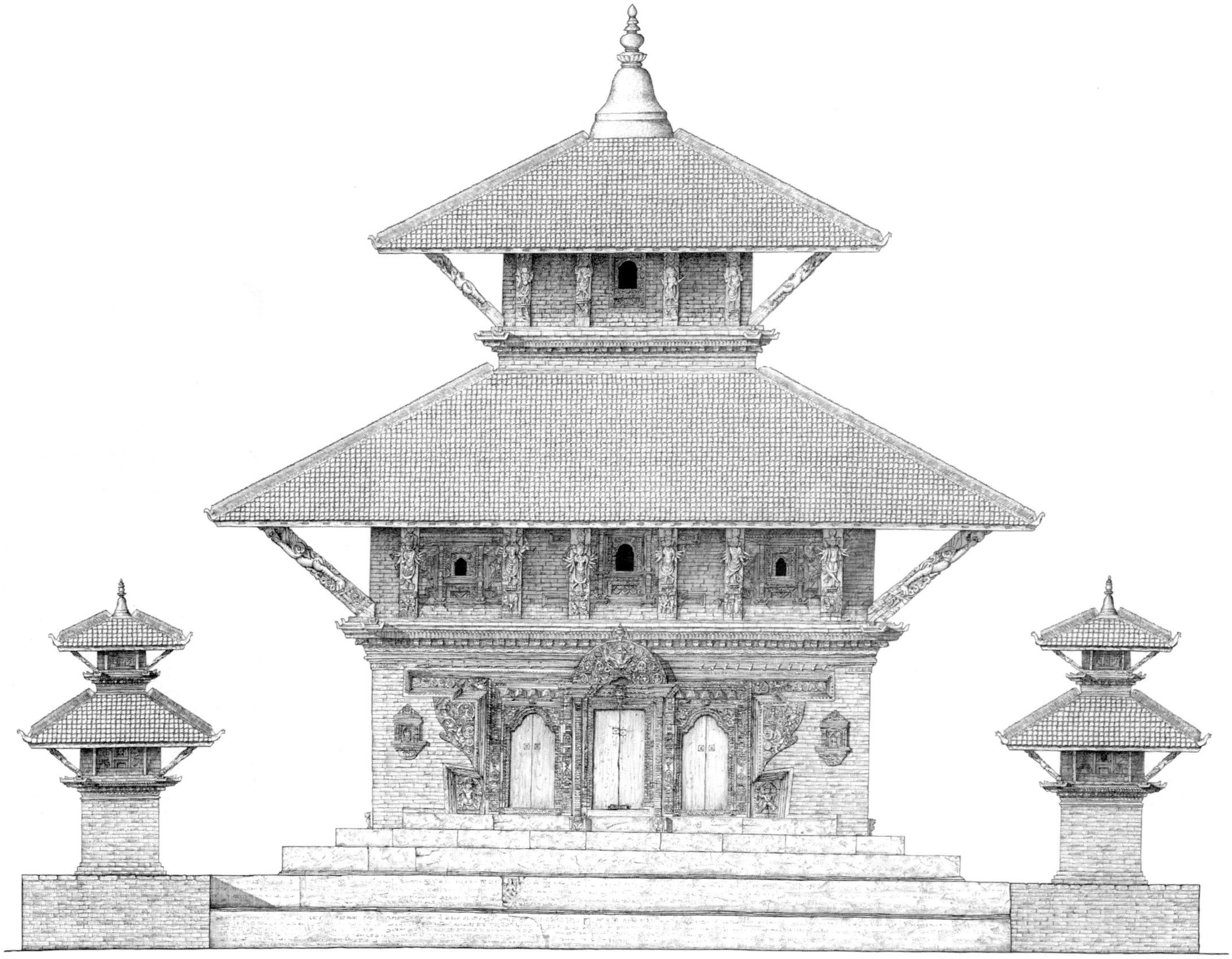

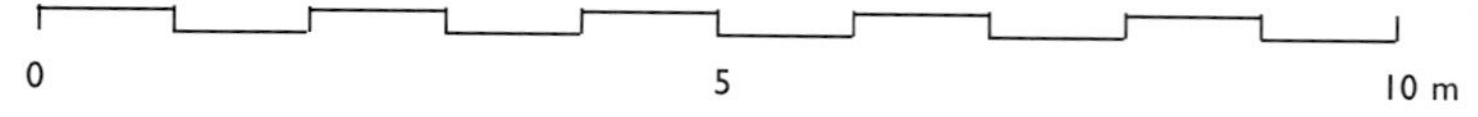



**Jagannath Temple, Hanuman Dhoka,
Kathmandu Darbar Square**
East elevation and ground floor plan

The seventeenth-century Jagannath
Temple typifies the early pagoda type: a
massive and sturdy two-tiered structure
in which the upper roof is carried by the
inner wall of a double-wall system.
Additional miniature temple structures
at the corners follow the traditional
Indian *pancayatana* diagram in plan.
The temple's intact and elaborate
woodcarvings, and its original
inscriptions and icons, make this a
significant example.
Drawing by Sushil Rajbhandari, 2000

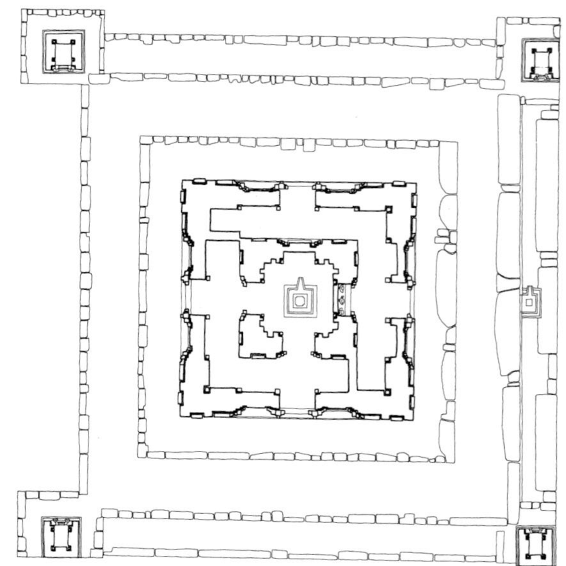



The Sulima Pagoda

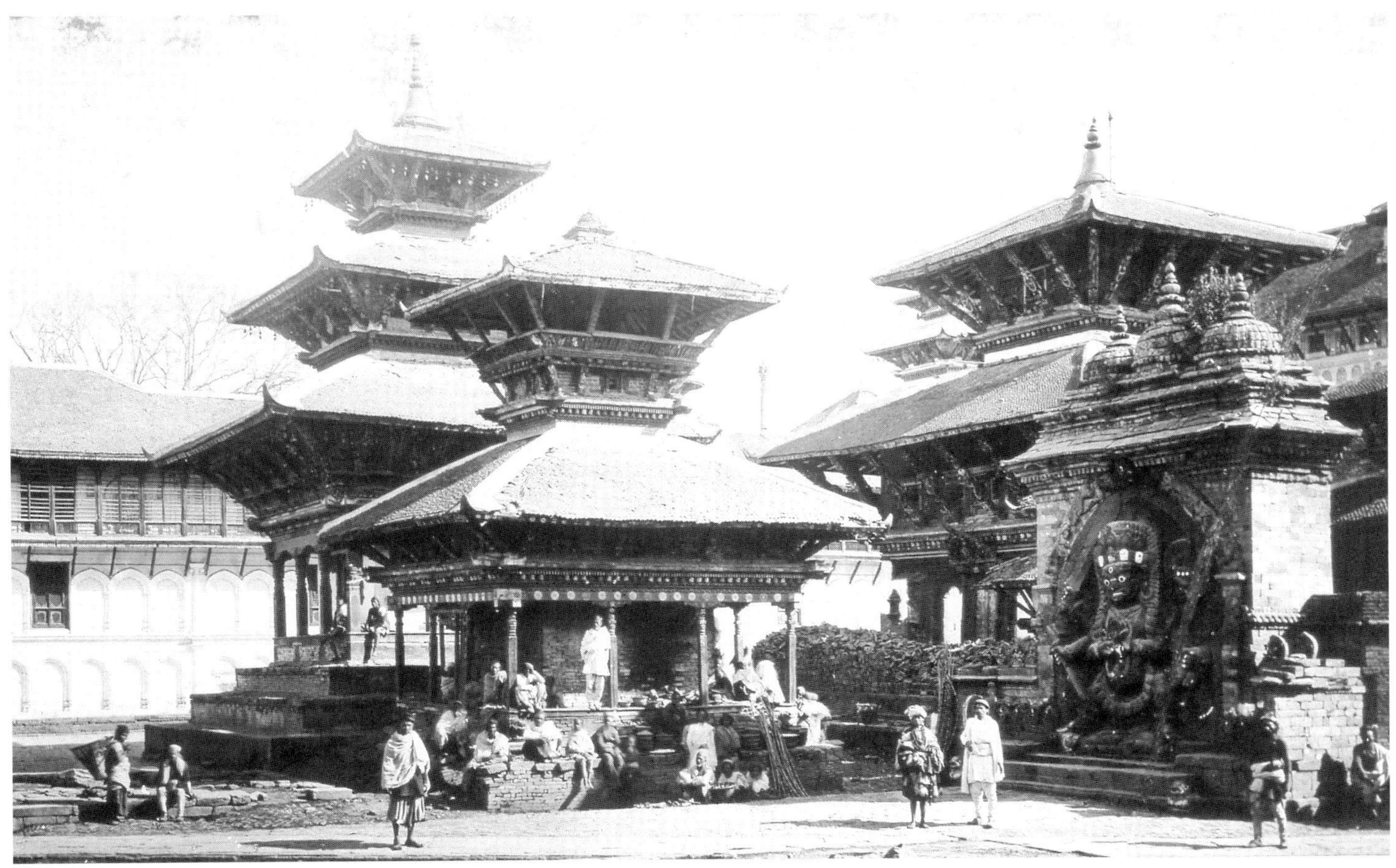

her discussion of the sculptural embellishments of Hindu temple façades. "This vituosity of organization of symbolic structure in all its intricacies gives final exposition of the power held to be inherent in the temple walls."[4]

The pagoda temple's refinements and multiplications are thus an eloquent architectural expression of importance. The temple not only houses the deity, but through its form manifests its significance, communicating a holy presence across the rooftops of neighboring quarters. The gilt pinnacle or *gajura* on top, representing the essence of the celestial world, crowns the composition like an antenna to spread and receive "the word."

**Kathmandu Darbar Square, before 1885**
**View of the principal temples outside the royal palace. The Jagannath Temple is to the right, behind the Kal Bhairav shrine. These three pagoda structures were partially rebuilt after the 1934 earthquake, but have since fallen into disrepair. They are the focus of an international restoration initiative (2000-2004) led by the Kathmandu Valley Preservation Trust.**

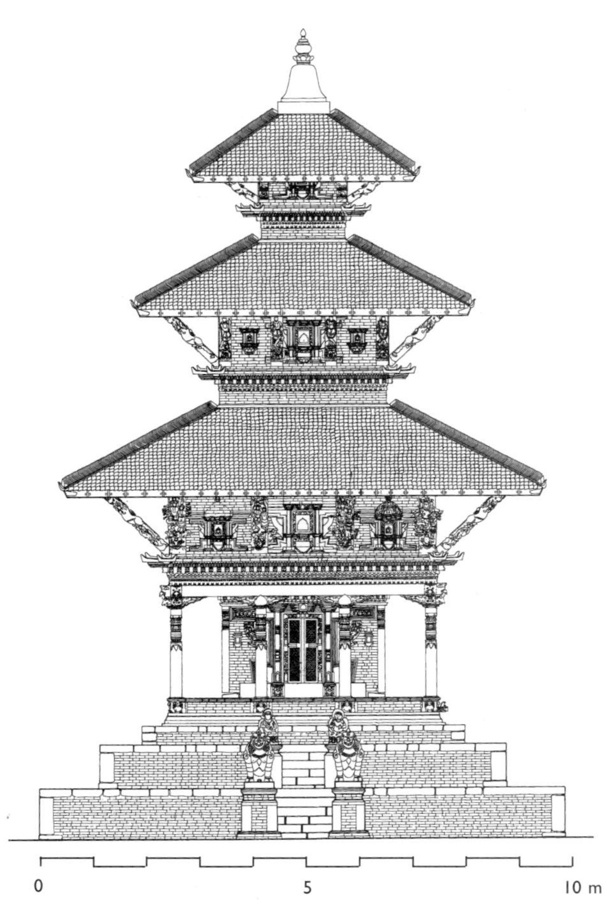
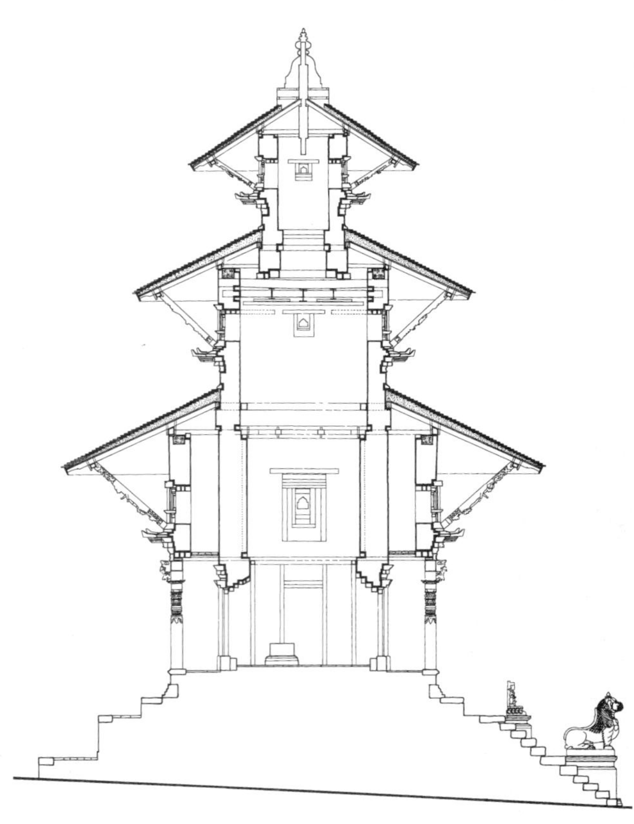
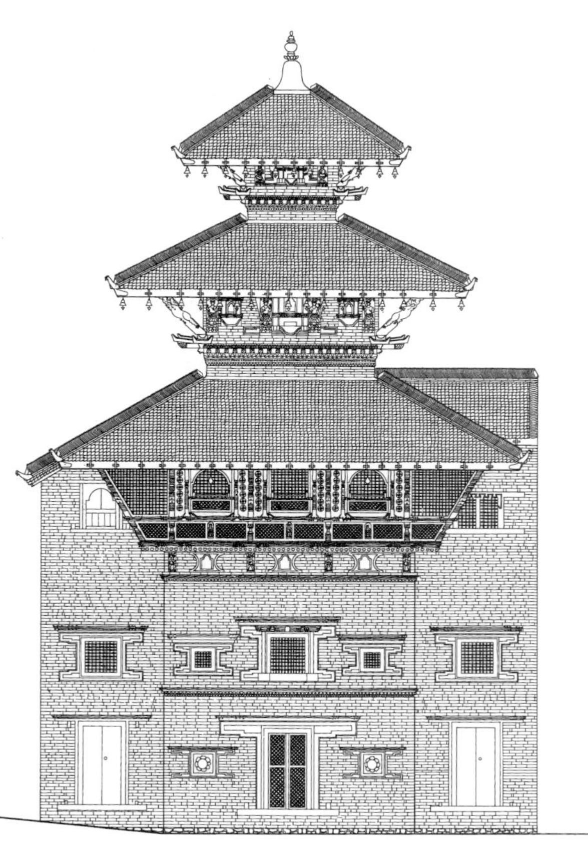
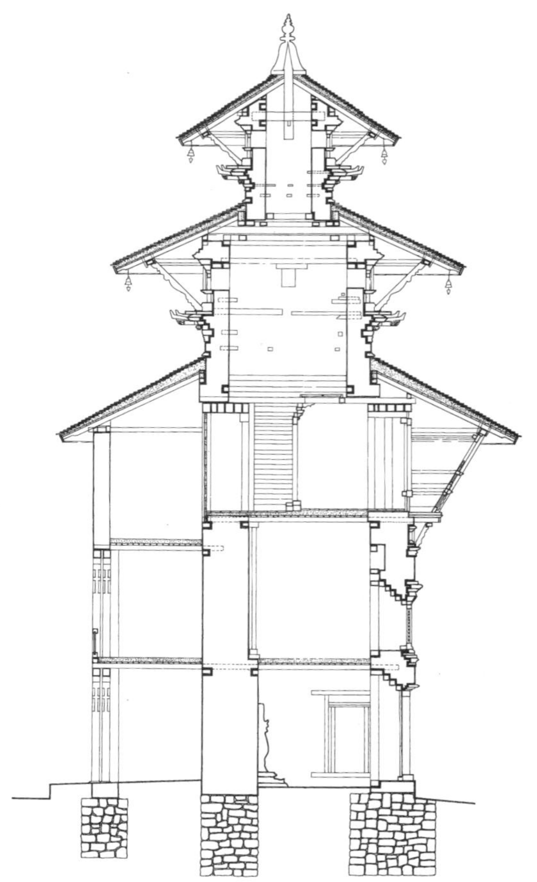





The Sulima Pagoda

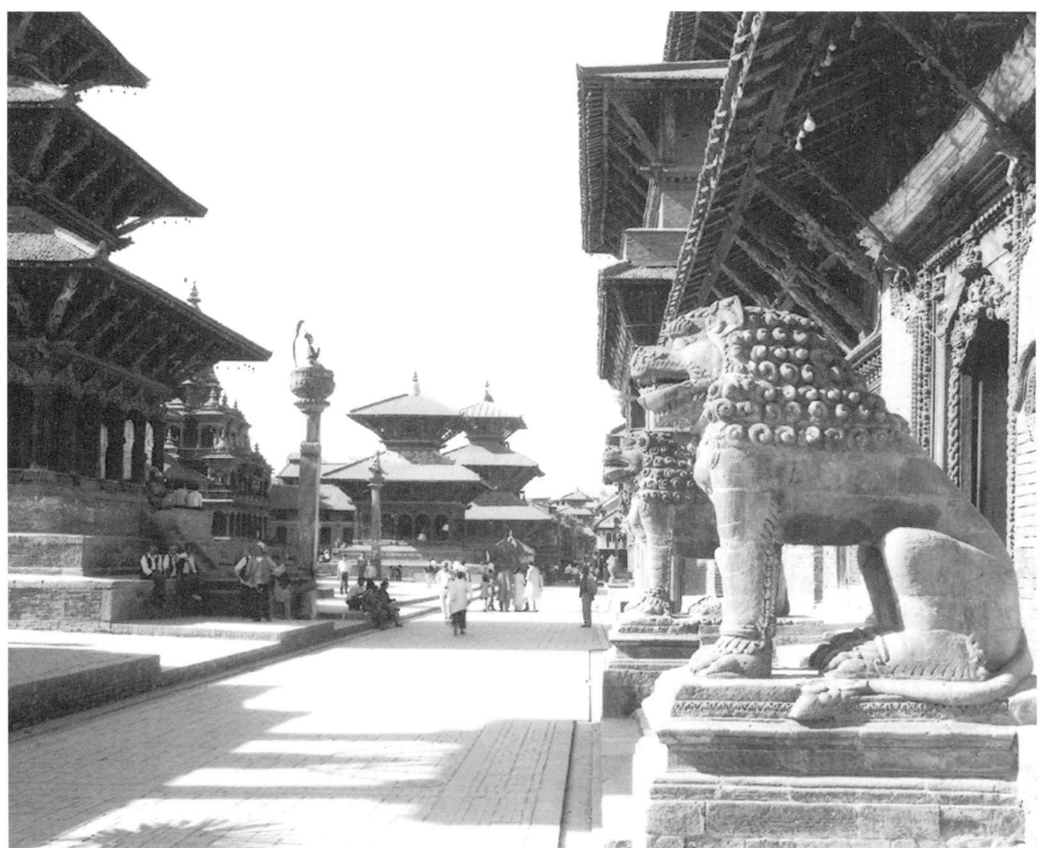

right: Architectural continuity
A field of pagodas at Patan
Darbar Square stands before the
royal palace complex. The
pagoda's striking form, created
by multiple roof overhangs, is
harmonious with surrounding
palace and residential
structures.

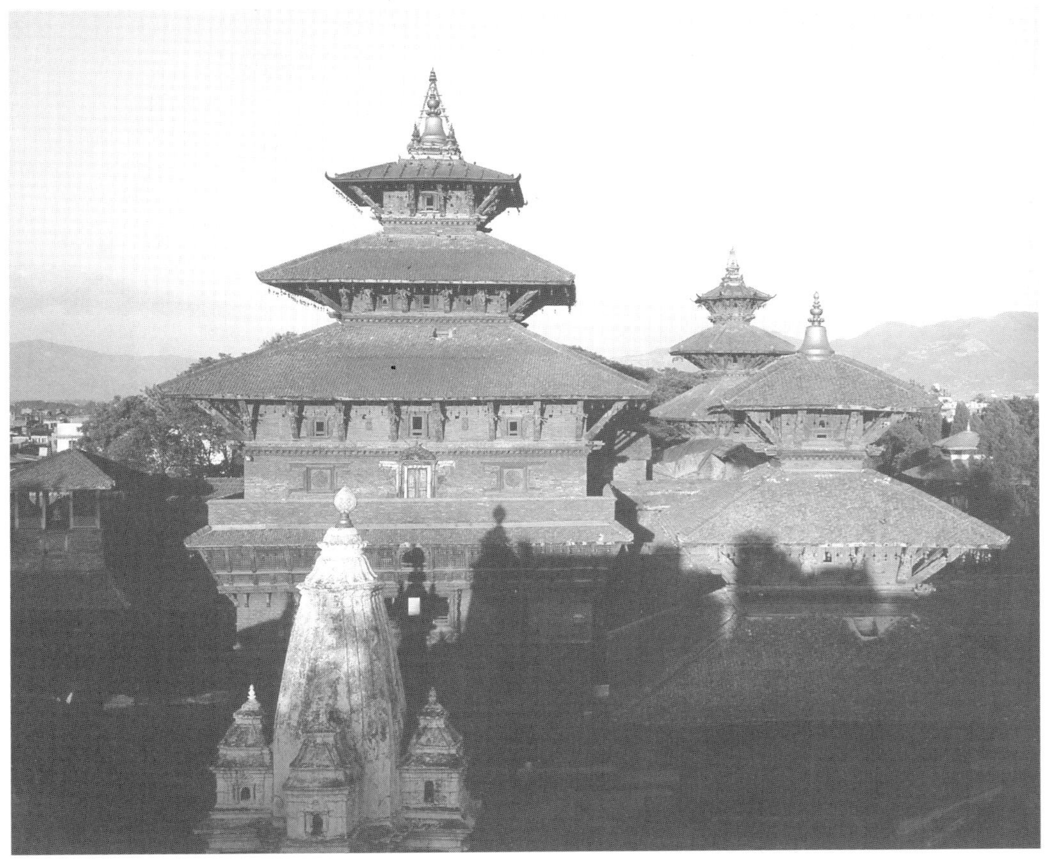

right: Patan Darbar Square
Seventeenth-century Patan kings
built the shrines to the tutelary
deities Degutale and Taleju.
These shrines were conceived as
superstructures crowning the
royal palace complex.

left: Typological variations:
These two seventeenth-century
religious structures have
identical stepping, tiered roofs.
The Radha Krishna Temple
(above) is raised by a massive
plinth, while at the Patukva
Agamchen, a private shrine
(below), the roof surmounts a
residential structure. This
superstructure houses the
esoteric shrine of a priestly
family, the detachment from the
ground symbolizing limited
access to the shrine. Both
buildings were restored by the
Kathmandu Valley Preservation
Trust, 1992-1996. Drawings by

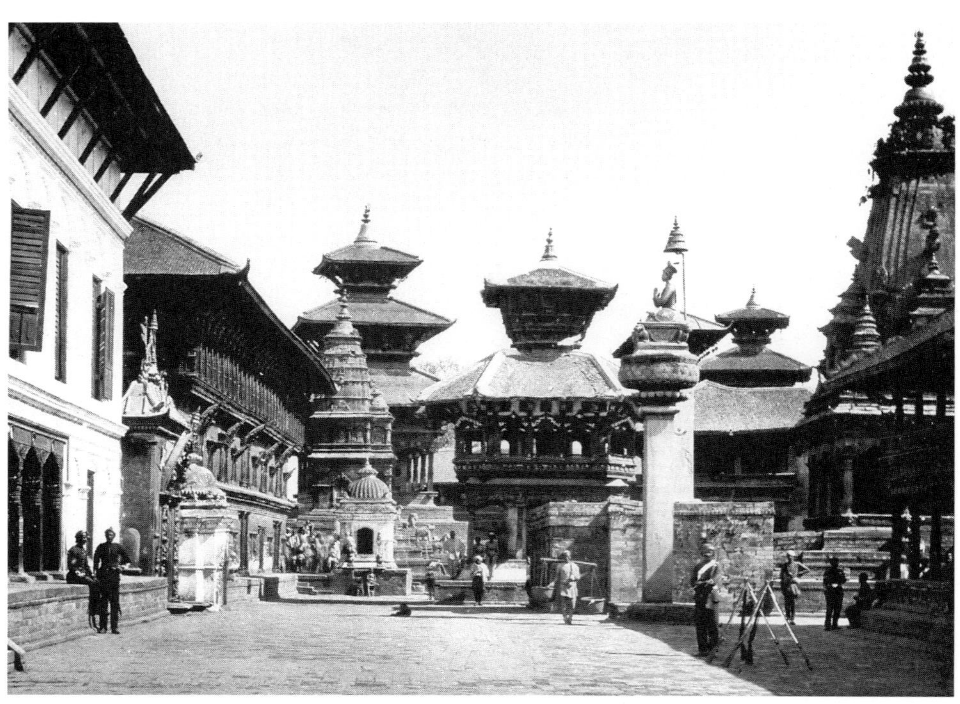

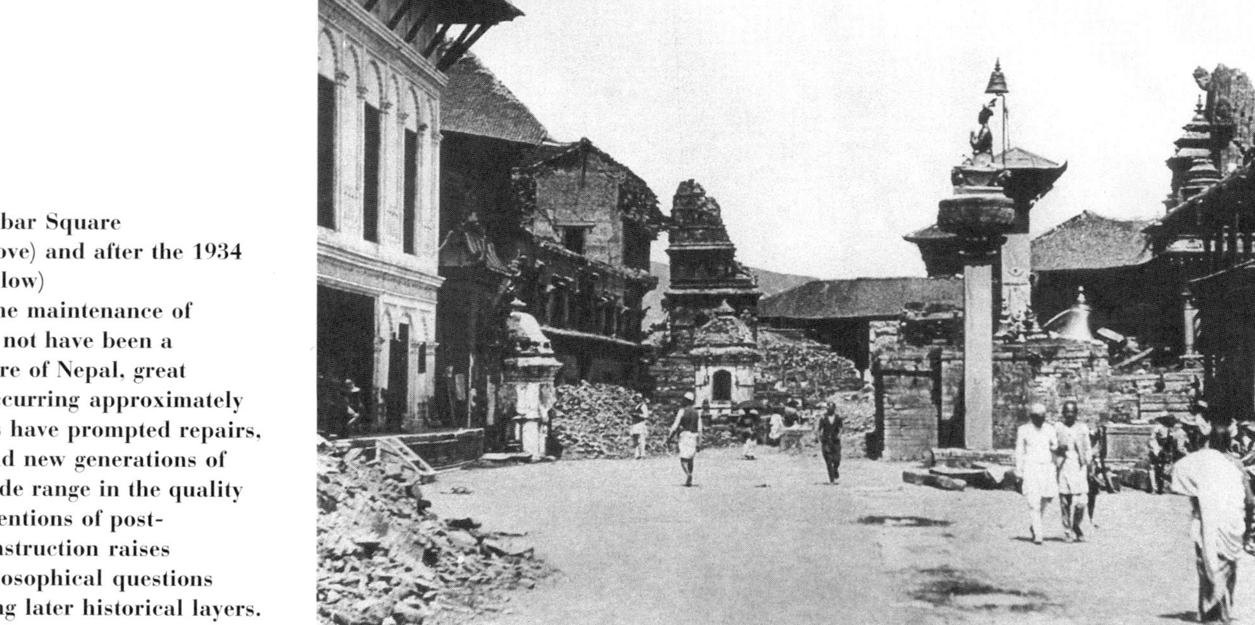

Bhaktapur Darbar Square
Circa 1921 (above) and after the 1934
earthquake (below)
Although routine maintenance of
structures may not have been a
historical feature of Nepal, great
earthquakes occurring approximately
every 100 years have prompted repairs,
renovations, and new generations of
buildings. A wide range in the quality
and artistic intentions of post-
earthquake construction raises
interesting philosophical questions
about preserving later historical layers.



The Sulima Pagoda

# Conservation in Nepal
## A Review of Practice

Niels Gutschow

## Techniques of repair and renewal in history

Very little is known about approaches to and techniques of maintenance and renewal of temples and houses in historic times. Countless inscriptions tell us of the construction of temples, *shivalaya*, *stupas*, and monasteries linked with agricultural lands whose returns were dedicated to maintenance, repairs, and rituals. These resources, however, seem to have been diverted from maintenance and renewal early on. Images of the Kathmandu Valley in the 1850s by Henry Ambrose Oldfield and the Schlagintweit brothers of Munich document a largely neglected townscape, with temples and *stupas* in urgent need of repair, sometimes even in ruins.

Oldfield reported that the local people complained that urban festivals had lost their grandeur. "There is not a tithe of the splendor exhibited, nor of the cost expended upon them, which were observed in the time of the Niwar dynasty."[1] Oldfield accused the "Gorkha Government" of taking no interest in festivals and concluded that in the course of another generation little of the festivals would exist except their names. One hundred and fifty years later we lament the dilapidation, although now it is part of a larger pattern of outright destruction commonly found in the urban centers of developing countries.

We have to ask how it differs from those glorious seventeenth and eighteenth centuries when the Newar kings were building up the squares in front of their palaces with temples, statues, and bells with the same intensity that we now see high-rise concrete frames rise. Were the historic buildings of those days maintained on a regular basis? Or were earthquakes the prime initiators of repairs and reconstructions?

Inscriptions often record *jirnnodhara* (repairs) such as the replacement of door panels or the pavement of a courtyard. In a Buddhist context such activities are important as a way to accumulate religious merit. It is hard to distinguish when and if the notions of merit and maintenance meet. A pavement job acquires merit for the donor, but does it reflect a need to repair or a wish for merit? We know surprisingly little about seasonal maintenance routines, such as removing grass from the roof after monsoon, undertaken in the past.

Such votive offerings have overtaken those traditional activities funded by dedicated agricultural lands. This is especially true since the nationalization of all private land trusts in 1962 created an ungainly centralized agency, the *Guthi Sansthan*, a national trust to administer land formerly owned by religious institutions. Proceeds from the land are meant to support daily rituals, seasonal festivals, and building maintenance.

## Traditional recycling in a seismic zone

The Newari building formula, bricks laid in mud mortar and timber frames assembled without the use of nails, allowed the reconstruction of structures after earthquakes to reuse as much as 80 percent of the bricks and roof tiles and 60 percent of structural

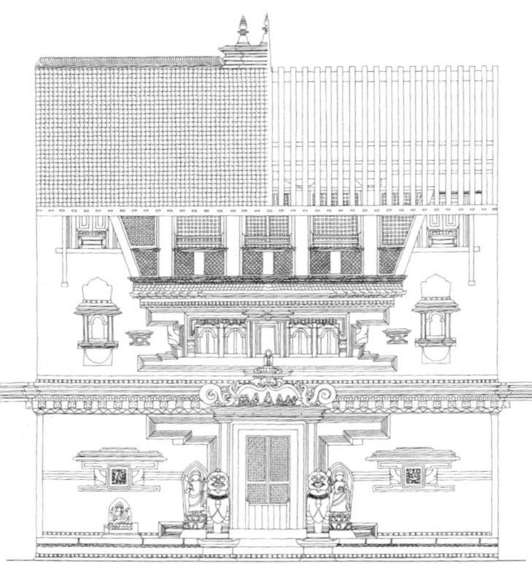

**Yetkhabaha Agamchen, Kathmandu**
**The building's seventeenth-century roof**
**struts were later reincorporated as the**
**vertical members of the projecting**
**latticed window. Principle elevation,**
**drawing by Anil Basukala, 1999**

timbers such as joists and rafters. We know that for generations timber components have been recycled: secondary installations have ranged from makeshift to inspired. The fine seventeenth-century roof brackets or struts of the Yetkhabaha Agamchen in Kathmandu, for example, were shortened and installed to create a new balcony instead of carrying the roof overhang. The eleventh-century blind window of Manjusri Degah in the courtyard of Sasunani, certainly among the oldest extant woodcarvings in Nepal, found secondary use in a single-storied temple rebuilt in 1737. This building was dismantled recently for a reconstruction primarily intented as a votive offering and not a preservation exercise.

Reconstruction in *reduced* forms to cope with post-earthquake scarcities must have always been a practice. The devastation inflicted on the Kathmandu Valley by an earthquake on January 18, 1934[2] is evident in existing detailed photographic surveys. The response, rebuilding on an ambitious urban scale, probably replicated activities following the earthquakes of previous centuries.

Even when virtually leveled by the quake, temples of great popular importance—like the Bhairav Temple in Bhaktapur or the Taleju Temple in Patan—were reconstructed close to their original forms. Temples of lesser importance were often reconstructed in reduced scale or form. The Bhaktapur palace, which was of no political importance in this century, was not rebuilt by the Kathmandu-based rulers. Its legendary 99 courtyards were largely reduced to a heap of rubble and cleared away, the main wing reconstructed using windows from another building. Only the names of the adjoining wings and courtyards are remembered today.

Questions of style and use also affected repairs. Many damaged pagodas and *sikhara* towers were replaced with domes in 1934, in keeping with the tastes of the ruling Rana dynasty. In front of the Bhaktapur Palace, the Rana governor rebuilt a public arcade in a new location to give the narrow square turning radius for his car. Many structures simply disappeared, their *spolia* sprinkled throughout the city in new buildings and repairs of old structures. Only a reduced platform survived from the Cyasilin Mandap in Bhaktapur, a historic pavilion of great beauty, until it was reconstructed in 1990. The reconstruction, however, was able to incorporate original elements that had survived in other structures. Two massive guardian lions near the pavilion bear witness to an even grander building, a three-storied pagoda on a huge multi-stepped plinth, also lost in the 1934 earthquake.

While assessing the historical buildings of the Kathmandu Valley, one can thus distinguish between earthquake repairs and the layers of votive offerings over the years. The well-documented and massive rebuilding effort after the 1934 earthquake must be recognized, in particular, for its preservation achievement. The Rana rulers of the time, fanatic builders of European-style palaces, were able to utilize their armies of building crews to effectively address the demands of reconstruction. Nearly 75 percent of the historic configuration and monuments of the Newar cities were effectively recaptured after nearly complete devastation.

## Early conservation practice by the Department of Archaeology (1956-1970)

The establishment of a Department of Archaeology in 1952[3] and the promulgation of the Ancient Monument Preservation Act of 1956 were institutional and legal models borrowed by the young, modern state from British India. The British focus on archaelogical sites in India would have deep and lasting significance for all monument maintenance throughout the Subcontinent. In contrast to the practices of the

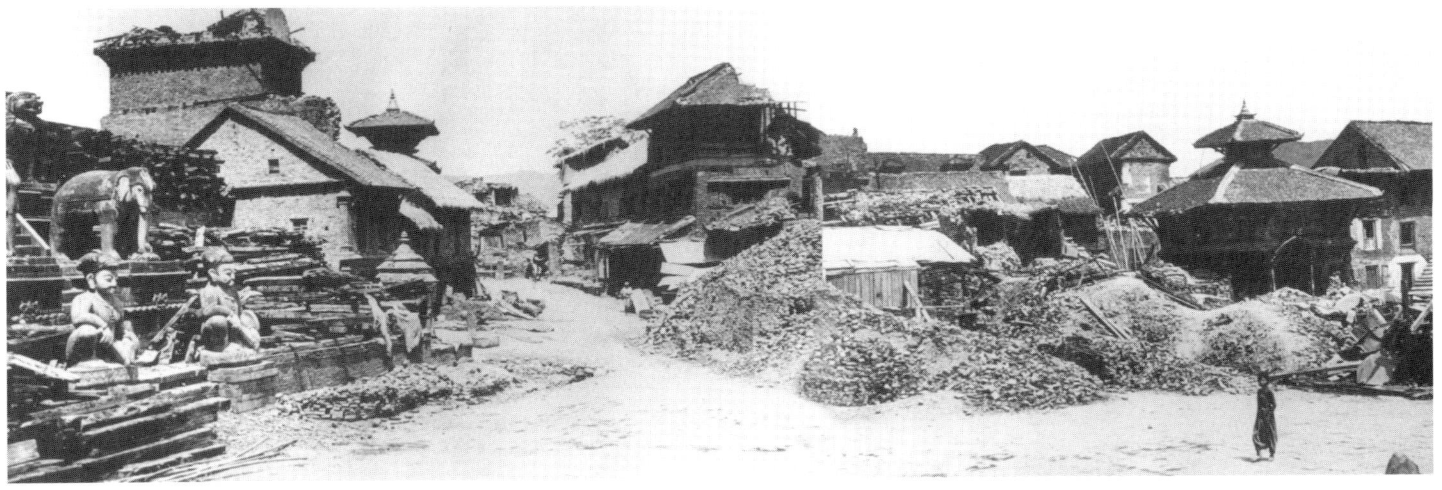

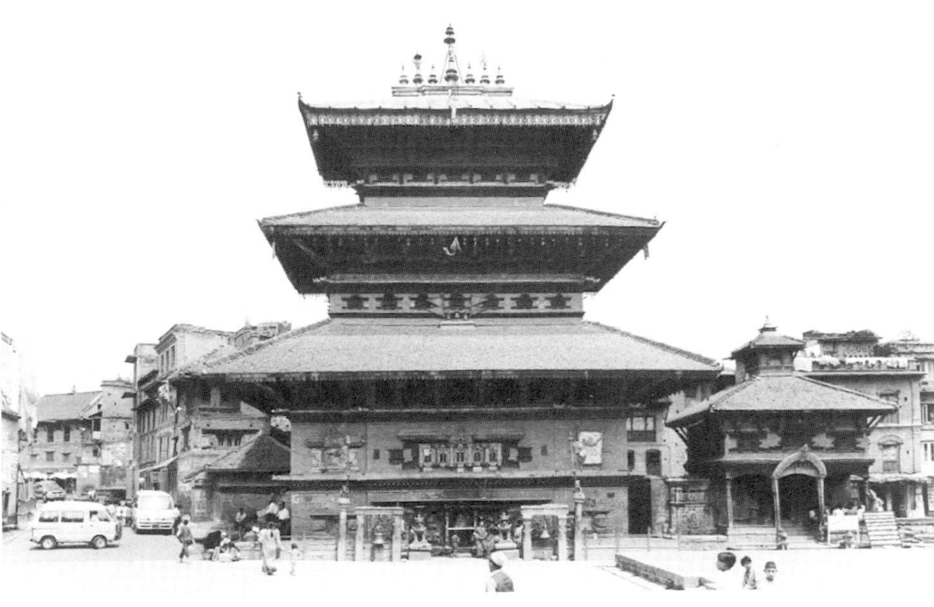



Archaeological Survey of India, the legal basis for the identification of monuments was never clarified in Nepal. Relevant legislation merely mentions an age of one hundred years for a structure to qualify as a monument, while a general notion about the public nature of a monument guided government policy. Any building owned by the king, the state, or the *Guthi Sansthan* was considered public and historical, and thus a monument. The first role of the Department of Archaeology was as an agent to repair trust properties in extreme cases of neglect, using the financial resources of the *Guthi Sansthan.*

Another Indian legacy was the relationship between government restoration projects and the Department of Public Works. Repairs were carried out by contractors on the basis of tenders and approved government rates, using the inappropriate rates of new construction. In most cases these activities involved replacing leaking roofs and repairing walls damaged by rising ground dampness. Retention of historical fabric was not a consideration. "Proper" rebuilding was the guiding principle, and the rates for new construction further encouraged rebuilding rather than repair.

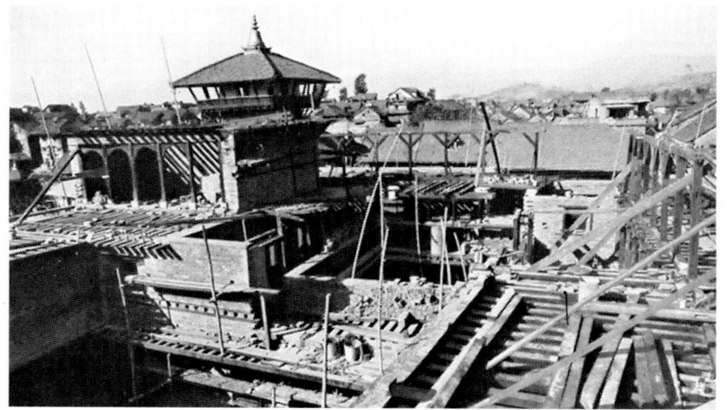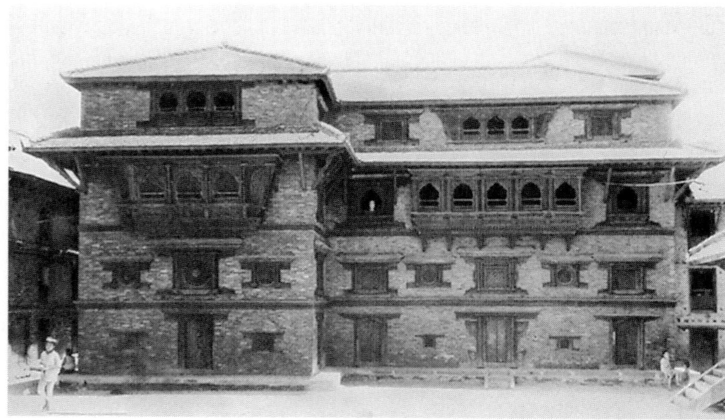

**Pujari Math, Bhaktapur**
*left:* **The entire roof was replaced and the northeastern wing was reconstructed.**
*right:* **Restored principal elevation, 1974**

As with the Archaeological Survey of India, archaeologists—not architects—were entrusted with architectural conservation. John Marshall's *Conservation Manual*[4] was published in 1923 and has been the bible of archaeologists from Lahore to Rangoon and from Kathmandu to Colombo ever since. Marshall stressed the importance of "annual repairs," but the focus of the manual was the conservation of ruins or dead monuments. He specifically says "to abstain as far as possible from any interference with the management or repair of religious buildings."[5] In contrast to India, Nepal's living culture has few ruins, and those are found only in the country's remote west. The Indian and colonial focus on archeological sites thus partially explains the inability of Nepali law to deal with living problems of ownership, encroachment, and modernization. Most significantly, private buildings, then and now, have remained outside the purview of conservation legislation and projects.

## The first bilateral project:
## Restoration of the Pujari Math in Bhaktapur, 1971-1972

An enlightened officer of the German Foreign Service, Heinrich Seemann, had the idea to make the restoration of a historic building the state gift in honor of the wedding of King Birendra Bir Bikram Shah in 1969. The Pujari Math in Bhaktapur, one of the most significant mid-seventeenth century buildings in the country, was chosen. From August 1971 to May 1972 the building was partly reconstructed and restored by a team of four German architects (Auer, Busch, Gutschow, and Kroger) in collaboration with the Department of Archaeology.[6] The building had suffered greatly in the 1934 earthquake; subsequent repairs had led to further decay.

The project revitalized dozens of traditional building techniques, including the production of the veneer bricks unique to these historical buildings. These bricks (Newari *datiapa*, Nepali *telia ita*) taper in section allowing hairline joints on the façade and a thicker layer of mortar behind. A traditional sealant *(silay)*, reproduced based on interviews with elderly masons, was also used on the thin masonry joints for the first and only time in modern practice. Similarly, a traditional roofing formula using flat terracotta tiles to span the rafters and carry the traditional mud and roof tiles was used here and never again. The structure's bulging walls were dismantled, rebuilt with cement mortar, as was the standard practice of all government work, and supervised by *Guthi Sansthan* overseers. Timbers were impregnated with a preservative, Xylamon TR, a modern, imported chemical that eventually proved useless. Rotted timber decorative elements were recarved following extant examples, although figurative carvings were generally not reproduced so as not to compete with surviving originals.



**The Sulima Pagoda**

## Restoration of the Hanuman Dhoka Palace

In 1972. UNESCO established an ambitious training project focus linked to the restoration of the Hanuman Dhoka royal palace complex in Kathmandu. From 1972-1974, portions of the complex around Nasal Chok were repaired and reconstructed with contributions from Japan, France, Italy and the Nepal-Britain Society. From 1975-1978, the Kirtipur and Bhaktapur towers were restored with German support. Finally, the Nautale Darbar, a nine-storied tower, was restored and transformed into a museum in 1980.

The ambitious aim of the project was the structural reinforcement of these large-scale structures *in situ*. The project architect, John Sanday, has explained in his project handbook that there are instances in the consolidation of an old and failing structure in which the use of concrete with all its properties is "indispensable."[7] Reinforced concrete ring beams, bounders, supporting beams, and wall plates were thus introduced to stabilize the structure.

Another innovation was the introduction of roof planking with a double layer of bituminous tar felt under the mud and tiles to increase durability. The introduction of timber planking instead of traditional flat tiles allowed for wider rafter spacing: this practice reduced roof loads and saved costs. This "modern" rafter spacing is common practice even today, having changed the traditional look of the roof overhang. The introduction of planking and tar felt has become general practice for government projects. Unfortunately, the use of unseasoned planking and low-grade tar felt has not made this modern solution particularly effective. Maintenance of the roofs thus remains a mandatory annual exercise regardless of the techniques and materials used.

Among the more important achievements of the project was the installation of new, carved roof struts in the Nasal Chok courtyard for the royal coronation in 1975. Although western conservation norms would have discouraged the production of new iconographic carvings, palace officials considered uncarved elements unacceptable. New loose interpretations of the lost carvings were rendered by local craftsmen, a commission that provided a critical springboard to carry these skills into the future.

## The Bhaktapur Development Project 1974-1986

Architectural conservation played a leading role in this twenty-year integrated urban-renewal project that also included water supply, sewage disposal, pavement, and small-scale industry development. In the first phase, some 170 buildings were repaired or restored. Project work, which generally included roof rebuilding and the introduction of ring-beams for seismic reinforcement, was modeled on the practices of the UNESCO project at Hanuman Dhoka. Some 30 more ambitious restorations included the dismantling and re-erection of buildings, sometimes using historical photographs to reproduce lost elements.

The most spectacular reconstruction was that of the *sattal* (rest house) in the middle of the Taumadhi Square, in 1976. The building was transformed into a café and was the first and most visible adaptive reuse of a historical structure for tourism.[8] In 1977, the single-storied Ram Temple in Bolachen was carefully reconstructed in its previous two-tiered pagoda form, using photographs and surviving building components. A later report stated: "The materials and the craftsmanship employed for the 're-integrated' (the term reconstruction was avoided) part conformed in every respect to historical practice." This emphasis on traditional craftsmanship remains a valid priority today: reconstruction of historical details is a means of supporting craftsmen who turn to other trades when there is not enough work.

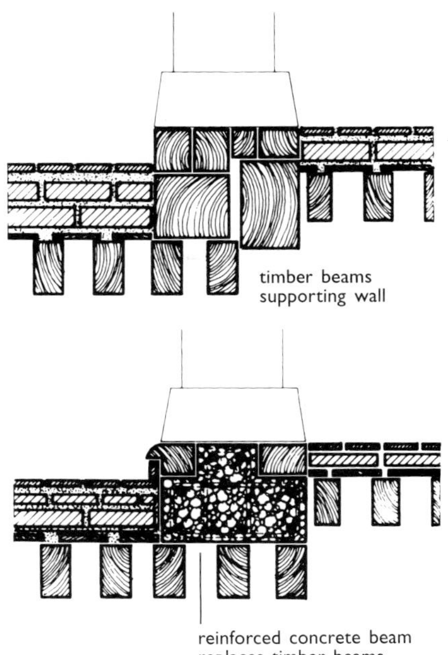



**Restoration of the Hanuman Dhoka Palace, Kathmandu (1972 to 1980)** These illustrations show the "method of replacing defective timber beams by casting a special *in situ* reinforced concrete beam" discussed by John Sanday in *Building Conservation in Nepal*. (Paris: 1978)

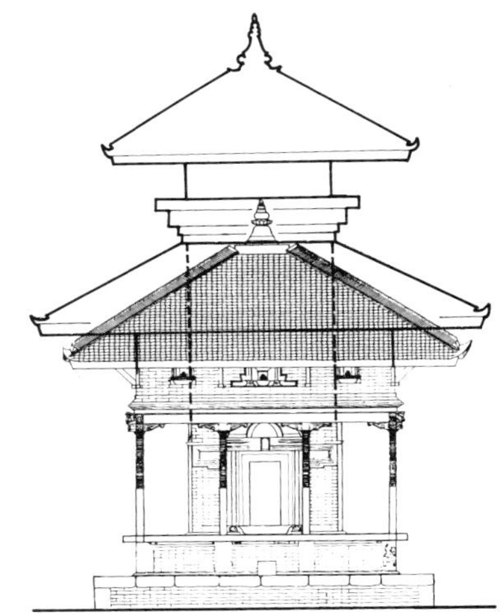

**Reconstruction of the Ram Temple, Bholachen, Bhaktapur** Using photographic evidence and surviving fragments, the original two-tiered shape was reconstructed by the Bhaktapur Development Project in 1977. Drawing by Niels Gutschow on the basis of Y. Parajuli, *Experiencing Preservation and Restoration in a Medieval Town* (Lalitpur: 1986, p. 145)

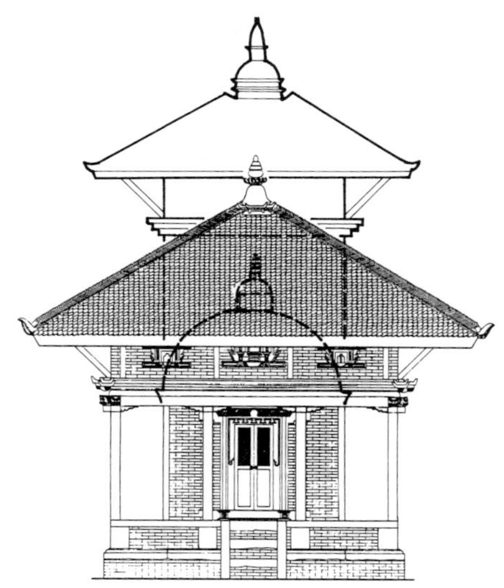

**Manjushri Temple, Nagpokhari, Bhaktapur, 1978**
Circa 1940, the original two-tiered roof on this diminutive pagoda was replaced with a domed structure. When the dome later collapsed, the community wanted to reconstruct the original roof that was known only from memory. Because no other evidence was available, the Bhaktapur Development Project architects designed and implemented a more modest reconstruction of only the lower roof tier.
Drawing by Niels Gutschow based on Y. Parajuli, *Experiencing Preservation and Restoration in a Medieval Town,* Lalitpur: 1986 p. 165

Another reconstruction at Nagpokhari, Bhaktapur documents an interesting compromise between the demands of the local people and international conservation norms regarding the reproduction of lost historical forms. Both roofs of the two-tiered pagoda of Manjusri Temple collapsed in 1940 and were replaced with a domed superstructure. In 1978, after structural damage necessitated repairs to the dome, the neighborhood proposed reconstructing the lost pagoda in its original form. Because historical evidence of the original configuration was limited to local memory, the project architects arrived at a solution to rebuild in "pagoda style," reducing the structure to a single tier with simplified decorative carvings. These gestures reflected their reservations about "faking" a historical structure.

## Department of Archaeology projects in the 1970s

In 1967, the *Guthi Sansthan* and the Department of Archaeology formed a committee, the *Guthi Jirnodhar Tatha Nirman Samiti,* to oversee conservation of architectural heritage. In 1973, it undertook the repair, restoration, and reconstruction of 60 structures in anticipation of the King's coronation. In 1974-75, some 34 monuments were repaired. Only in 1976 did the Department of Archaeology receive its own budget for restoration and repair projects. At the same time it attracted foreign funding to carry out projects. These included the reconstruction of the Mandap at Yashimhkel, Bhaktapur[9] with support from the Netherlands in 1974; the re-roofing of the Balkumari Temple, Panauti with French support in 1976; and the restoration of the Narayanthan Temple, Banepa with Belgian support.

At the same time a multi-disciplinary team from UNESCO led by Eduard F. Sekler, a preservation consultant active in Nepal since 1964, prepared the *Master Plan for the Conservation of the Cultural Heritage in the Kathmandu Valley.*[10] At its Cairo meeting in 1979, the World Heritage Committee added a collective listing consisting of seven sites in the Kathmandu Valley to the List of World Heritage Sites. The submission was prepared by W. Brown Morton III. Nepal subsequently received UNESCO support for the stabilization of Svayambhunath, one of the seven sites, after a devastating landslide in 1981. UNESCO also funded the rebuilding of collapsed roofs of the Visvanath Temple, Patan Darbar Square, in 1991 and the re-roofing of the adjacent Taleju Temple in 1996.

The early inclusion of the Kathmandu Valley on the List of World Heritage Sites was laudable. Differences between local and international norms and expectations, however, have been problematic ever since. An expert review mission organzied by UNESCO in 1993 proposed inclusion of the Kathmandu Valley sites on the list of *World Heritage in Danger.*

## Reconstruction of the Cyasilin Mandap in Bhaktapur, 1987-1990[11]

The reconstruction of the eight-cornered pavilion on Bhaktapur Darbar Square was a state gift from Germany to the people of Nepal on the occasion of Chancellor Helmut Kohl's 1987 visit. Consulting architects Gutschow and Hagmüller selected this project to demonstrate how the reconstruction of a lost historical structure could be used to recapture qualities of urban space.

The pavilion had stood in the center of the Bhaktapur Darbar Square, once a rich ensemble of temples and palaces, many of which disappeared because of the 1934 earthquake. The reconstruction of the pavilion incorporated earthquake-

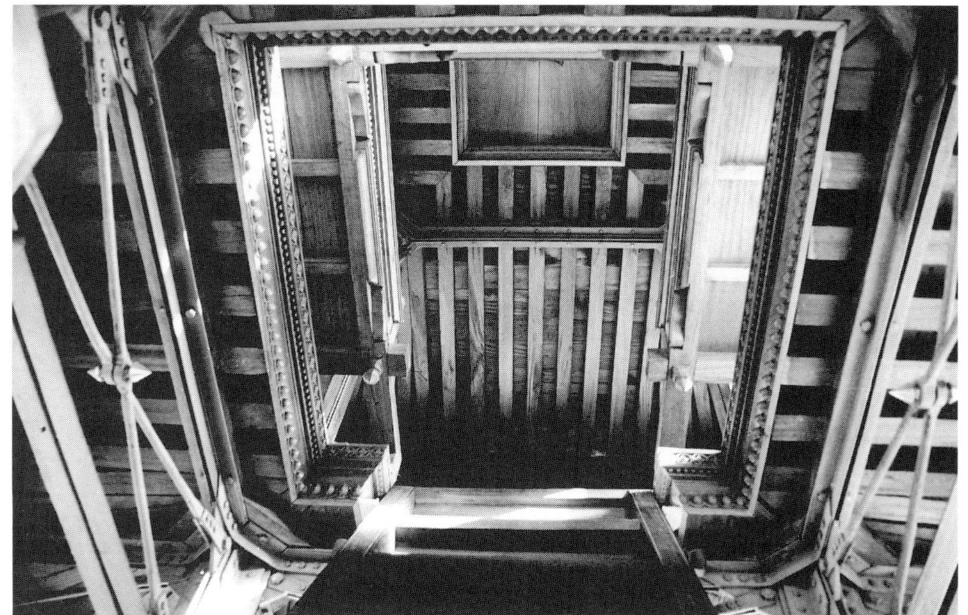

Details of the Cyasilin Mandap,
Bhaktapur, reconstructed 1987-1990
Traditional timber framing and new steel
members are juxtaposed in the ceiling
of the pavilion's open ground floor.

strengthening measures to protect the top-heavy building from another quake. This
led to the decision to introduce a rigid steel frame into the reconstructed historical
building. The partially visible frame offended some Nepali colleagues in its
unapologetic demonstration of western technology in an eastern building.

However, in the handling of another design question, that of replacement
carvings, the architects followed the wishes of the craftsmen and people of Bhaktapur.
While a western approach to new elements would require a visible indication of old
and new, here new figurative carvings were commissioned and blended into the
historical elements. It was the first time new figurative carvings were intentionally
commissioned by a bilateral project to complete a building's ambitious iconographic
and narrative program. This was despite notable gaps in the historical evidence that
made some of the new carvings conjectural.

Meanwhile, the Department of Archaeology was also carving replacement
elements for its numerous temple repair projects, such as the 1976 restoration of Uma
Maheshvar Temple at Patan's Kulima Square. Foreign conservationists tended to
disregard these practices—there were two schools of thought regarding replacement
carvings and no dialogue between them. The Department of Archaeology projects
demonstrated continuity in design and craftsmanship, even if quality was highly
variable. Foreign conservation professionals, on the other hand, felt inhibited from
following the local practice of replacing carvings, often inserting plain substitutes in
their efforts to conform with international norms.

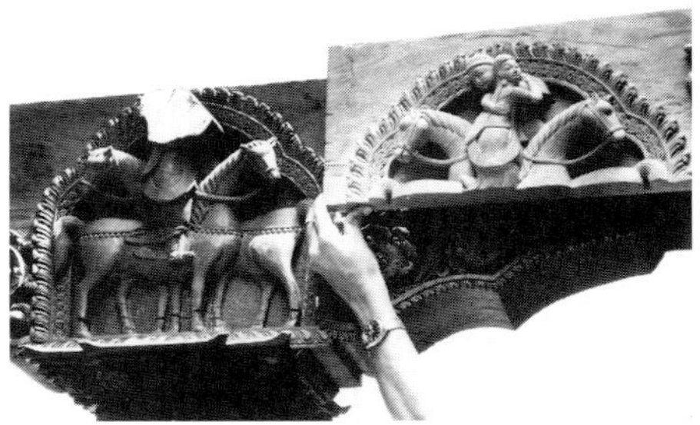

Details of the Cyasilin Mandap original
and replacement pavilion carvings. The
design of lost features, such as these
figures on horseback, was left to the
artistic and narrative abilities of the
carvers, who produced eight different
versions.

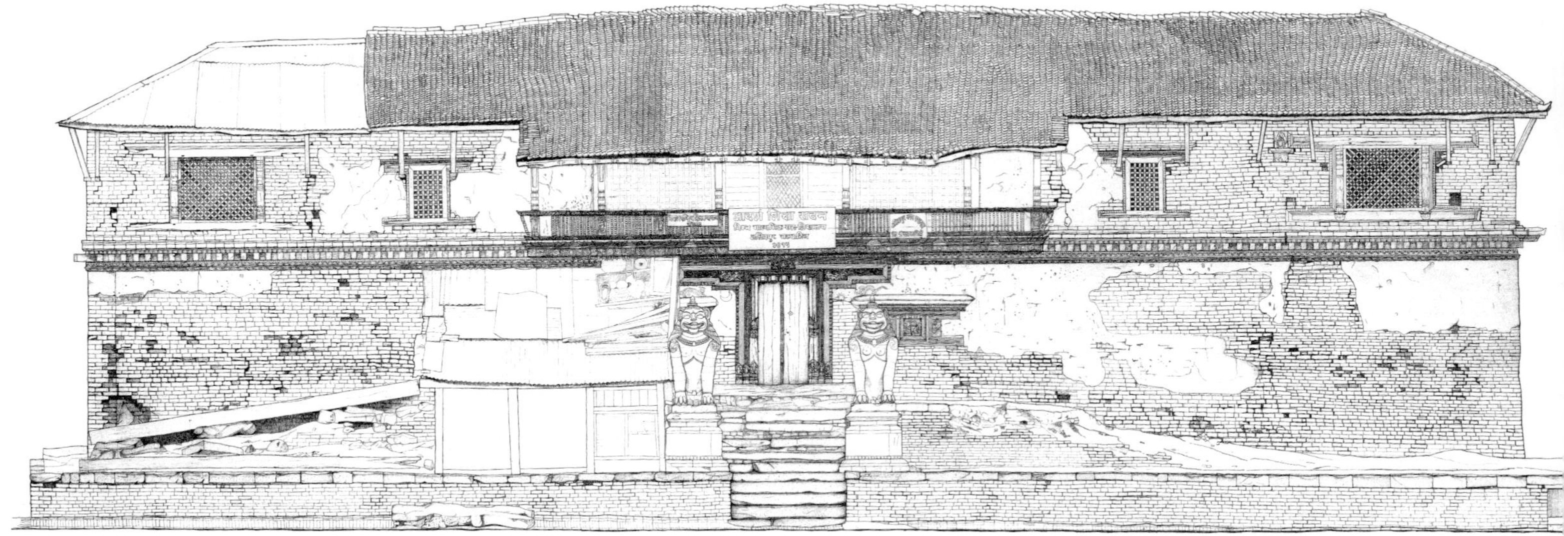

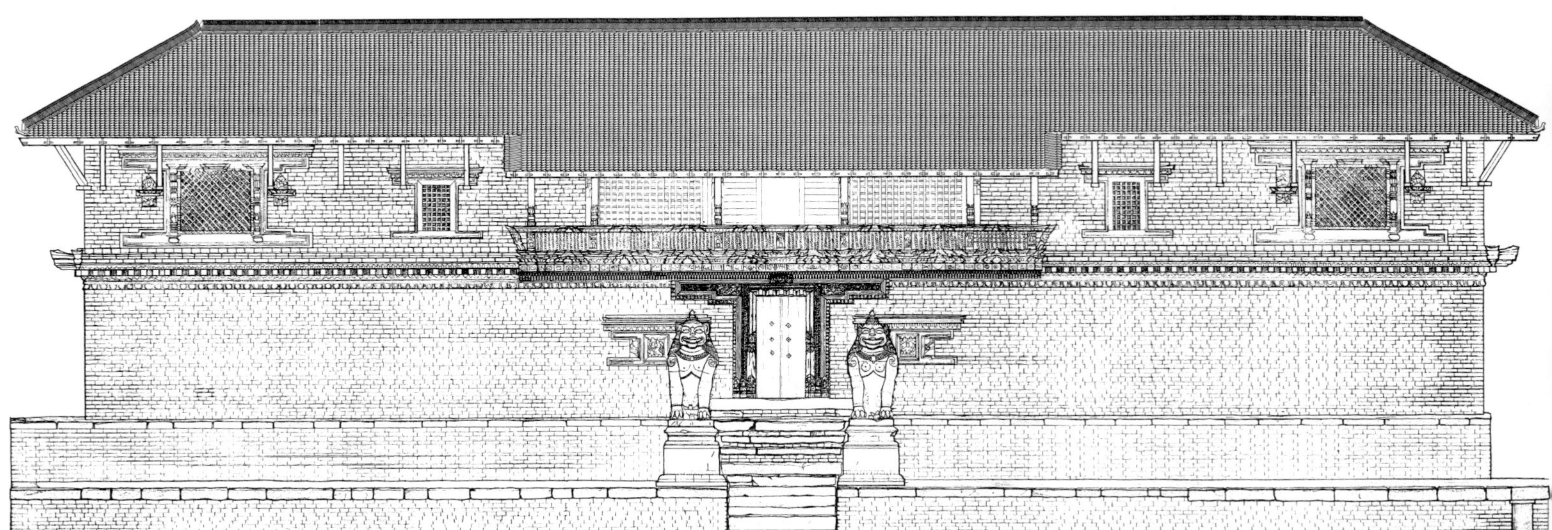

Ibaha Bahi, Patan, principal east
elevation before and after restoration,
from *The Royal Buildings and Buddhist
Monasteries of Nepal*, Nippon Institute
of Technology, 1985



The Sulima Pagoda

## New foreign initiatives in the 1990s

The 1990s saw the advent of several new bilateral and international efforts that prompted a review of conservation strategies in general. With Nepali-French cooperation a number of historical *pati*, small rest houses for pilgrims and neighborhood use, were dismantled and re-erected in Panauti as part of the comprehensive redevelopment of the small town from 1993-1996. This effort was modeled on the Bhaktapur preservation approach some ten years earlier, which favored rebuilding over repairs. The replacement of the twelfth-century Indreshvara Temple roofs and the subsequent rehabilitation of all structures within the temple compound, another project component, constituted a major contribution appropriate to the historical significance of this temple complex.

From 1990 to 1995, Japan's Nippon Institute of Technology undertook the first restoration of a Buddhist monastic building, Ibaha Bahi. Architects Katsuhiko Watanabe, Jun Hatano, and Takayuki Kurotsu[12] dismantled the ruined building after the most detailed documentation ever done in Nepal. The reconstruction included numerous thoughtful approaches to timber conservation, most notably hybrid solutions mixing Nepali and Japanese techniques of timber repair, which are discussed later in *Techniques in Architectural Preservation in Nepal*. These examples suggest that the conservation philosophy of the donor country leaves an indelible stamp on historical buildings.

The Austrian-funded restoration of a royal palace in Patan (1983-1997) and its adaptation into a museum has similarly left its mark, in this case testament to an individual design philosophy.[13] Viennese architect Götz Hagmüller expanded the project beyond the narrow confines of a conservation exercise to a more ambitious design challenge, a state-of-the-art museum synthesizing eclectic, contemporary, and traditional features. This fusion of Newari and Viennese ideas, a bold interpretation of a historic building, will have a lasting impact on conservation practice in Nepal and is discussed in several contributions in this volume.

In 1992 a German project, the Patan Conservation and Development Program, began with the ambitious goal of integrating conservation planning within a comprehensive urban development plan. Architects Gutschow, Hagmüller, and Theophile identified pilot projects and initiated the first comprehensive inventory of monuments of national and local importance, carried out in collaboration with the Department of Archaeology. Among 12 conservation and repair projects implemented, a notable achievement was the design of seismic strengthening measures in timber for a Buddhist *agamchen* (shrine) at Vambaha in 1993. The lost tower of this Buddhist monument was also reconstructed at the same time on the basis of photographic evidence.


## The Kathmandu Valley Preservation Trust

The Kathmandu Valley Preservation Trust (KVPT), based in the U.S.A. and founded in 1991, is the first international charity dedicated exclusively to safeguarding Nepal's architectural heritage. During the past decade, the Trust has built expertise in repair, stabilization, and documentation techniques through a dozen building conservation projects in the Patan Darbar World Heritage Site. The project framework was novel: with projects fully funded by private donors, they could be executed on a turn-key basis that avoided the government tender process. This classically American private-sector emphasis has enabled the Trust to develop a fundraising base in Nepal. Projects are typically funded through matching local and international sources, a promising direction for future endeavors.

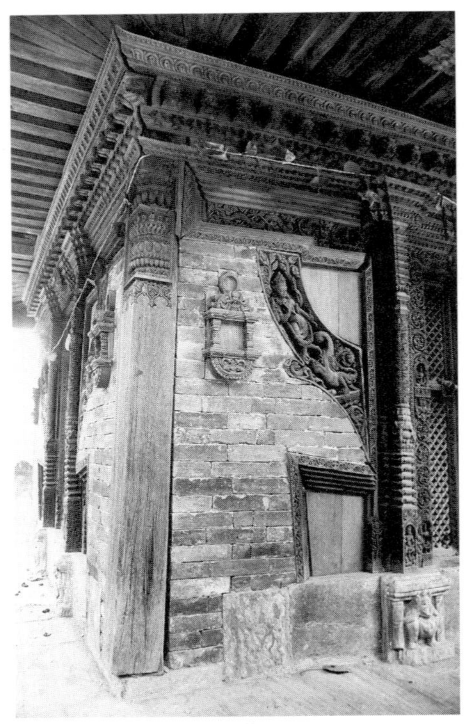

**Detail of Radha Krishna Temple, Patan
Certain new panels and niches were left
plain as there was no historical evidence
of the lost figurative carvings.
Restored by the Kathmandu Valley
Preservation Trust, 1991-1992**

The first Trust project, the restoration of a pagoda at Kvalakhu Square in Patan, included seismic strengthening measures. Trust architects Theophile and Ranjitkar identified vertical structural discontinuities and top-heaviness as structural deficiencies typical of the pagoda structure. In this case, the design of a reinforced timber ring[14] beam to strengthen existing timber elements was introduced to improve earthquake performance.

In 1992, the restoration of the three-tiered Radha Krishna Temple at Svatha Square offered another test case to build experience in the design of seismic reinforcements. Other preservation challenges included the design of replacement carvings and the maintenance of historical patina. The architects decided to recarve some but not all of the lost decorative and figurative elements. Weighing religious, aesthetic, and philosophical considerations, the architects wrote that although "the communities who continue to use these temples...would of course always demand a restoration of religious figures which can be seen and worshipped, we in some cases decided to follow Article 9 of the Charter of Venice that demands 'to stop at the point where conjecture begins'."[15]

With more than a decade of experience, the Trust has built up a Nepali team of private-sector professionals skilled in documentation, building repair, fundraising, and publicity. It is developing the Nepal Architecture Archive to assemble materials related to architecture history and conservation practice for scholars, students, and practitioners.

## Technology: East meets West

The consequences of importing modern structural solutions should be closely examined. Traditionally, damaged buildings were dismantled and rebuilt from the ground up, but western technologies allow the *in situ* consolidation of structures using reinforced concrete and steel. We know little, however, about how modern structural materials will ultimately affect historical fabric.

Already, certain modern improvements, such as the use of timber planking in roof cover, can be mentioned for negative effects on the visual character of the rebuilt roofs' wider rafter spacing. Certainly, new technologies and materials should still be considered, but authentic building practice must not be forgotten. In some cases one might abstain from modern interventions in order to retain the "authenticity" of traditional techniques. Returning to the use of mud mortar after decades of modern cement mortar in conservation projects is one example.

In September 1994, a training workshop organized and funded by the UNESCO/Japanese Trust Fund proposed the use of stainless steel "split-ring connectors"[16] developed by the British Timber Research and Development Association. Such devices would allow the reuse of damaged rafters and joists to maximize retention of original fabric. Such *in situ* splicing of damaged timber members, however, has never been the practice of local carpenters, who would simply replace them.

If local building practice is itself a consideration of a monument's authenticity, then such a technical solution favors material values, *i.e.* building fabric, over cultural values. To save authentic material with an expensive, imported technology would change traditional carpentry and seems a western imposition.

# Current local practice

A remarkable change occurred in the Nepali preservation scene in 1996, when the Bhaktapur Municipality began to charge visitors an entrance fee. This measure suddenly produced considerable funds to help maintain and preserve the city's rich architectural heritage. The achievements of the Bhaktapur Development Project were expanded upon, suggesting that it takes a decade or two for certain ideas to arrive and bear fruit. The Bhaktapur Municipality repaved the main roads in brick, rebuilt the roofs of the most prominent Bhairav and Nyatapvala pagodas, and repaired the Yaksheshvara Temple at Darbar Square in 1999. The Municipality also repaired the Dvarikanath Temple on Darbar Square in 2000, just 21 years after the Bhaktapur Development Project had renovated it. The overseers of the municipality still follow the repair techniques (including wide rafter spacing) developed in 1974, but time will probably allow the introduction of more sophisticated solutions.

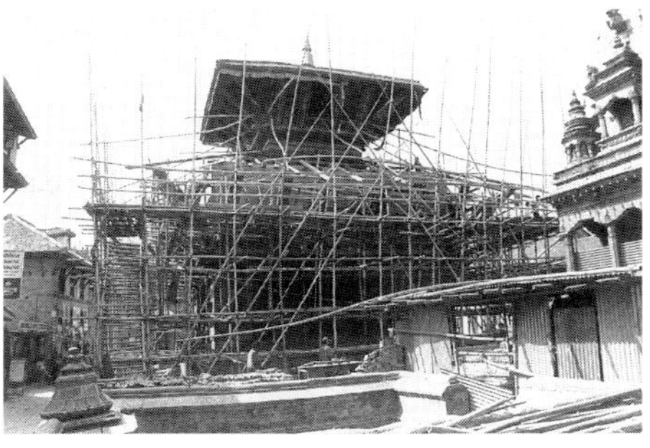

**Yaksheshvara Temple, Bhaktapur Darbar Square: Restoration by the Bhaktapur Municipality, 1999**

The availability of funds allows the Municipality to act, while the Department of Archaeology, theoretically the lead government agency, remains an observer. The Kathmandu Municipality has also become more active, although hundreds of threatened structures remain unattended. For example, the lower roof of the monumental Tripureshvara pagoda in Kathmandu collapsed in August 1997, but repair plans are yet to be implemented.

The model practices in Bhaktapur deserve more detailed discussion. In 1997-98, the Municipality achieved the ambitious rehabilitation of Siddha Pokhari, a man-made tank from the sixteenth century with many later interventions. For more than a generation the tank, nearly dry, had been abandoned except for ritual use during *Indrajatra* (September) and *Dasain* (October). The rehabilitaton recaptured the tank's original splendor.

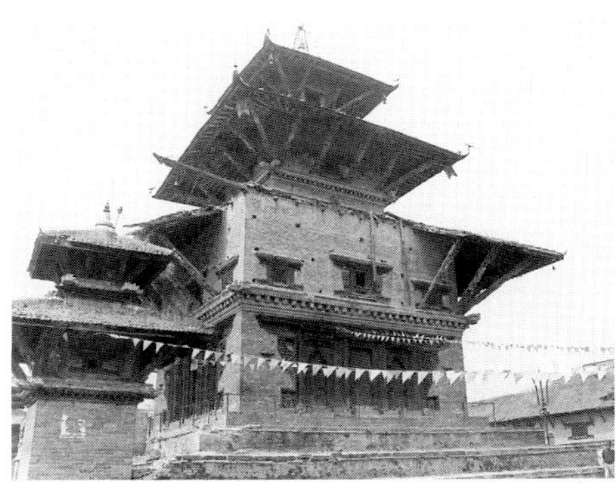

**Tripureshvara Temple, Kathmandu The lower roof of this monumental nineteenth-century structure collapsed in 1997. Repairs to this important temple were not completed until 2002.**

The early nineteenth-century eastern gateway was dismantled and fully reconstructed without using surviving historical fragments and by replacing some of the original Mughal detailing with Newar designs. While the nineteenth-century baluster columns typical of Mughal and colonial India were faithfully reproduced for the reconstruction, the arched panels between the columns were replaced with Newar-style brackets following seventeenth-century designs. This replacement of Indian features with local design solutions is intentional and suggests that the local canon is considered more politically correct even if ahistorical.

Another project, the reconstruction of a Ganesh shrine at Lalachen Square, is an interesting example of local approaches to reconstruction and replacement of lost carvings. This two-tiered pagoda survived the 1934 earthquake, but collapsed in 1965. Only the ground floor and lower roof were rebuilt, using the struts that formerly supported the upper roof. In 1998, the ward chairman secured funding from the municipality to reconstruct the original two-tiered design prepared by B.R. Koju.

The surviving struts depicting the protective *Ashtamatrika* (mother goddesses) were then moved back to support the upper roof. As not all survived, several missing struts were carved by Gopal Krishna Silpakar from neighboring Yachen Square. Silpakar, who comes from a long line of carvers, had no difficulty in rendering the missing mother goddesses, who are known to everybody in Bhaktapur. He received a modest lump sum payment for each strut and produced satisfactory results. A limited budget forced the project to leave the new lower roof struts uncarved.

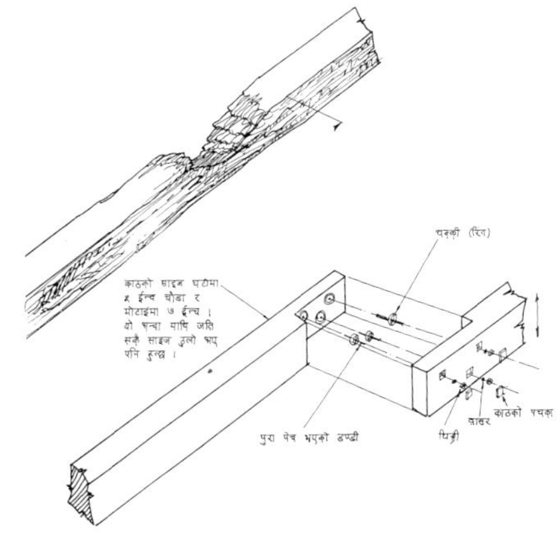

**Split-ring connectors for the repair of damaged rafters and joists D. Michelmore, *Training Workshop*, Kathmandu 1994 (not published)**

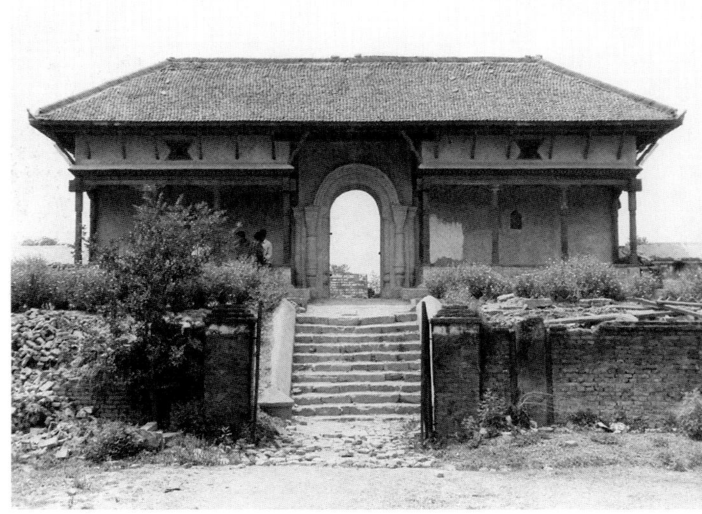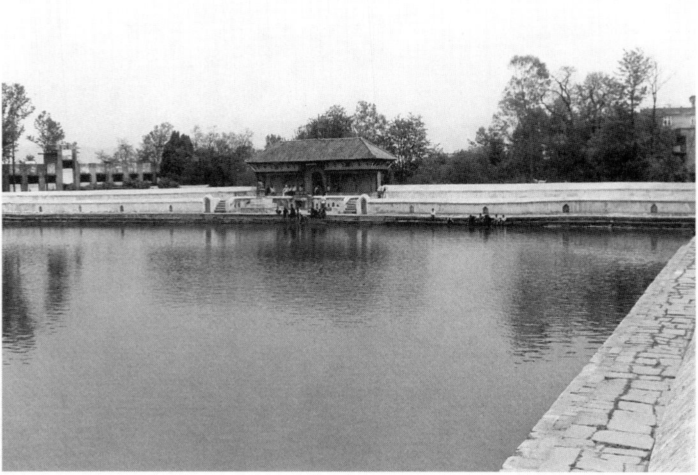

**Siddha Pokhari, Bhaktapur**
This medieval tank, which had been reshaped in the early 1800s, fell into disrepair. The tank, nearly dry, was only used for ritual purposes twice a year. The revitalization of the tank (1996-1997) by the Bhaktapur Municipality brought water to the neglected monument; much of the historical fabric was reconstructed.

The organization of the restoration workforce notably broke from tradition in order to save money. The designer, carpenters, and masons, all members of the farmer caste, were chosen over professional, hereditary carpenters *(Silpakar)*, and masons *(Awal)* because their rates were lower. This affected the quality of building because the farmers lacked the expertise of those who have benefited from the passing down of skills from generation to generation.

The reconstruction also introduced new cornice bricks above the ground floor that did not match historical prototypes. Traditionally such elements were custom

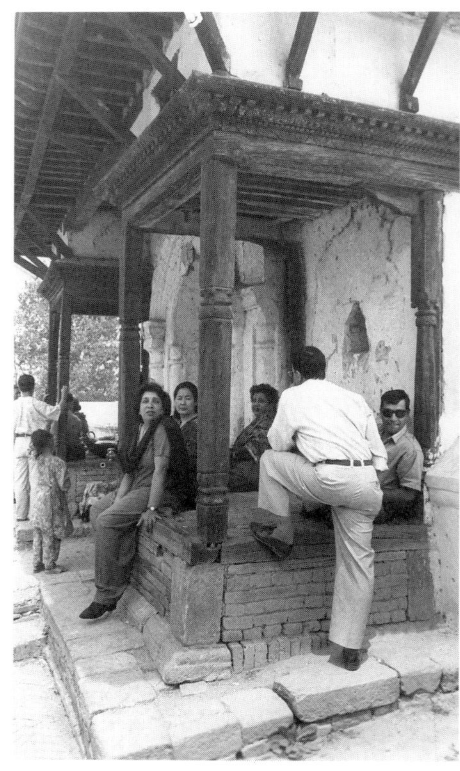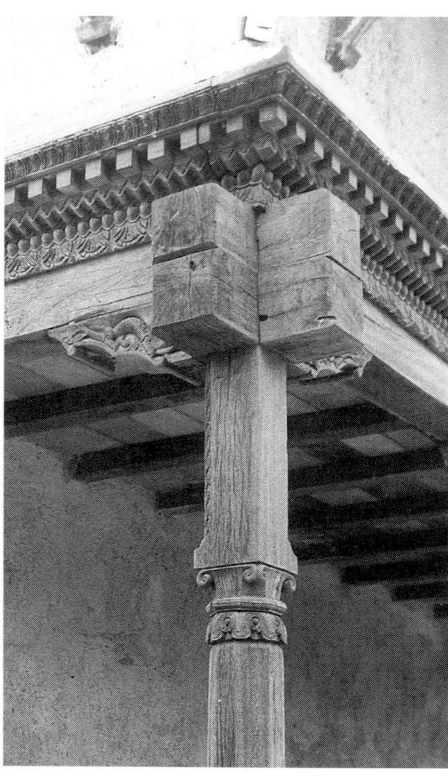

**Siddha Pokhari eastern gate**
The rebuilt gate replicates the historical pillar design but introduces a traditional carved bracket instead of replacing the lost arched panels, typical of Anglo-Indian influence in the early nineteenth century.

made for a particular building, but in this case the project made use of readily available stock. Since 1993, decorative bricks of various designs have been mass-produced for commercial projects; anyone in a hurry must rely on those bricks that are in stock. This commercial influence on design, like the use of less expensive tradesmen, demonstrates how architectural restoration has evolved from a votive offering into a competitive business.

## Design control within the Bhaktapur World Heritage Site

Although local regulations to control the height and style of new structures within the historic core area were proposed by the Bhaktapur Development Project in 1975, little attention was paid to this western notion of townscape preservation. The scene began to change after the advent of democracy in 1990, when the absolute majority of the Nepal Workers and Peasants Party in Bhaktapur gave local authorities more power. In 1996, awareness of the city's tourism potential encouraged the Municipality to enforce strict building bylaws within the World Heritage Site, the boundaries of which were even extended in 1997.

In 1997, Samanta Raj Sakya of Inacva, Bhaktapur, started to rebuild his house but the ward chairman forced him to apply for a building permit. Not only did he have to pay a considerable sum for the permit, he was also forced to pay for the municipal photographer to document the historical building and for the muncipal overseer to design the new building. The owner's vision included large windows, a cantilevered second floor, increased ceiling heights, and an additional floor, but he was forced to abide by rules that could not accommodate any of these features.

Similarly, when the house next to the Nyatapvala pagoda was rebuilt in 1998, the owner was forced to hide the reinforced concrete frame with traditional brick veneer. In recent years a new pseudo-Newar style has emerged and dresses every new concrete frame structure with a variety of vaguely traditional details. This is especially true for the new shopping arcades in and around the Darbar Square, which have been built by affluent individuals to expand their tourist trade.

In most cases, these developments also reflect changes in social topography. Business people acquire properties from less affluent families in these prime areas and replace ancestral homes with commercial structures. In the summer of 2000, five such structures stood in the Darbar Square area and, although pleasant to the tourist's eye, have dramatically compromised the historical authenticity of the neighborhood.

In 1998, *Visit Nepal Year*, the Municipality and local politicians decided to construct new city gates at major access points to the town. Although primarily an urban beautification project, the new gates loosely recall the city's early fortifications, of which only one gate survives. The new gates are tourist attractions of sorts with historic connotations, but different from any precedent in proportion, style, and scale.

These gates, like the houses discussed above, demonstrate how a new architectural style related to tourism impacts the historic city. Do these houses preserve the notion of a historic environment? The visual continuity of the revivalist style may be preferred to the more modern infill projects of previous years, but compromises in historical detail, loss of authentic building fabric, and the relocation of families from their ancestral homes must be noted. The frightening uniformity of

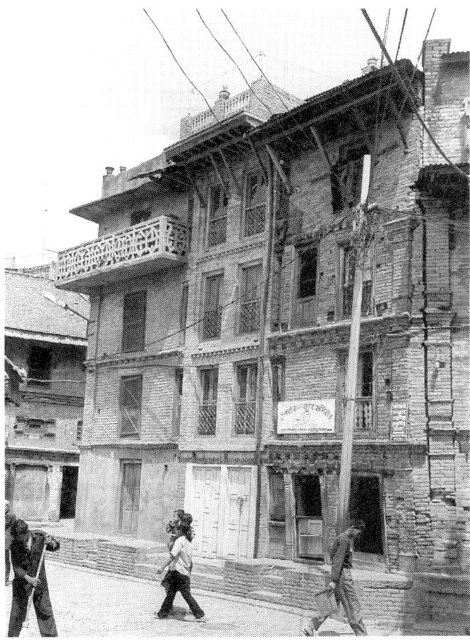

New house in Bhaktapur's extended World Heritage Site, Inacva Square, built in 1998; the owner had to abide by municipality guidelines that forced him to match the eavesline of the neighboring buildings and follow the proportions of historical windows.

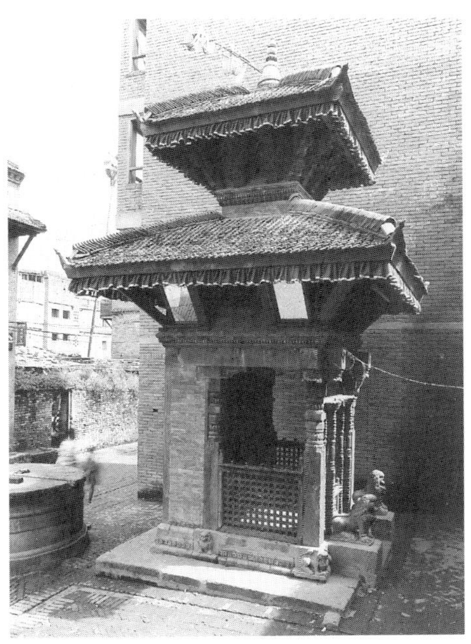

The Ganesh Temple at Lalachen Square reconstructed by the Bhaktapur Municipality in 1999

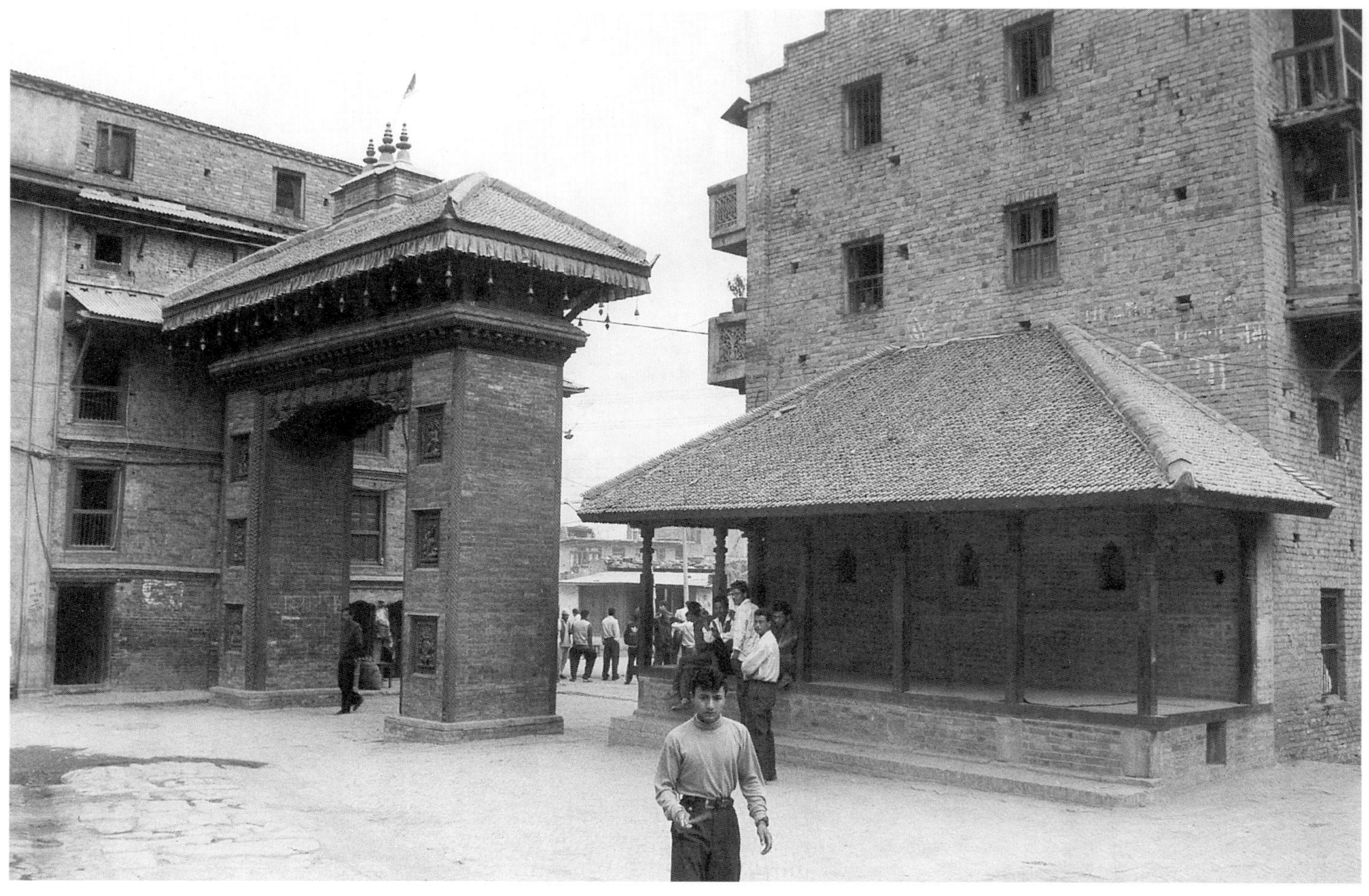

**Byasi, Bhaktapur**
The *pati* (resthouse) on the right was restored in 1997. The gate on the left was built in Kathmandu for *Visit Nepal Year 1998*. It was later dismantled and re-erected in Bhaktapur as part of the municipality's program to place monumental gates at all major access lanes leading into the city.

the new "traditional" façades also contrasts with the richness of Bhaktapur's vernacular, suggesting that strict guidelines are no panacea for historic town preservation. The story of Bhaktapur is representative of similar developments in the centers of Kathmandu and Patan, also World Heritage Sites where tourism offers an economic incentive to preserve, but is also inseparable from larger social and functional changes.

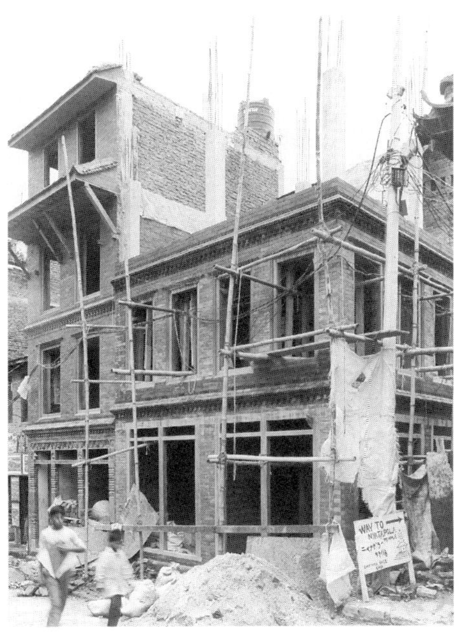

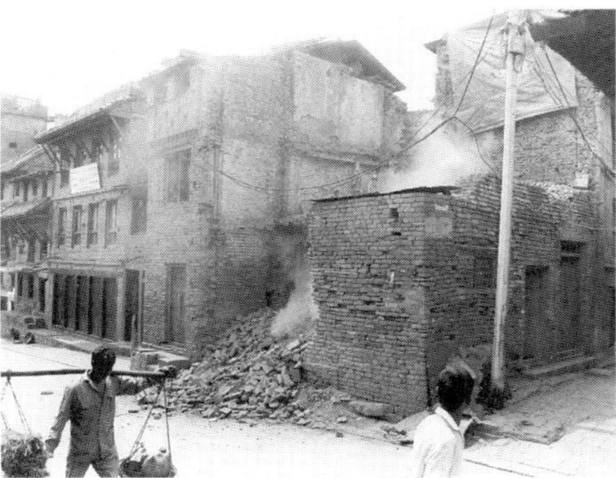

Sakotha, Bhaktapur
Demolition and new construction of two houses in Bhaktapur within the World Heritage Site, 1999. A pseudo-historic facade with nineteenth century window proportions and projecting eaves in front of a reinforced concrete structure are stipulated by the Municipality.

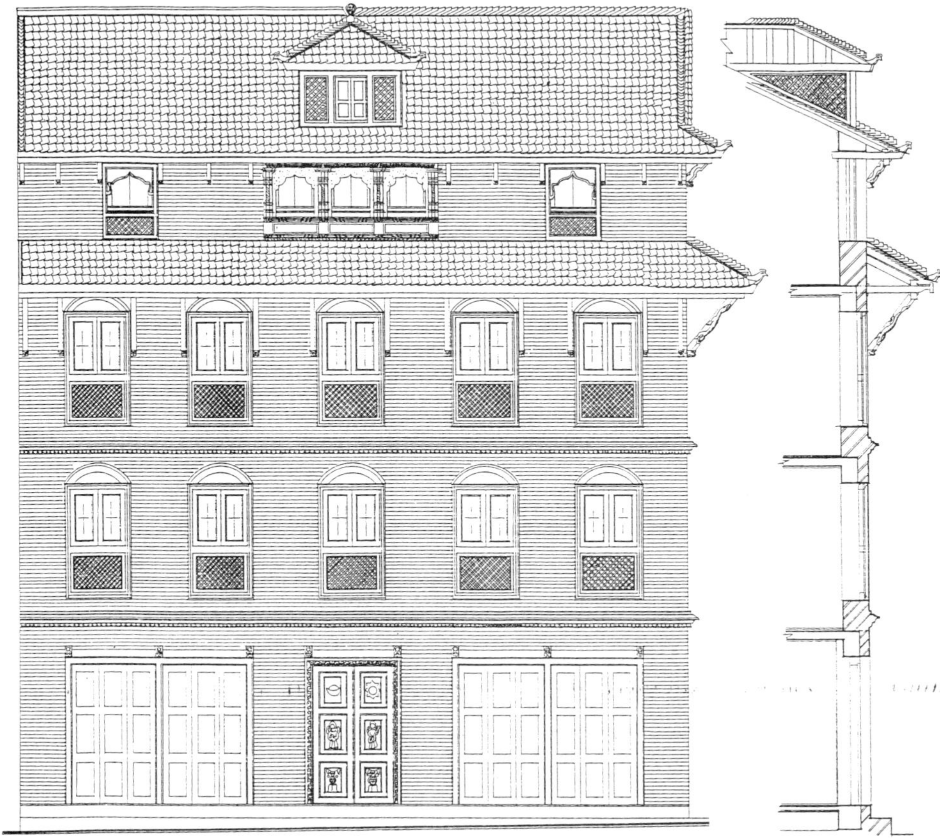

Main façade for a new house at Taumadhi Square, Bhaktapur, within the World Heritage Site; designed by Gopal Prajapati in 1998 and completed in 2000

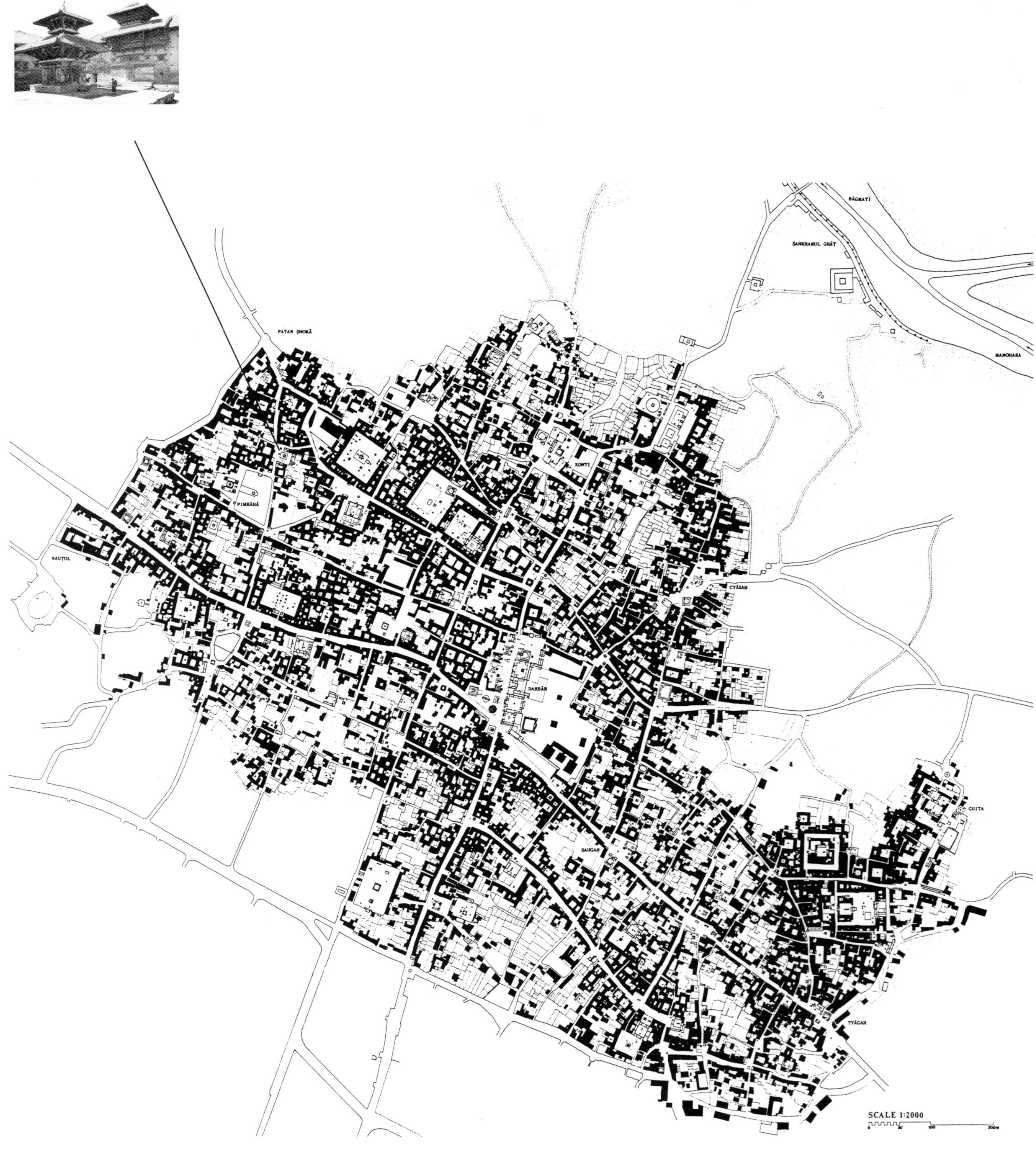



Map of historic settlement, Patan,
showing the location of Sulima Temple
Niels Gutschow, 1994



**The Sulima Pagoda**

# THE SULIMA TEMPLE

## The Conservation Project

Erich Theophile and Rohit Ranjitkar

## Background

The Sulima Temple is a two-tiered shrine to Ratneshvara Mahadev, a form of the Hindu god Shiva, housing a stone *linga* in its sanctuary. The temple is notable for its surviving, original timber wall carvings including niches, doors, windows, and cornices. These can be dated stylistically to at least the fourteenth century. Until three decades ago, the building preserved numerous roof struts of similar age and quality. These were stolen in the 1970s but, fortunately, were documented by photographs and written descriptions. The correspondence of the surviving carvings with the scale of the masonry structure suggests that the present overall building configuration is original. The combination of intact elements and documented lost struts makes for a fairly complete picture of the early building. Only a handful of buildings in Nepal preserve so much early carving in this complete an assembly.

The temple stands in the center of a small square in the northwest precinct of the historic urban core. The city quarter, called Sulima, although one of the most historical pockets of Patan, is not a protected monument zone. None of its buildings, which date from fourteenth to nineteenth centuries, are listed as municipal or national monuments. The Patan Darbar World Heritage Site lies some ten blocks away, protecting a complex of royal structures, some with early foundations, but most dating to the later expansion of the city in the seventeenth and eighteenth centuries. In addition to the Sulima Temple, the other structures defining the square have been studied in detail and are discussed in the following section about Sulima Square.

Dilapidated since 1980, the temple's rehabilitation had been discussed since 1992, when the entire square was proposed as an additional monument zone by the authors. This was in the context of the Patan Conservation and Development Program, an initiative funded by German Technical Cooperation. In 1994, a local repair initiative erected scaffolding and even started to carve replacement elements, but interest dwindled and work stopped. The 1994 cost estimate prepared by a local overseer proposed replacement of all the time-worn carving with new carvings.

Finally, in 1996, the Kathmandu Valley Preservation Trust negotiated with the temple's *guthi*, neighbors, the Patan Municipality, and the German Patan Program to combine efforts. The principal goal, as identified by the Trust at the time, was to document the extraordinary historical woodwork and conserve it to the highest possible standards. A generous pledge by Himalayan Bank Limited, Nepal, was the first step in funding the project. This contribution from a private corporation was a critical precedent and augmented local and municipal support. The significance of this combination of donors and the historic value of the monument was the justification for a matching grant by the Robert W. Wilson Challenge to Conserve our Heritage program, under the auspices of the World Monuments Fund.

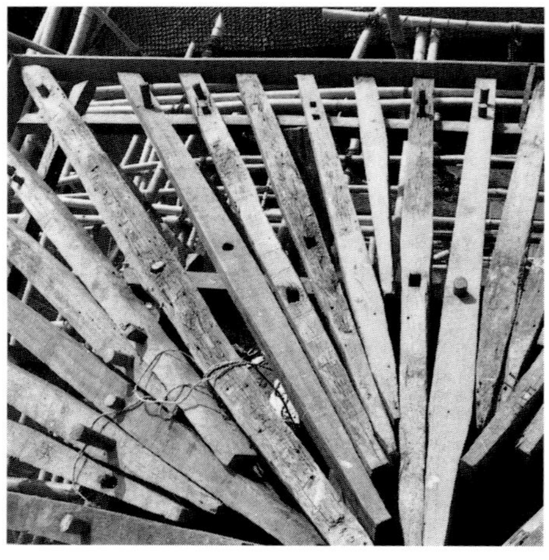

**Radha Krishna Temple rafter assembly restored in 1958**
This photograph, taken during the 1992 restoration, shows a good example of how closely the rafters were traditionally spaced. Too often, pagoda roofs have been rebuilt in haste and with low quality materials and techniques, compromising the quality of the timber joinery.

## Recipe for restoration

The repair and restoration of the Sulima Temple presented challenges similar to those the Trust faced in other projects during the past decade. Typical problems include fragile roof cover, insensitive earlier repairs, art theft, and damage from the monsoon rains.

The massive roofs of the Nepali pagoda are the most vulnerable feature of the traditional construction. The traditional roof cover consists of a fragile terracotta tile laid on a mud bed without fasteners, and is easily susceptible to movement and breakage. Subsequent leaks commonly cause deterioration of the timber roof structure below. At the Sulima Temple this cycle of damage had resulted in the partial collapse of the roof structure. The necessary rebuilding of the roofs followed the historical configuration precisely while introducing new invisible moisture barriers and strengthening measures, which are discussed below under seismic issues. In addition, the mud bed was treated with a herbicide to inhibit weed growth. Old tiles were reused wherever possible because new tiles are of inferior quality.

The masonry wall structure is typically much more durable. Significant damage was found only in those areas just below the damaged roof. Repairs to the damaged masonry (*e.g.* veneer brick, decorative terracotta elements, and tile and stone pavement) replaced only structurally damaged or lost elements. Newer layers of cement pointing, a common and damaging "beautification" techniques of recent decades, were removed.

While the structural timber of the roofs was universally damaged, the woodcarvings were largely intact and in good condition. Documentation, study, repair, and careful *in situ* cleaning of all historical timber carvings were the first priorities of the restoration program. Simple and conservative cleaning methods using water and soft brushes proved effective in all cases. Modern preservative treatments were not used as our experiments have shown their penetration to be minimal in the resilient sal hardwood used for carvings in the Kathmandu Valley. Small decorative elements had broken off in many places. Repairs were undertaken to replace these fragments while trying to maintain as much of the adjacent historical fabric as possible.

## Tricky questions

Several restoration design questions unique to this building merited special consideration. The temple preserved a significant nineteenth-century intervention, the refacing of the upper wall levels in common brick covered with whitewashed mud plaster. This substitution for the historical veneer brick surface is a common feature of nineteenth-century renovations, symbolic of the newly established Gorkha dynasty's efforts to leave its mark on the monuments of the Valley. Here at Sulima the royal fashion trickled down to a local renovation, most likely a rebuilding after a major earthquake in 1832.

A "period restoration" would reface these walls with the appropriate veneer brick. This is, for example, common practice in recent restoration projects by the Department of Archaeology. Here we considered the retention of another historical layer not only as an important demonstration for local practice, but also because the brightness of the plaster much improved the visibility of the upper level woodcarvings. Shadows from the deep roof overhang were brightened by the whitewash, and one could actually *see* the carved detail from the plinth below.

Another question arose regarding the detailing of the rebuilt roof cover. The lost, historical solution of 5 x 10-inch terracotta tiles bridging closely spaced rafters

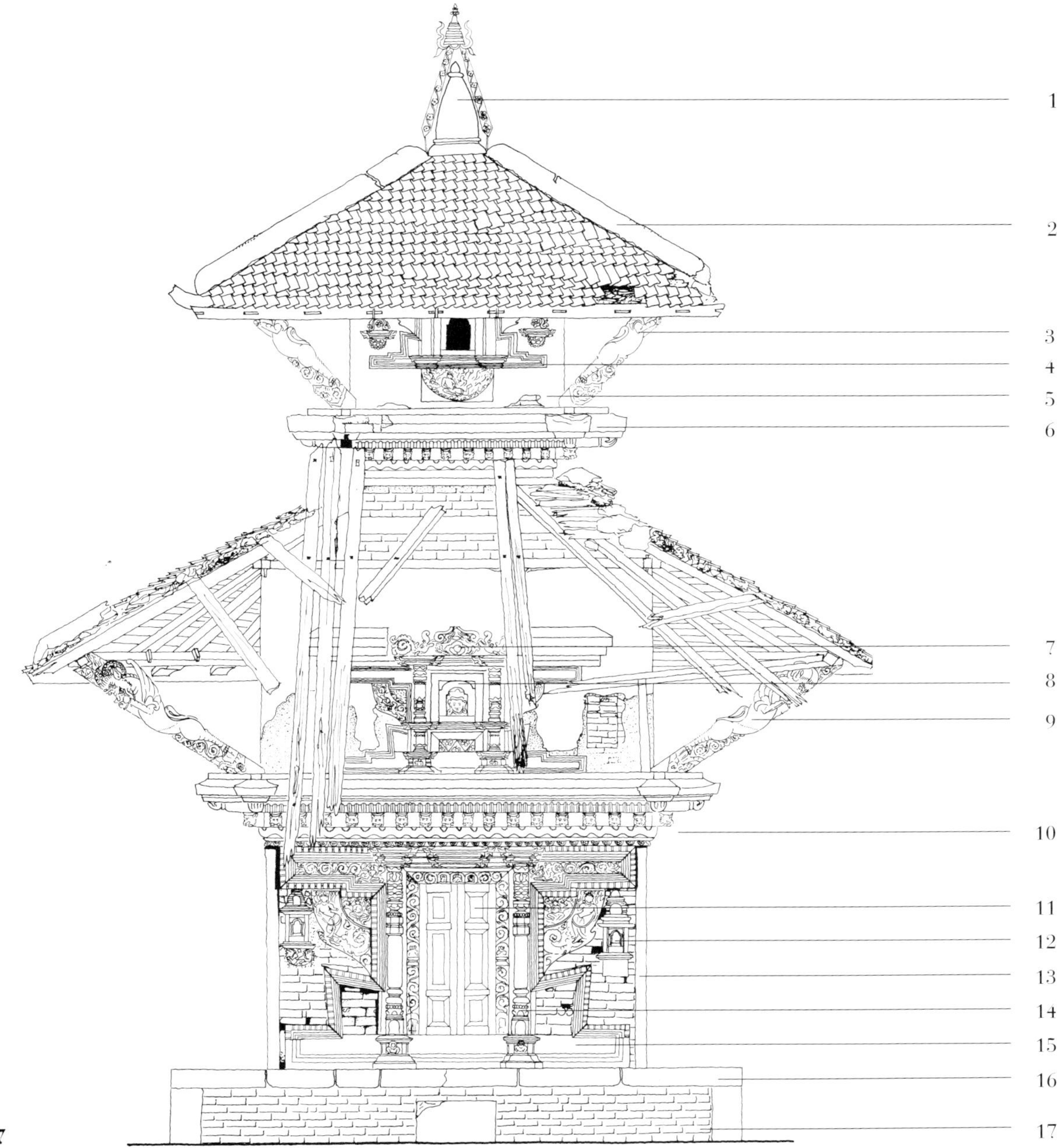

West elevation:
existing condition
Drawing by Asharam
Twayna and
Gyanendra Joshi, 1997



1 Gilt copper pinnacle replaced by plaster copy in 1974, historical decorative surround survives.
2 Roof cover: terracotta roof tiles, mud bed, and underlying pine planking extensively damaged: stacked ridge tiles are covered with lime *surkhi* plaster.
3 Roof struts: two corner struts are fourteenth-century originals, two are nineteenth-century replacements. Six of the eight regular struts were stolen in the 1970s; the two surviving struts are in fragile condition and are in storage.
4 Decorative timber carving: all four original fourteenth-century windows are in good condition. Three of the eight flanking niches were stolen in the 1970s.

5 Wall plaster: whitewashed mud plaster is in fair condition, probably dating from the nineteenth century.
6 Cornices: timber and masonry cornices are broken off on all four corners at both levels but otherwise in good condition.
7 Upper *torana:* the bottom survives intact.
8 Windows: four original fourteenth century windows structurally sound: five of the eight flanking niches were stolen in 1970s.
9 Roof struts: three corner struts are fourteenth-century originals, one is a nineteenth-century replacement. Eight original regular struts were stolen in the 1970s
10 The *torana* was stolen in the 1970s.
11 Latticed door shutters: principal entrance

was replaced by modern door. Wet rot damaged the lower third of all latticed shutters on the other elevations.
12 Niches: Six of eight partially survive; some flanking colonettes and upper carved pieces missing on three façades.
13 Corner columns: no originals survive.
14 Door frame and carvings: mostly complete with worn pieces on base: all carved portions are intact except for extended sill panels of main door with figures (surviving fragments in storage).
15 Stone threshold: in good condition
16 Plinth edge: original stones were replaced by non-matching yellow stone and bricks.
17 Plinth wall: the veneer bricks are damaged and patched with cement.

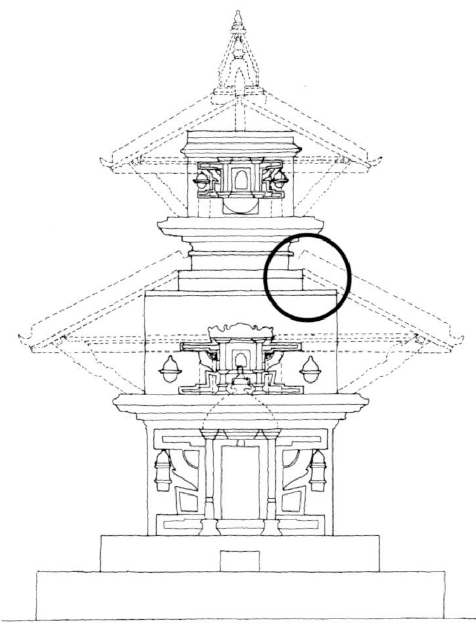

as a surface for the mud bed might be the most historically accurate, but had not been revived in modern practice, which substitutes timber planking. Drawbacks to the tile solution are that it does not provide an irregular surface to "hold" the mud, and that it is quite heavy. The modern detail uses lighter planking with timber battens above to key into the mud bed. Another alternative, a common traditional solution also of venerable age, is a crude layer of lathe made of random sticks and split bamboo.

While the reintroduction of one of these traditional roof covers had been a goal in past projects, we have never been able to achieve it. In several cases our seismic strengthening measures were able to take advantage of the planking as a rigid membrane. In others, the local donors were opposed to the use of less expensive lathe. At Sulima we decided that the lighter and structurally consolidating planking solution was strategic in order to reduce the seismic risks: the protection of the historical woodcarvings was more important than the traditional materials of the roof cover.

## Seismic reinforcement

Given the seismic activity in Nepal, any restoration project must consider both the reinforcement of existing structure and the introduction of new structural members to withstand earthquakes. This is balanced against the desire to maximize historical fabric and configuration. In other projects we have introduced concealed, reinforced concrete, and steel ring beams to reduce seismic risk, based on seismic risk analysis.

In light of our experience with other pagoda structures, and given the very small scale and three-story height of this structure, we decided that major interventions were not necessary. We thus used as a model the KVPT reinforcements of Uma Maheshvar Temple, which was designed together with engineers Manohar Rajbhandari and Prayag Joshi in 1992. Interventions were limited to numerous small-scale reinforcement measures in the timber roof structure to help the historical timber frame to act as a brace for the overall structure. These measures included concealed bolting and steel angles at critical joints, bolting of the rafters to the wall plate (while maintaining the visible traditional timber-peg connection), and careful quality control of all timber joints.

This solution restores the historical configuration of the roof frame while adding a distinguishable layer of reinforcements, a self-conscious layering of interventions. Such layering is consistent with local building practice in which original structures were often buttressed by later props, secondary beams, and doublings-up, although these were traditionally executed in timber. In a recent review by visiting structural engineer Robert Silman, the efficacy of the custom-fabricated iron angles and stainless steel bolting was confirmed, the timber-to-timber joinery identified as the weakest link in the structural assembly.

In addition, the maintenance of *mud mortar* in the masonry structure of the pagoda is a key feature, both as a traditional material and as a damper to earthquake shocks. The soft mud is able to absorb the shock of the earthquake without fracturing adjacent bricks and other wall areas.

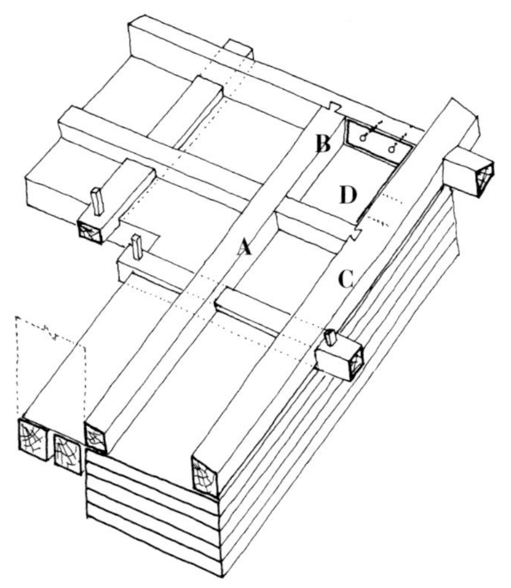

**A timber ring beam**
**Reinforcing the corners with timber and steel bracing allows the historical configuration of double wall plates to act as a ring beam, tying together the tops of the walls on which the rafters rest. Every third rafter is also bolted to the wall plate, and the timber planking above the rafters is nailed in a regular, closely spaced pattern to increase the rigidity of the timber structure.**
**Drawings by Sushil Rajbhandari and Rohit Ranjitkar**

**A  outer wall plate**
**B  inner wall plate**
**C  metal corner brace**
**D  timber brace**

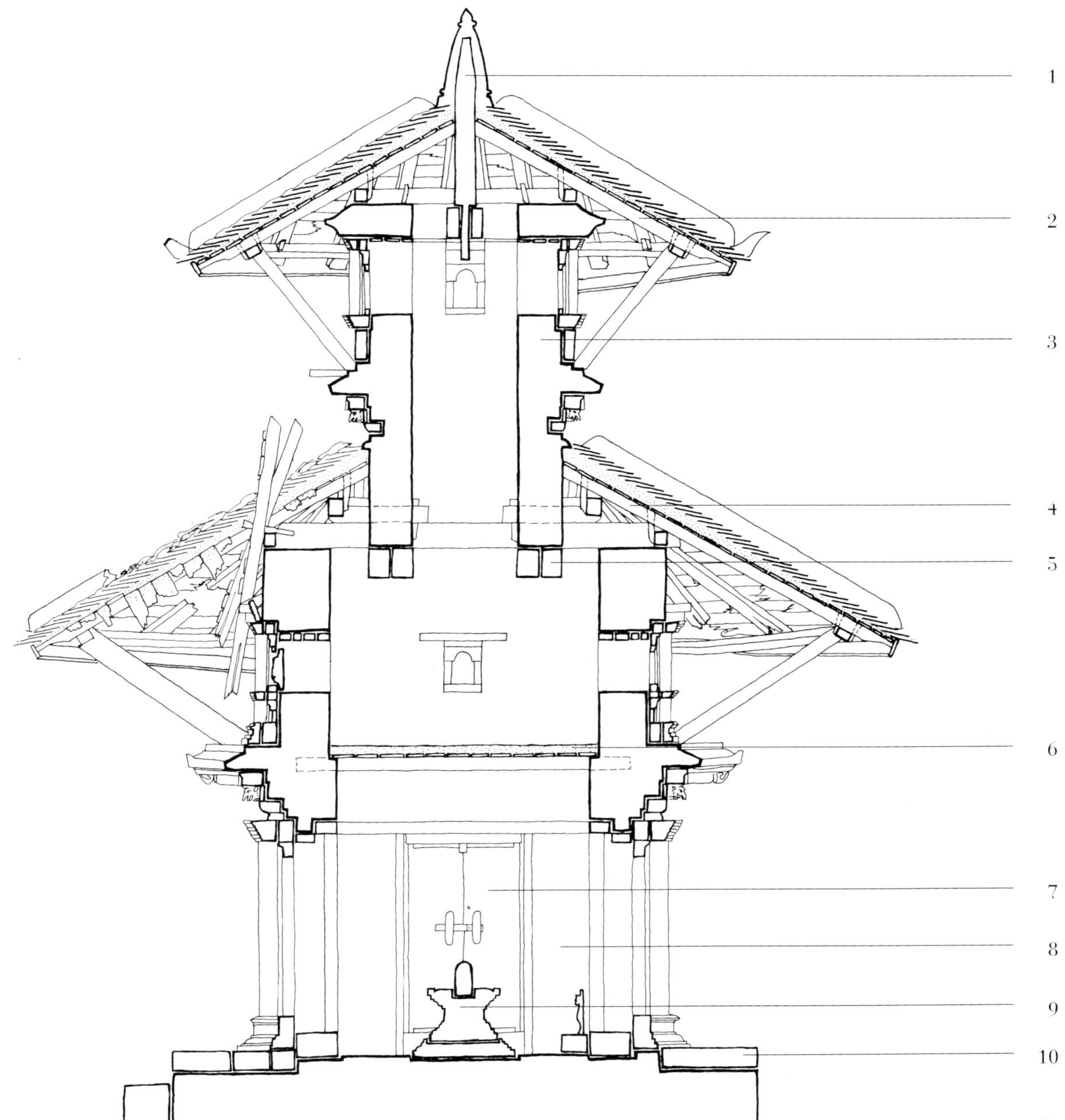

East-west section:
existing condition.
Drawing by Asharam
Twayna and
Gyanendra Joshi,
1997

1 King post and supporting beam: sal wood, satisfactory condition, nineteenth century.
2 Upper timber roof structure: pine rafters, purlins, wall plates of mixed age (30-60 years old), and sal eavesboards rotten from exposure.
3 Brick masonry wall: common brick in mud mortar in good condition, probably nineteenth-century repairs.
4 Lower timber roof structure: pine rafters, purlins and wall plates of mixed age (30-60 years old) fully rotted from exposure.
5 Timber beams: *sal* wood principal and secondary beams in good condition.
6 Floor: mud plaster over timber planking damaged by rainwater penetration.
7 Inner doors on four sides in good condition.
8 Interior: Spalled bricks on lower half of wall from rising damp. *Telia* tile floor badly cracked, 40 percent of tiles missing. Repaired in 1970s with cement patching.
9 Ratneshvara Mahadev: stone image of main deity, original fourteenth century, in good condition.
10 Upper plinth: most of the plinth wall repaired, rebuilt, and pointed with cement. Thirty percent of *telia* tile pavement survives, largely cracked.
11 Lower plinth: the veneer brick of the western plinth wall survives. All other sides rebuilt with mismatched brick and crude cement patches.

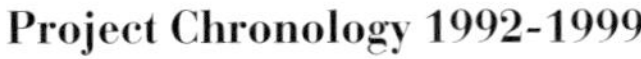



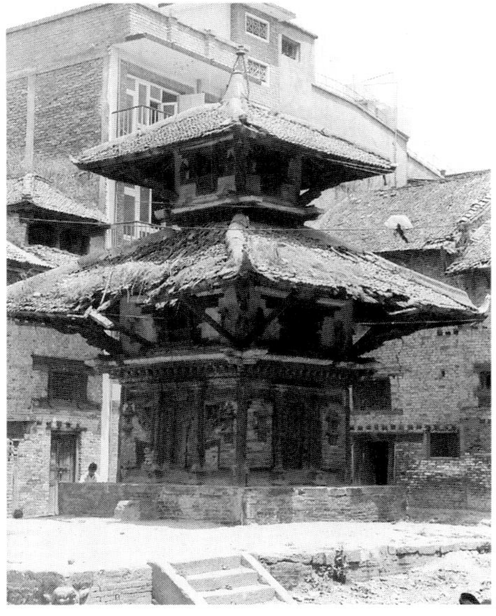

1992      Documentation of Sulima Square, supported by German Technical Cooperation (GTZ).

1993-94   Scaffolding for the repair of the temple erected by the community. Timber for roof rebuilding and carvings purchased. All corner horses recarved.

1994      Kathmandu Valley Preservation Trust undertakes research and documentation for its proposal to restore the temple. Fundraising drive begins. Photographs of lost struts located.

1995      Detailed restoration design and documentation for project implementation.

1996      Historic strut from upper roof recovered.
Funding from Himalayan Bank and other local donors obtained.
Start-up of restoration including new scaffolding, structural timber preparation, and masonry wall repairs. Ongoing study for design of strut replacements.
Upper roof structure rebuilt, copper roof pinnacle fabricated.
Cleaning of carved elements *in situ* at upper level.
Inspection by KVPT chairman, professional photographic documentation.
Second historic strut from upper roof recovered.

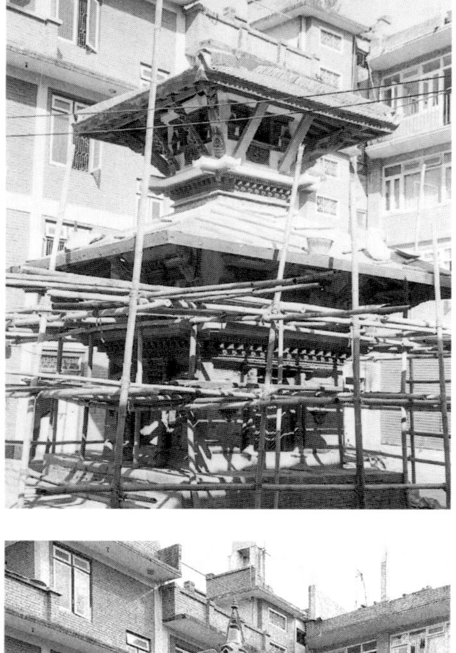

1997      Recarving of replacement struts begun.
Lower roof structure rebuilt.
Cleaning of carved elements *in situ* on lower level.
Pavement of surrounding square with the support of GTZ.
Work stopped due to funding shortage.
Matching funds from the Robert W. Wilson Challenge to Support Our Heritage (World Monuments Fund) granted.
Installation of roof tiles completed.

1998      Installation of copper roof pinnacle completed.
Replastering of upper walls, repair of lower level masonry walls and repair of plinth completed.
Installation of carved roof struts and repair of carved timber windows and niches finished.

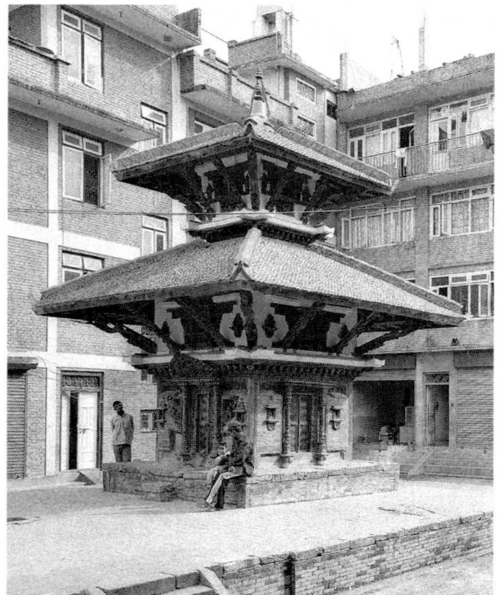

1999      Attempt to steal one of the new struts.
Design research for, and carving and installation of, *torana* replacement completed.
Carving and installation of niche colonettes finished.
Professional photographic documentation completed.
Visit from World Mouments Fund representatives.
Sulima Strut Conference held in November.

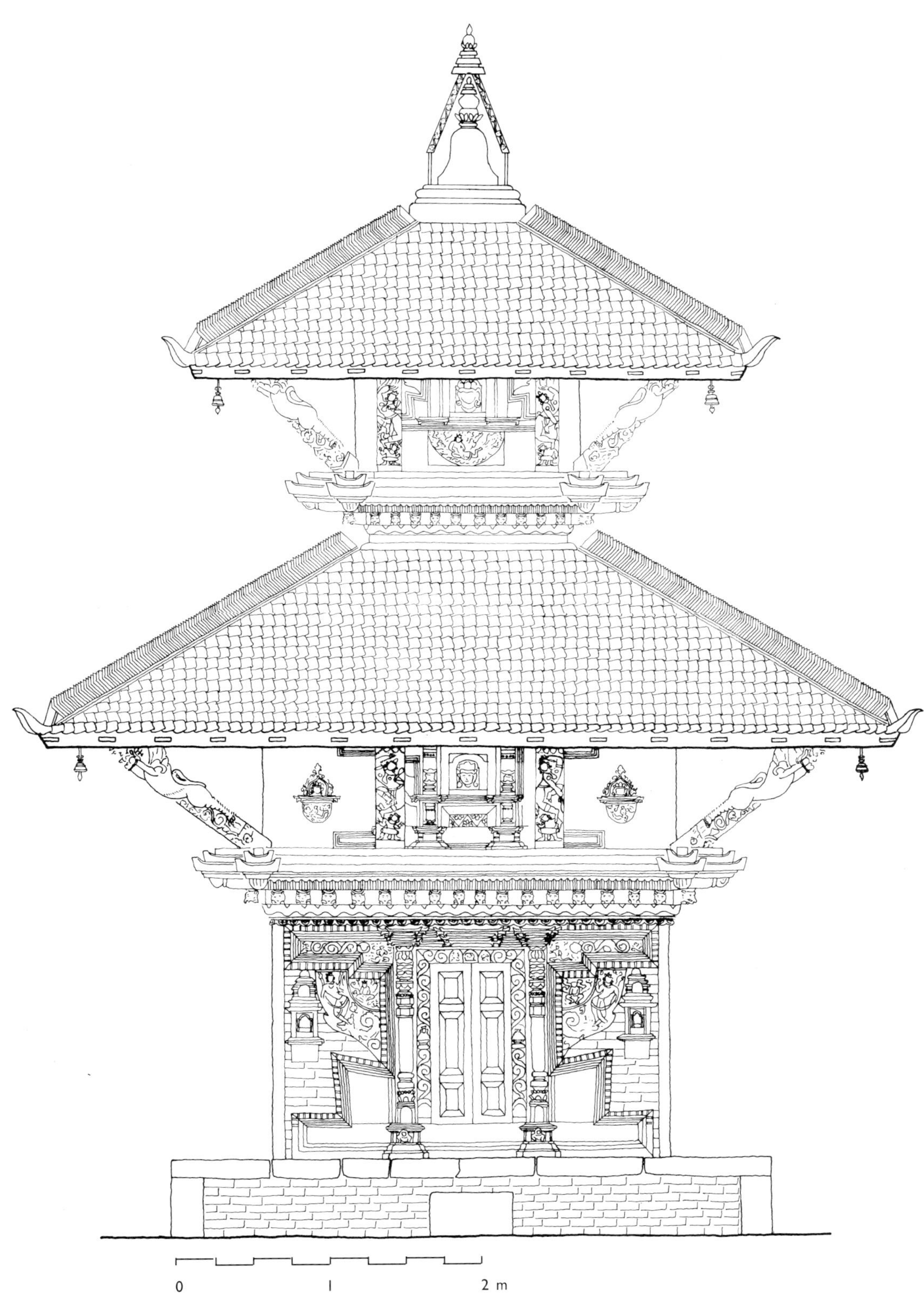



The restored west elevation
Drawing by Sushil Rajbhandari

*opposite page, top to bottom:*
The Sulima Temple before, during,
and after restoration

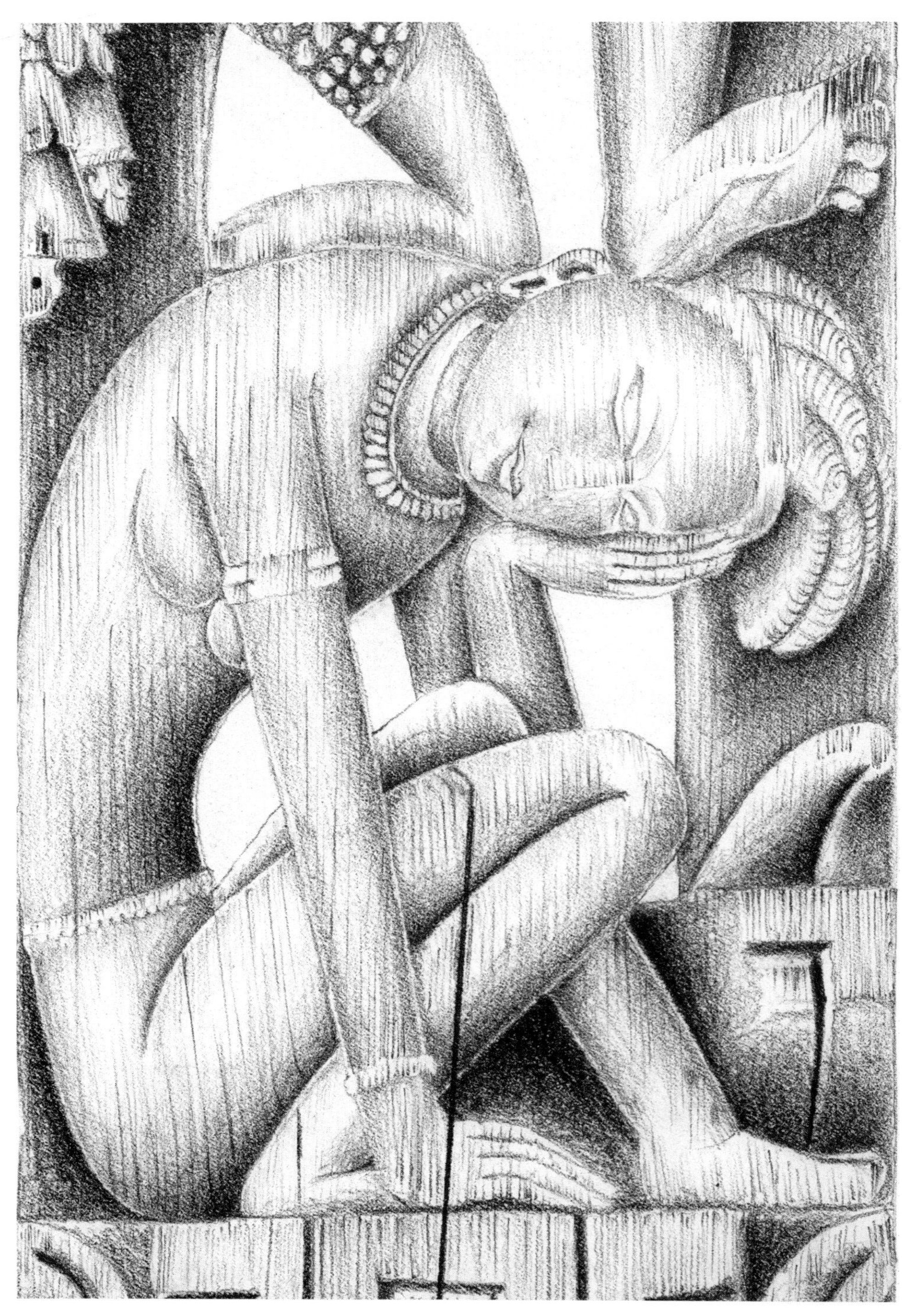

Detail of the recovered historical upper
roof strut depicting a female caryatid
Drawing by Bijay Basukala, 1997



**The Sulima Pagoda**

# Documentation of Woodcarvings

Erich Theophile and Rohit Ranjitkar

The recording of Nepali architecture presents the architect and the draftsman with a daunting task: not only is there a profusion of sculpture detail, but the typical inventiveness of the traditional craftsman rarely repeats a detail twice. Thorough documentation thus includes both typical architectural drawings as well as specialized detail drawings that attempt to capture the richness of the building.

The architectural elevations record the overall structure and include line drawings that approproximate the forms and decorative motifs of the woodcarving. These remain diagrammatic at the 1:20 scale of the architectural drawings. The angle of the roof struts and the roof's overhang, which obscure the upper ranges of wall elements, further make the orthographic elevation a limited record of the carving program.

Detailed drawings of a number of the significant carved features of the temple were prepared at 1:1 or 1:2 scale. Preparing the measured drawings and renderings of the detail and surface texture of the uppermost window, for example, was a four-month assignment for Bijay Basukala. Basukala is the most accomplished limner of South Asian architecture and has worked in the field with Niels Gutschow for ten years. Eight such detailed rendered documentation drawings of temple elements and artistic comparables were made; some of these drawings are included in this and following chapters.

The rendering of surface textures, such as wood grains and cracks, in the detailed documentation drawings grows out of Robert Powell's work. Powell, an Australian painter and architect based in Kathmandu, is internationally renowned for his photo-realistic architectural drawings. His pencil renderings can record more detail than a photograph. Documentation also includes photographs of every architectural element and component carving with iconographic identifications by Nutandhar Sharma. Artificial lighting was used for many of the shots under the roof overhang.

As other essays in this publication suggest, this investment in manpower and documentation represents more than a scientific exercise. The opportunity for Nepali students of architecture to devote significant time to a rigorous study and documentation process creates human connections and a deep knowledge base, both of which will play a role in Nepal's long-term preservation strategy.

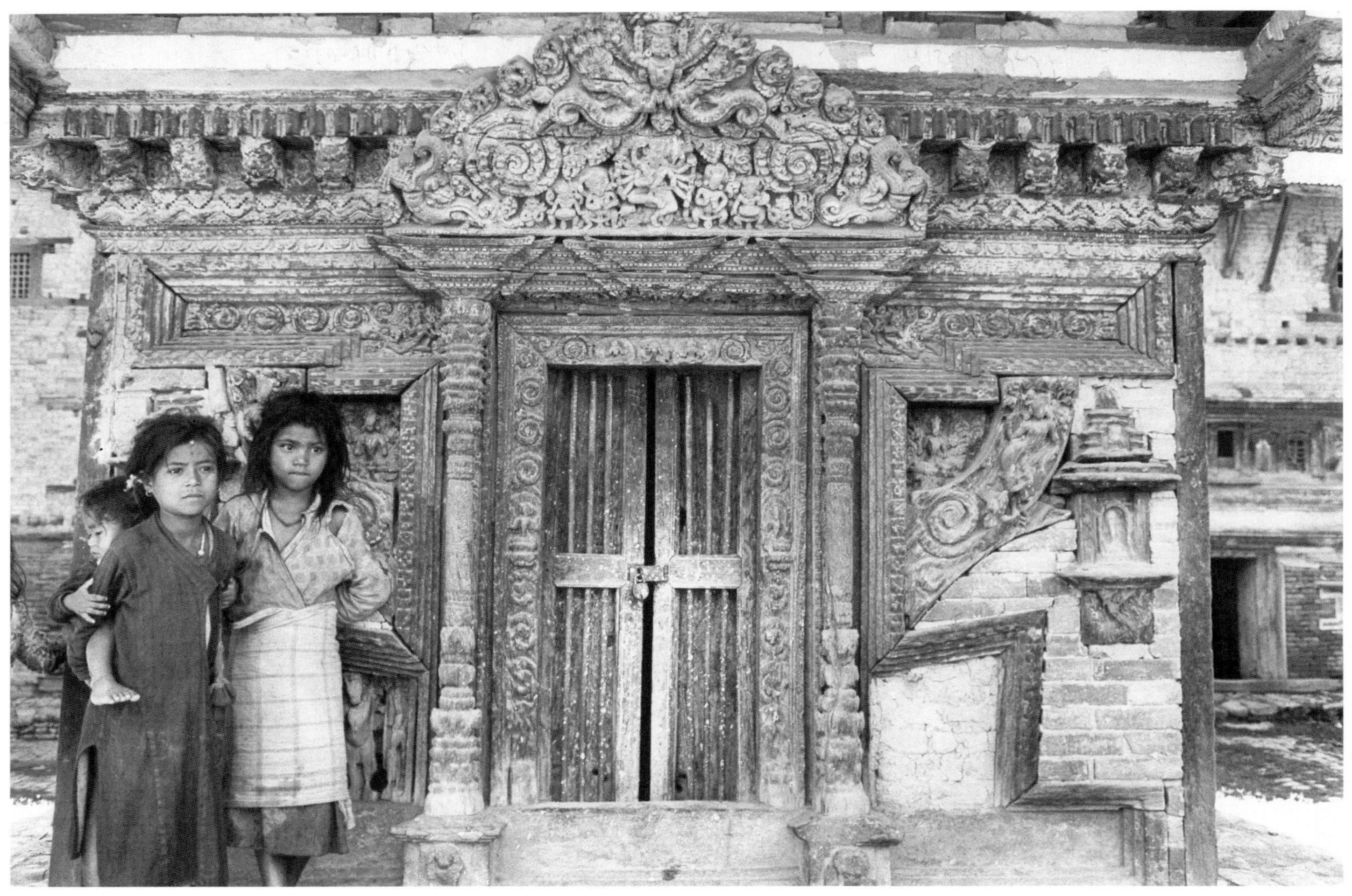

**The historical evidence**
Detail from Mary Slusser's 1968
photograph, which served as the principal
historical record for the restoration and
the basis for the recreation of the *torana*



**The Sulima Pagoda**

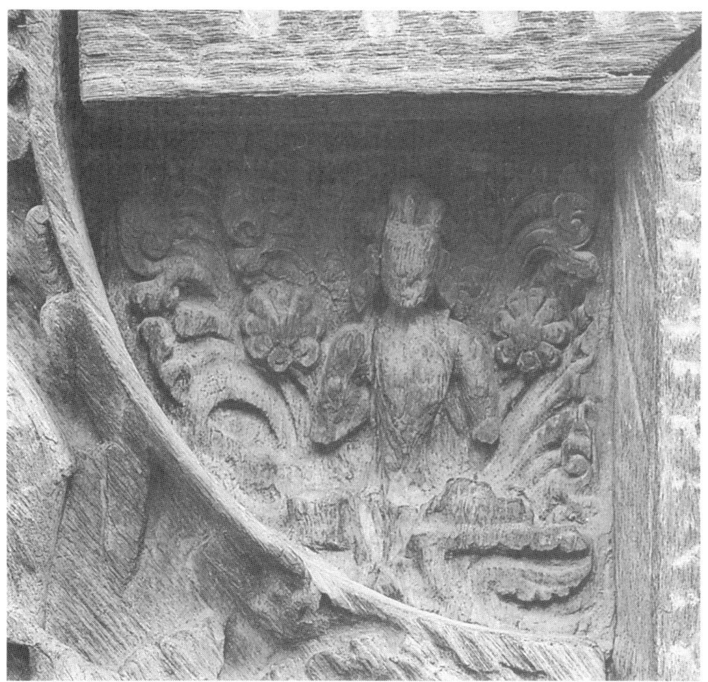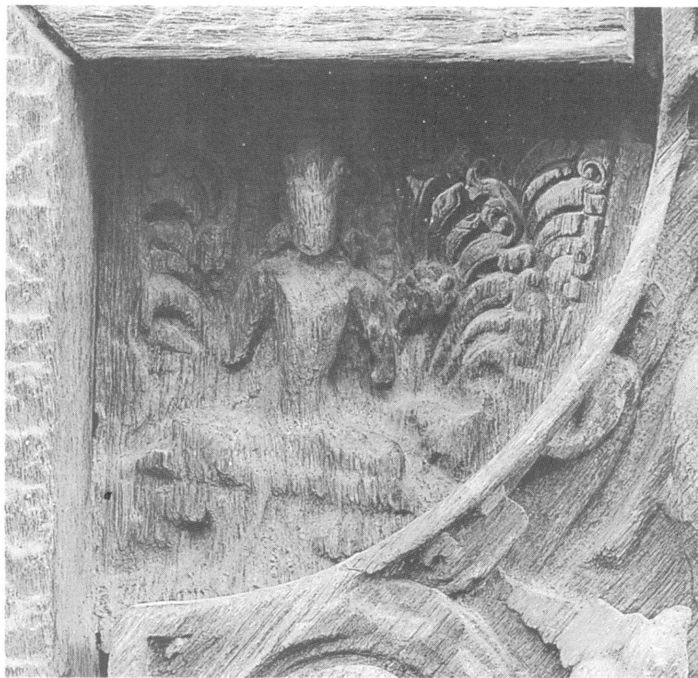

Quarter round panels, depicting Chandra
(left) and Surya (right), flanking the main
door

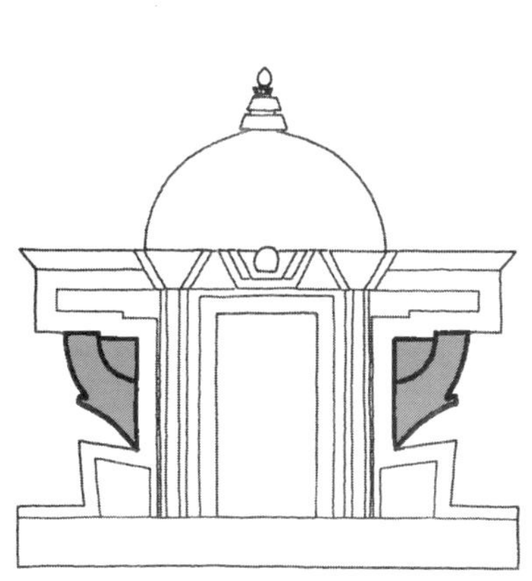

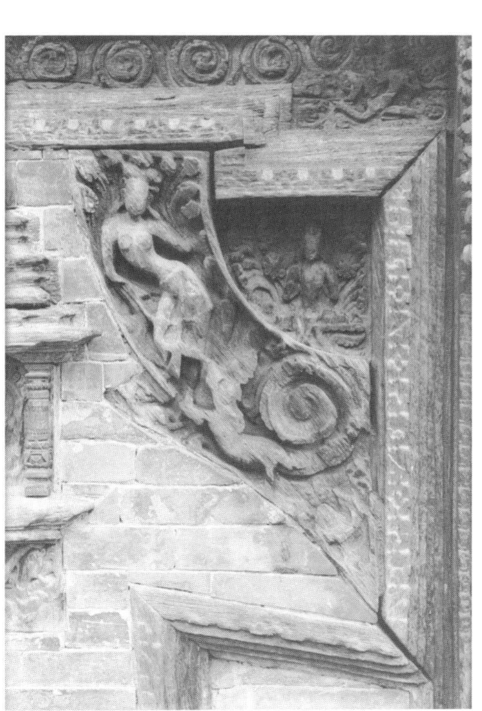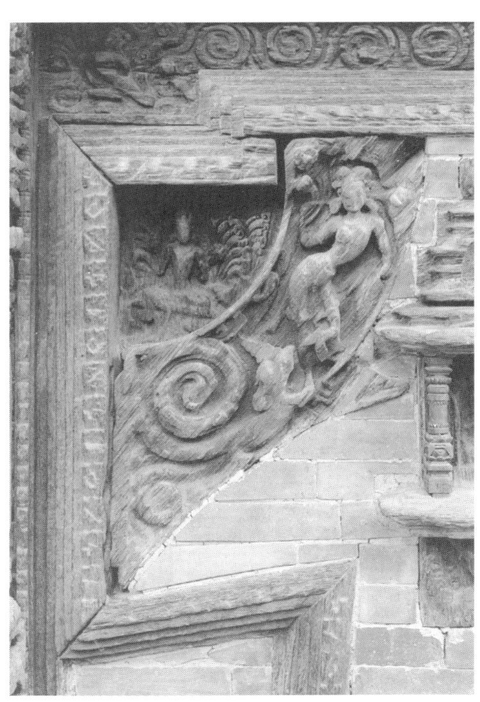

Curved wall brackets depicting Ganga
(left) and Yamuna (right); both figures
are supported by makara.

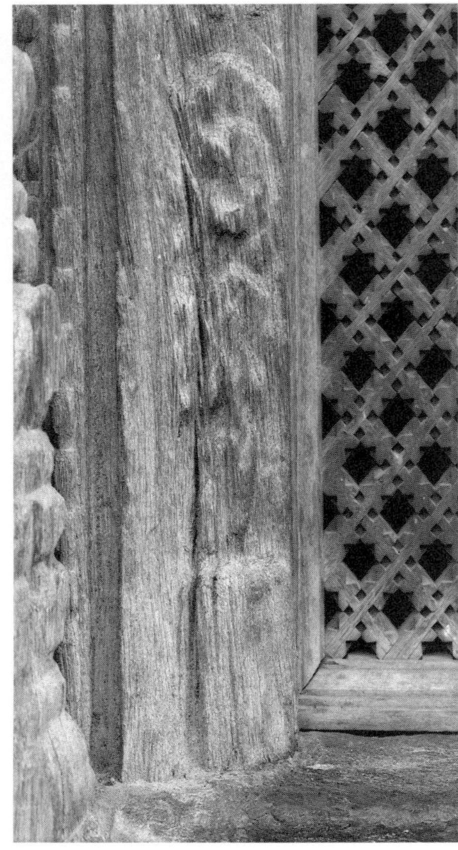
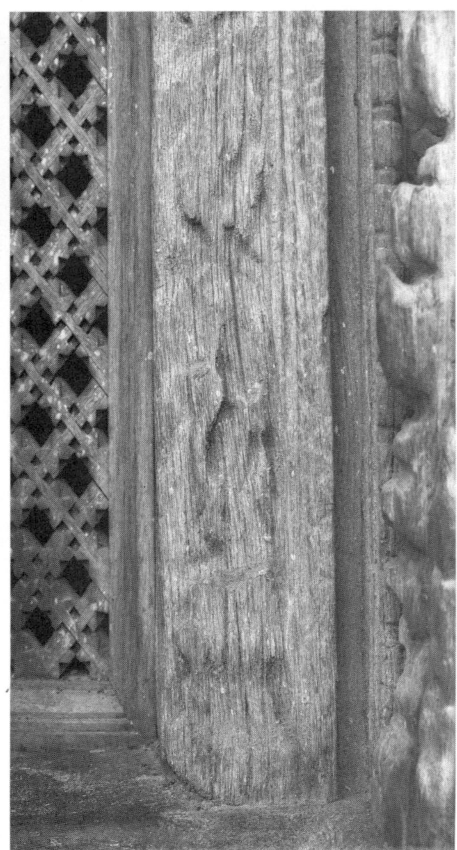

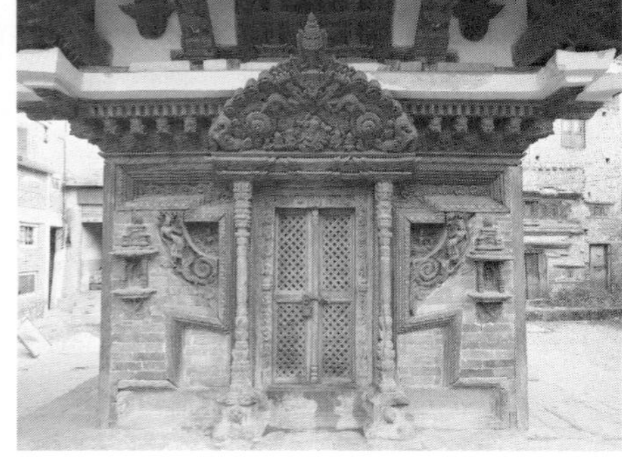

Door jamb, west elevation
Nagraja (left) and Nagini (right)

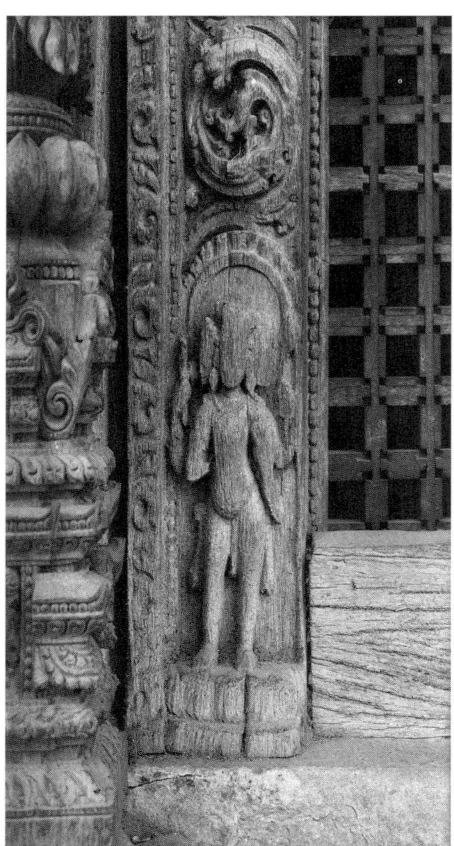
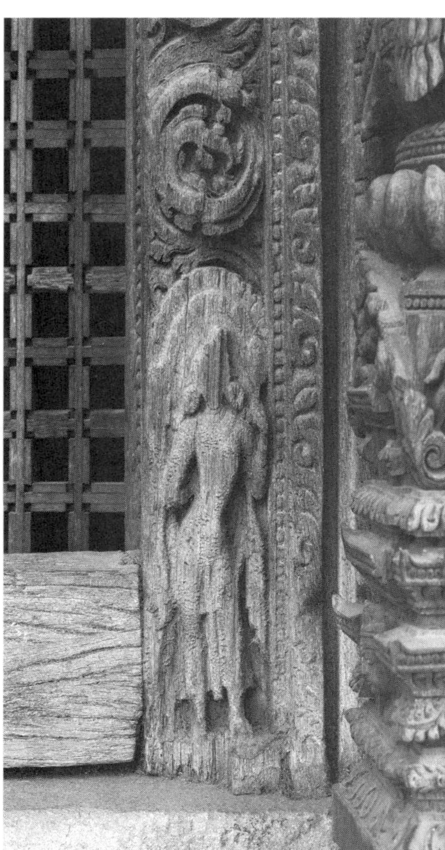

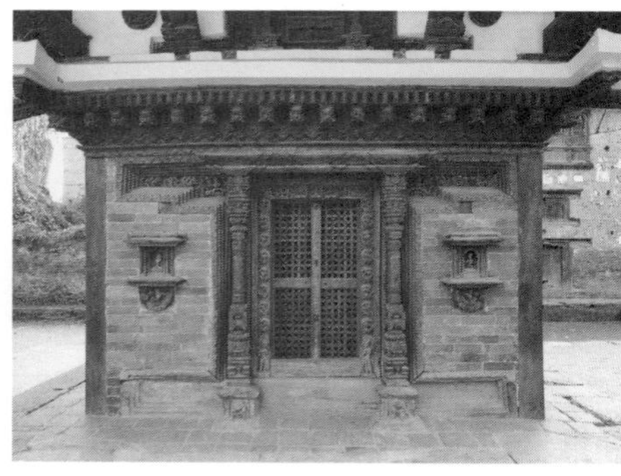

Door jamb, north elevation
Shiva Pratihara is depicted on both sides.

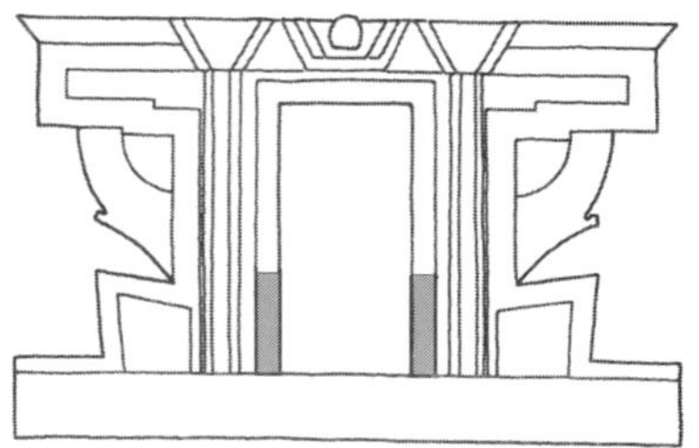



The Sulima Pagoda

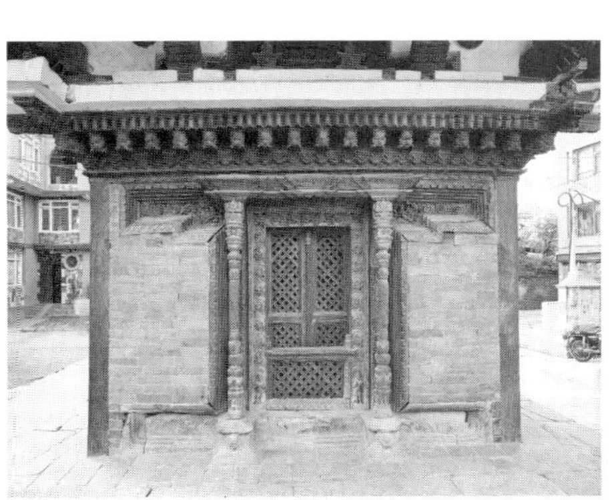

**Door jamb, east elevation**
Unidentified three-headed god (left), Shiva
Pratihara (right)

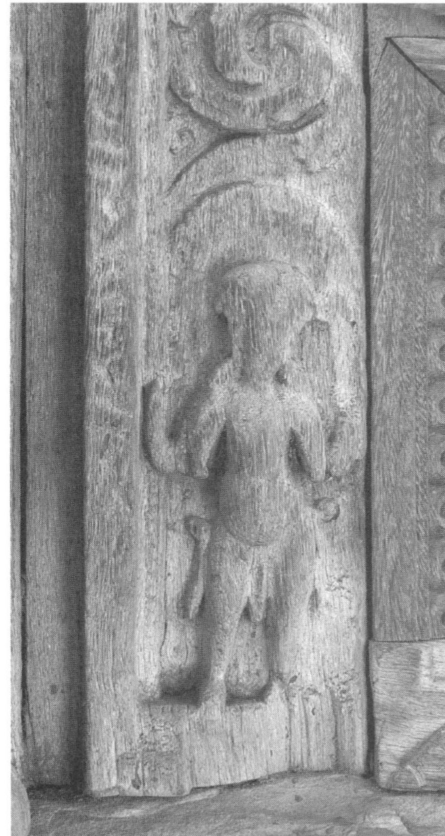

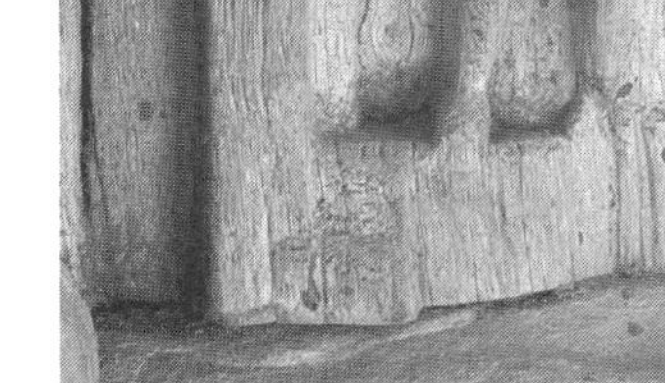

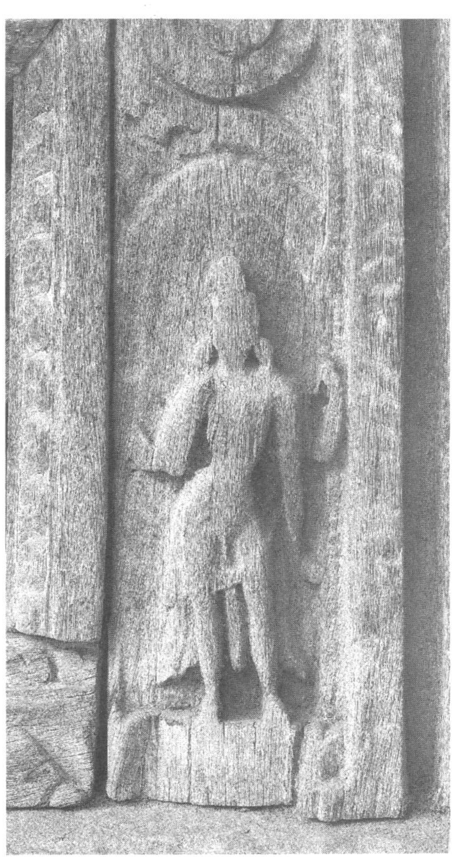

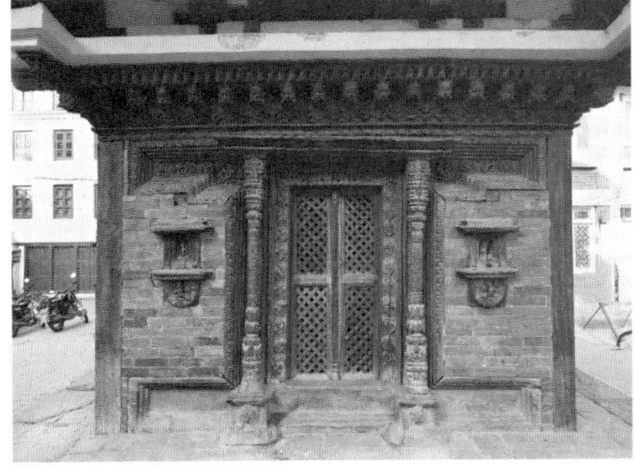

**Door jamb, south elevation**
Unidentified three-headed god in dancing pose
(left), Shiva Pratihara (right)

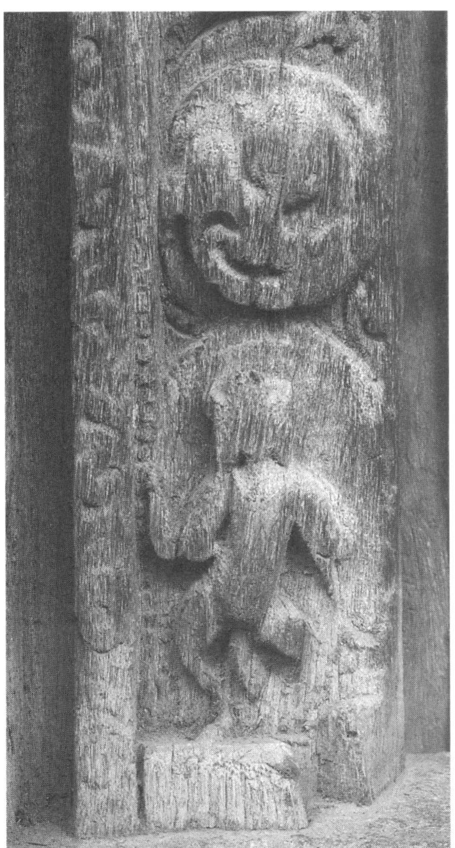

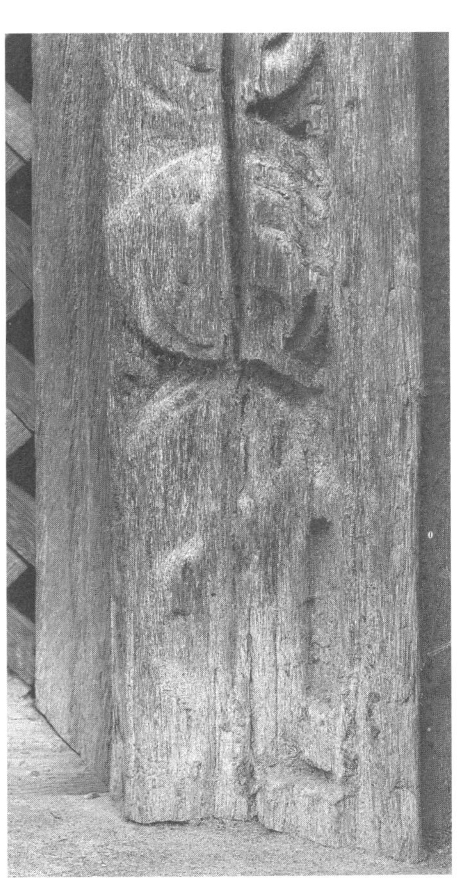

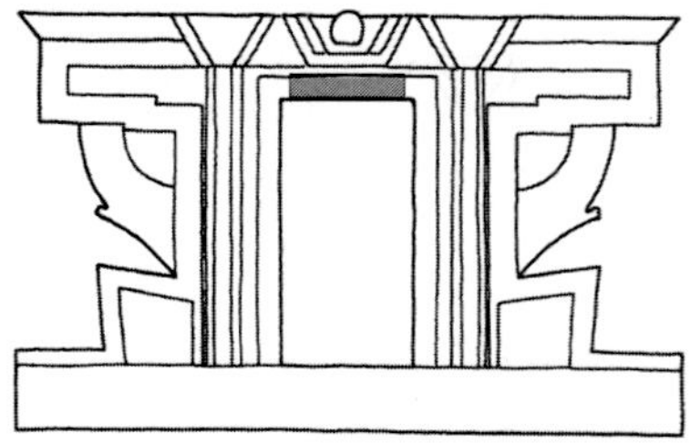

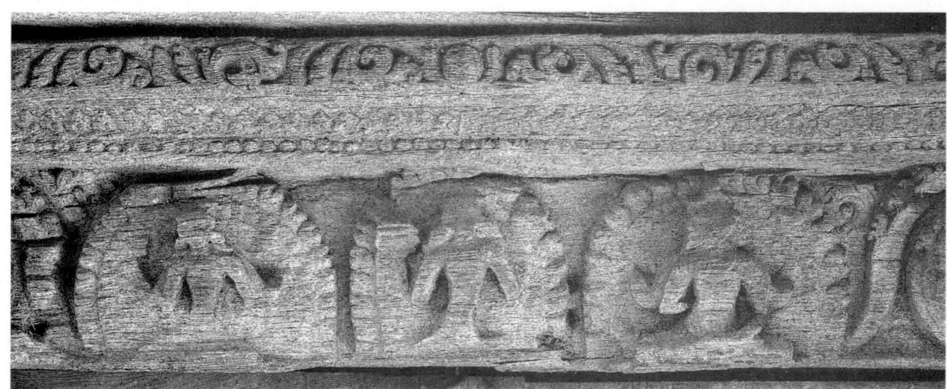

West:
Brahma, Surya, and Maheshvar

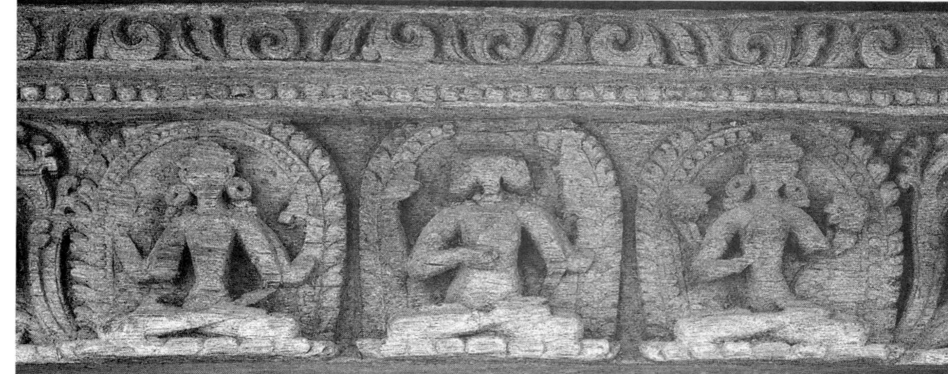

North:
Devi, Shiva, and Surya

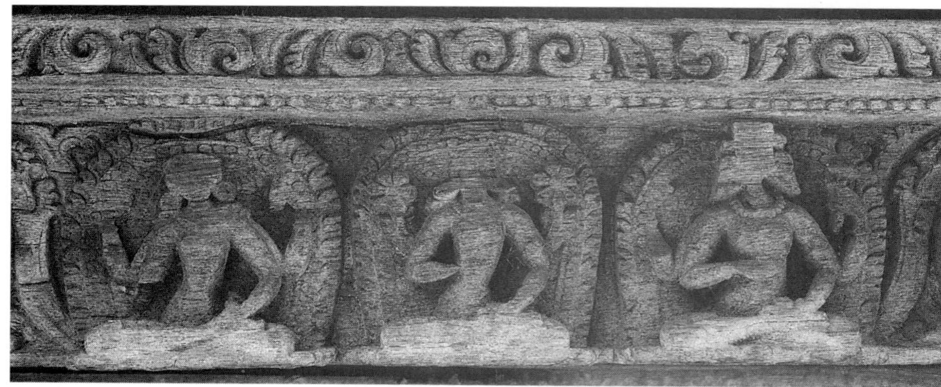

East:
Devi, Surya, and Shiva

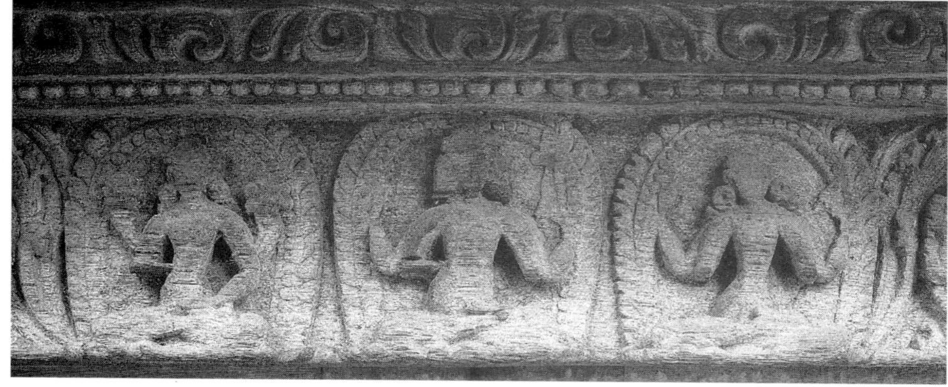

South:
Surya, Shiva, and Devi

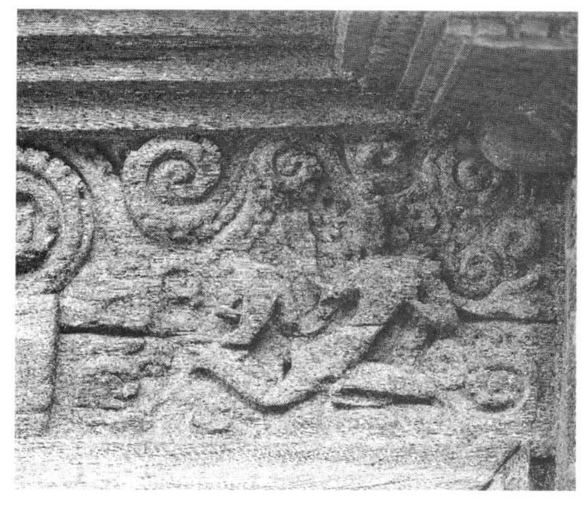
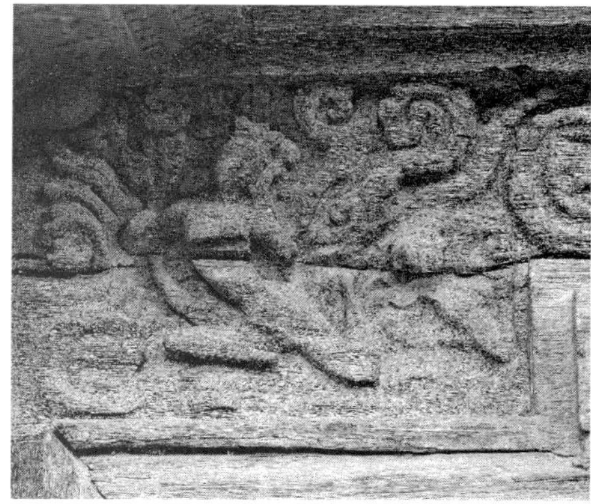

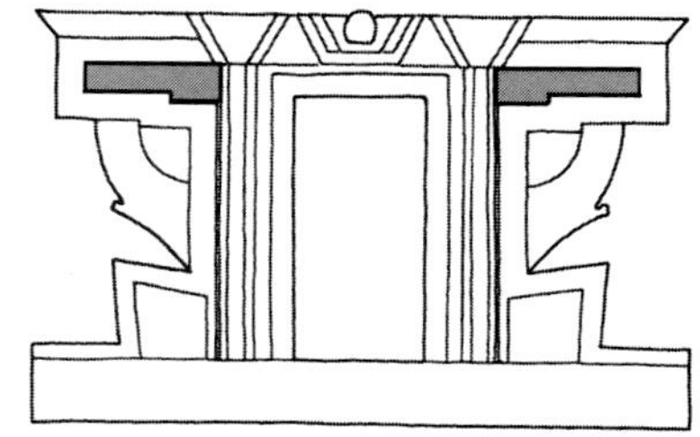

Extended door lintels depicting
Vidyadhara carrying flower garlands

West

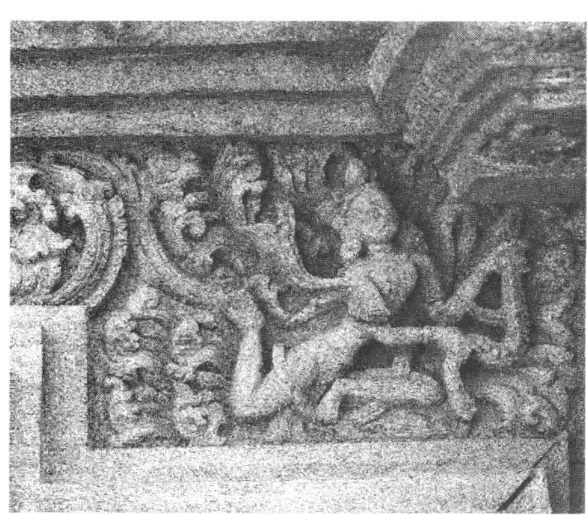
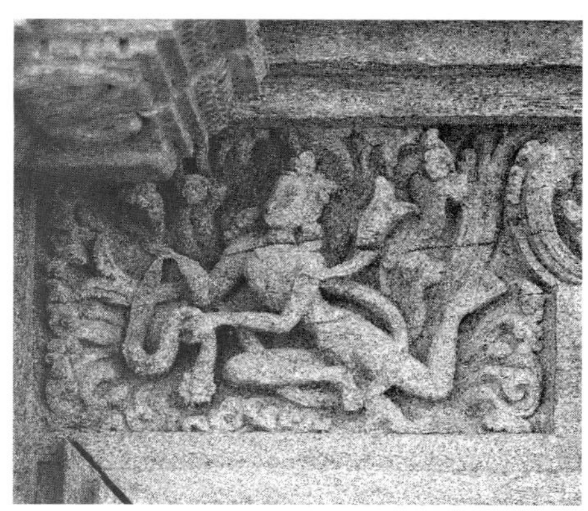

North

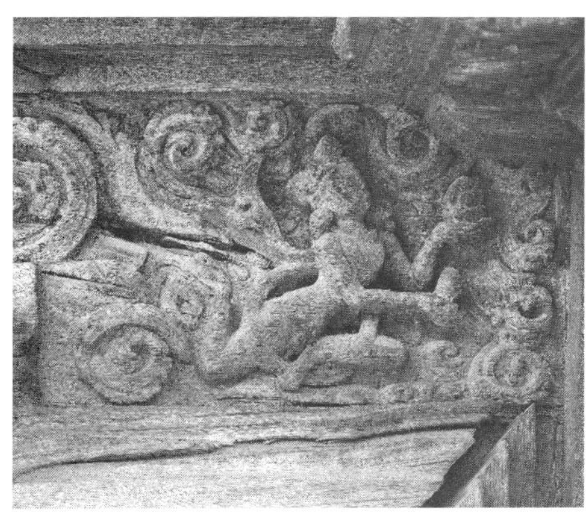
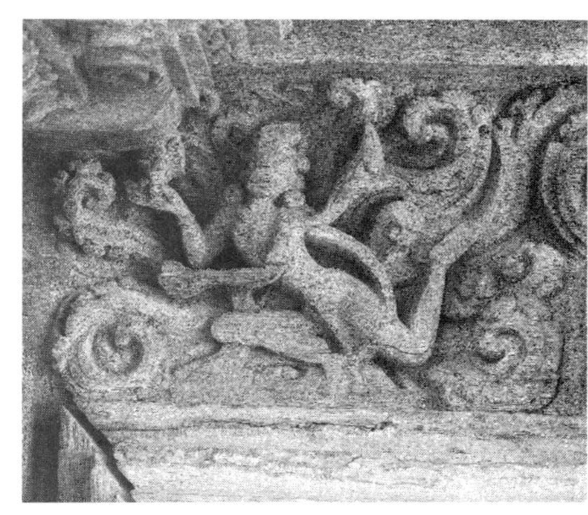

East

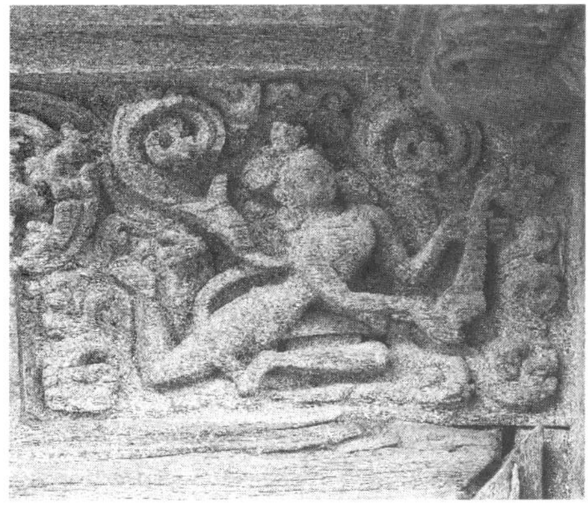
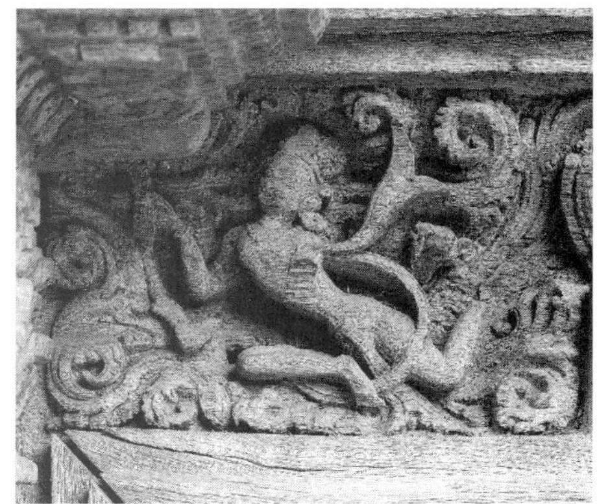

South

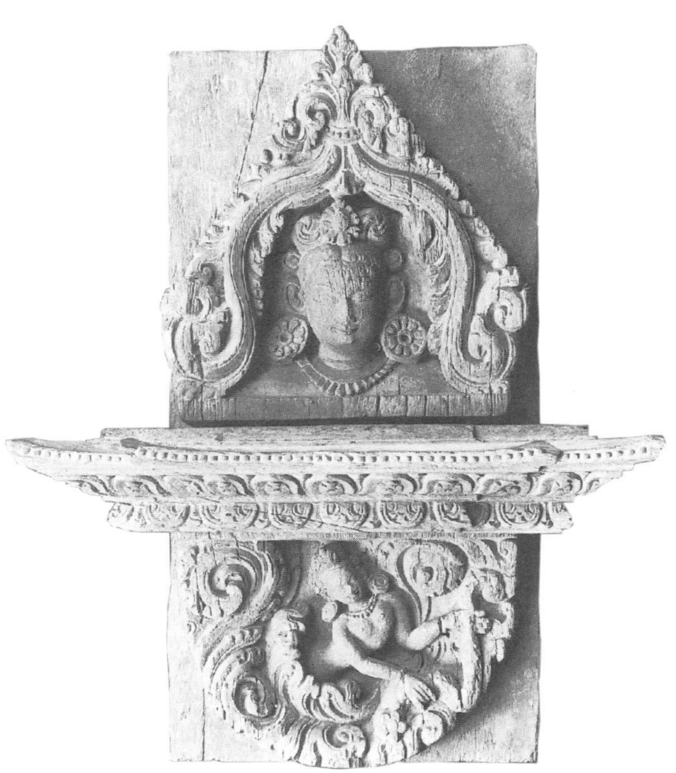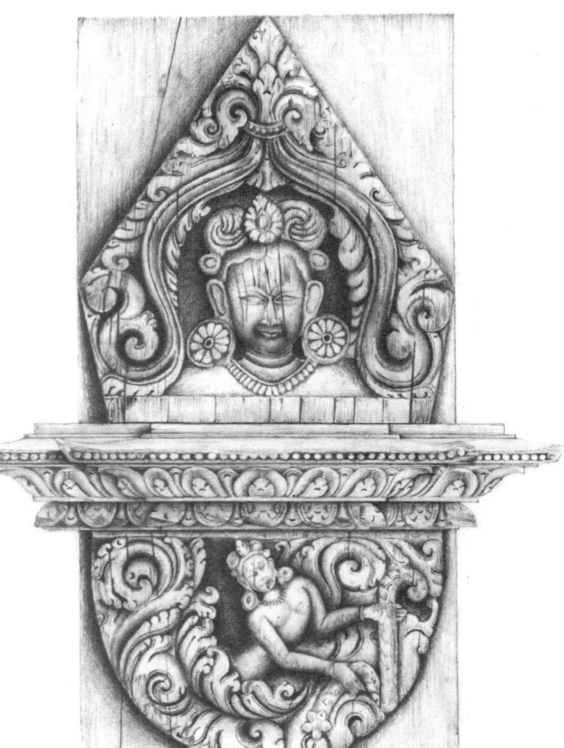

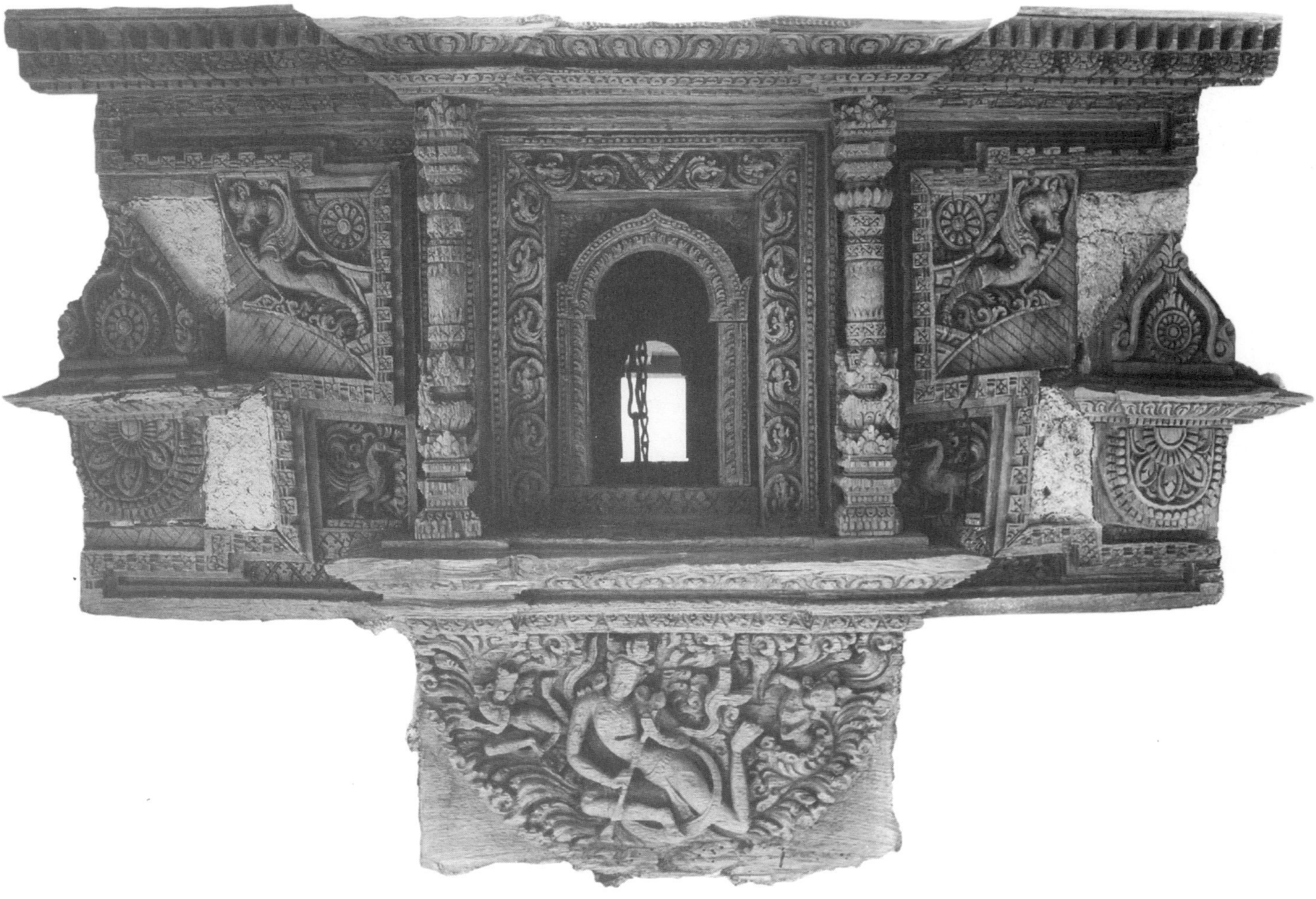

**The Sulima Pagoda**

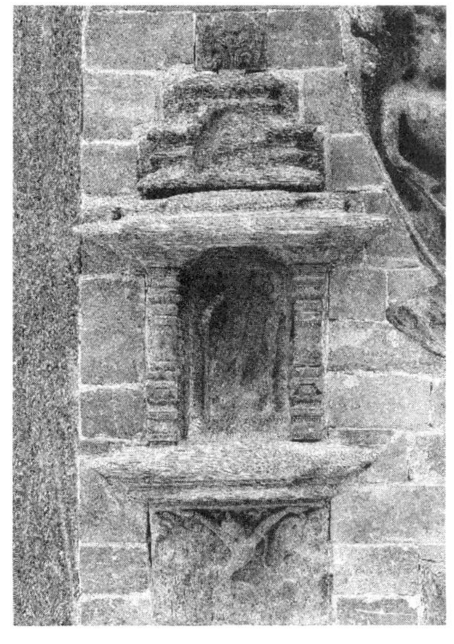 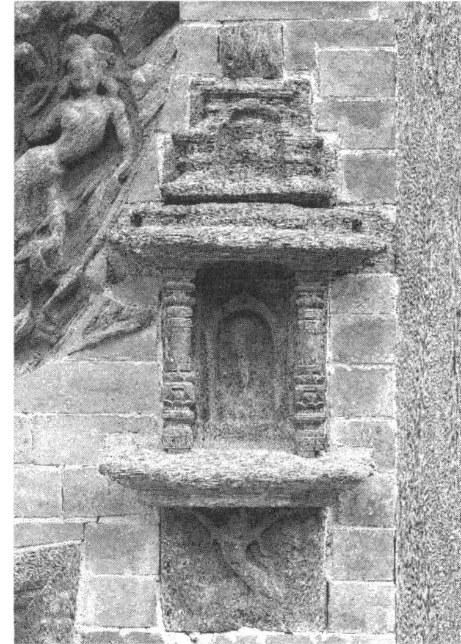

left: Ground floor niches
The composition of these *gahjyah* (blind window) consists of a multi-layered niche with a roof-like feature above and a half-round base block below. The varying seated niche figures are unidentifiable except for Garuda (west, left). Gandharva figures fill the lower panels.

West

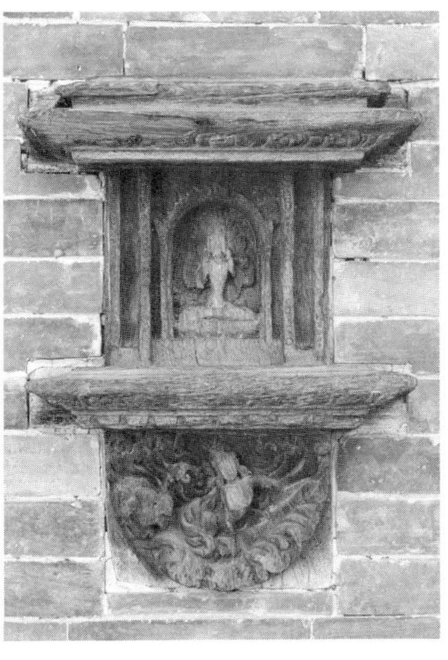 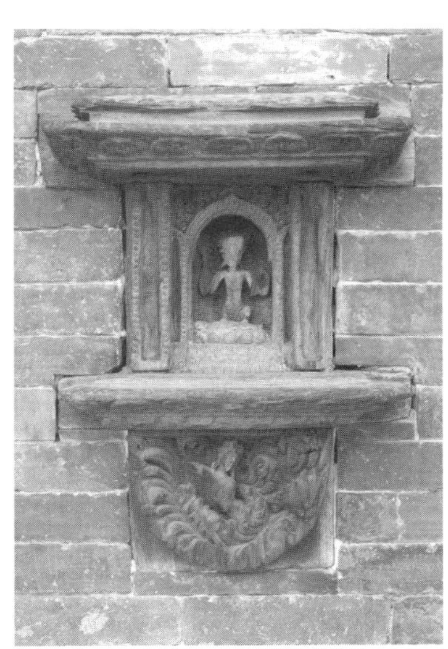

North

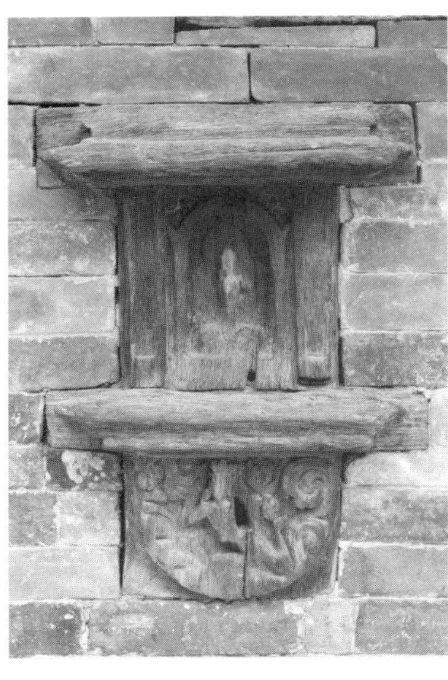 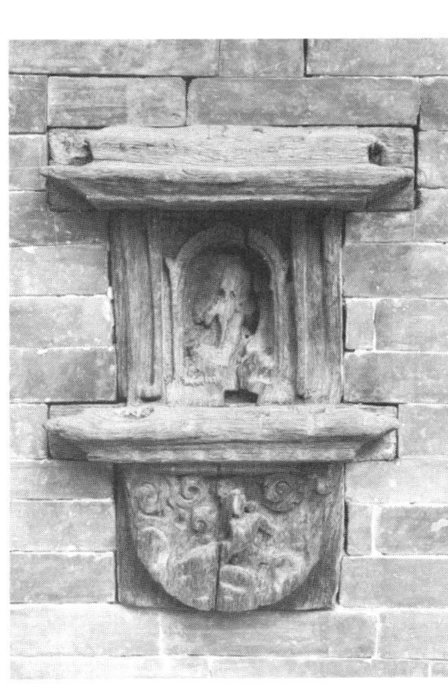

South

opposite, top:
Historic blind window below the lower roof, with *gandharva* above and *vidhyadhara* bearing garlands below
Drawing by Bijay Basukala

opposite:
*Gahjyah* on the upper level
This extraordinary composition sets niches within and at the sides of a pillared window opening. Unicorns and geese flank the colonnettes. Apsara amidst cloud patterns in the base carry the composition. Lotus flower motifs decorate the subsidiary niches.

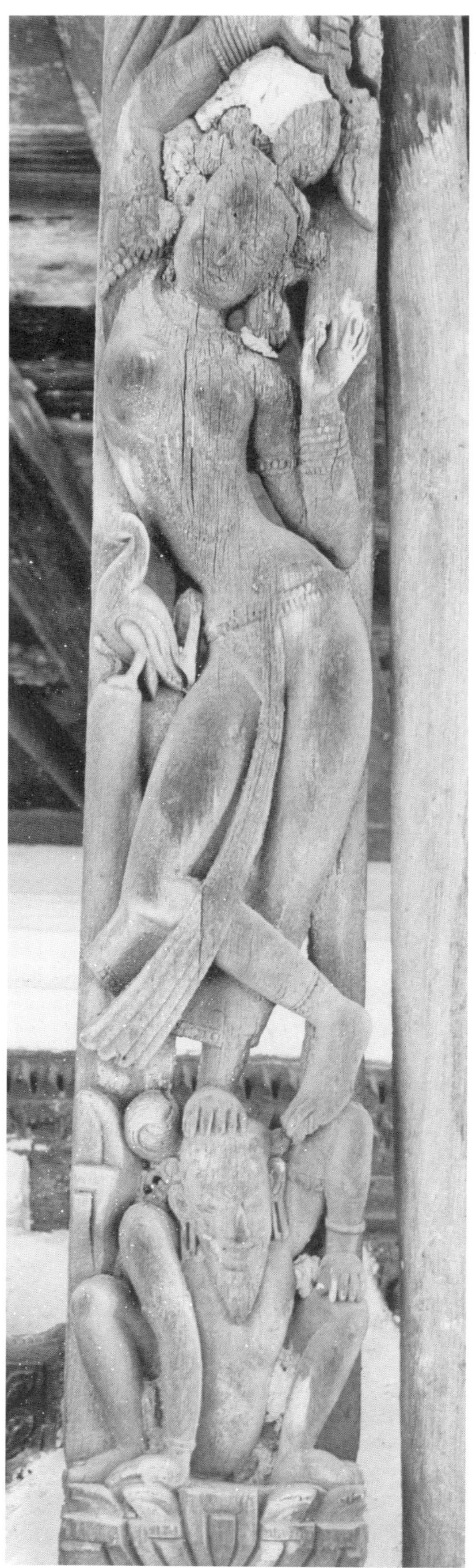

Lower roof struts
documented by Mary
Slusser in 1968
*Yaksini* are depicted above
yaksi, the demi-gods are
shown in different poses on
each strut.



The Sulima Pagoda

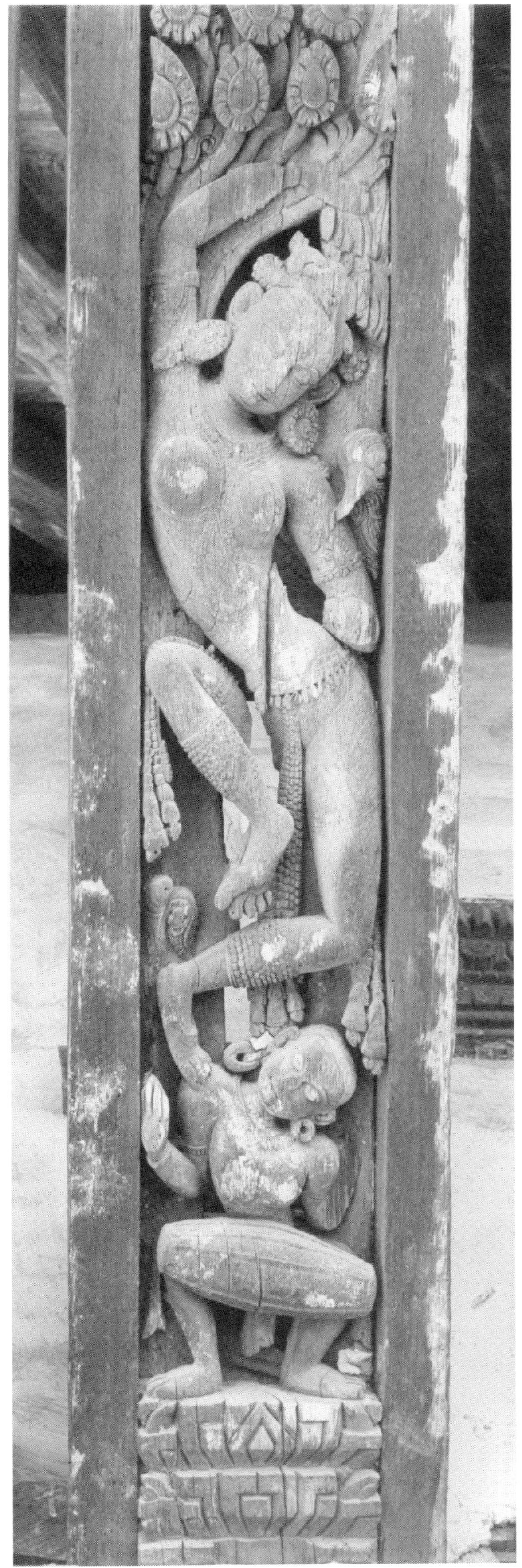 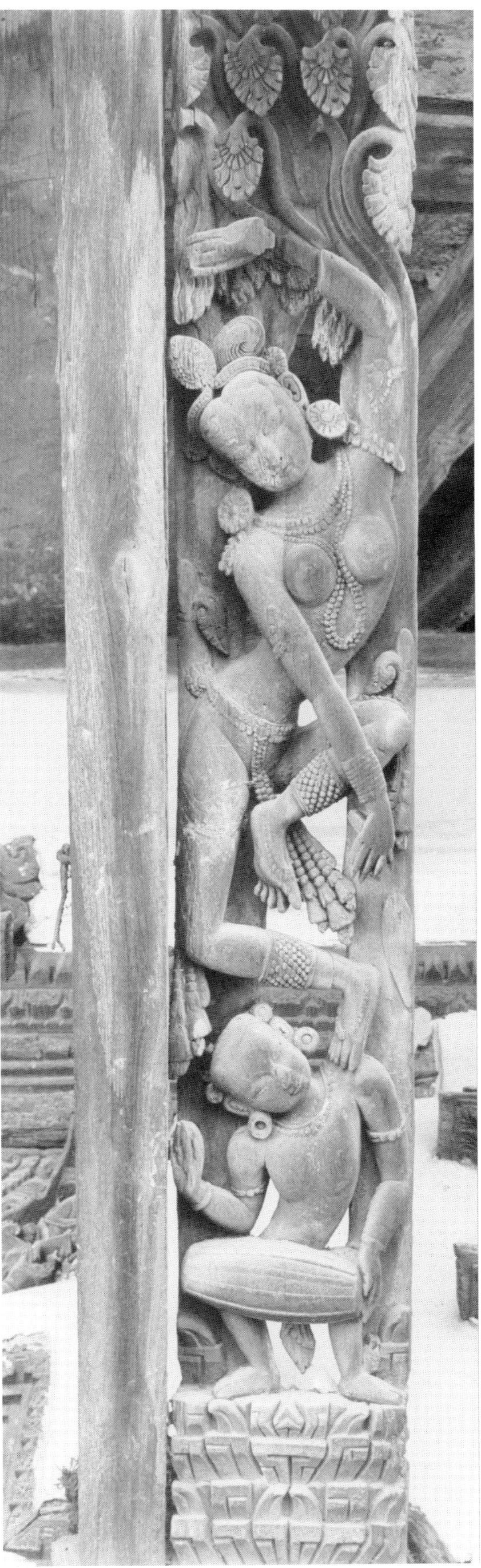

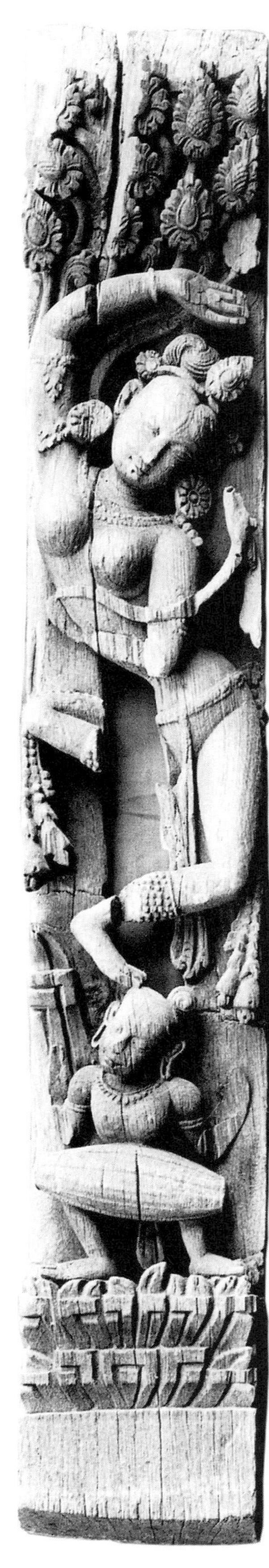
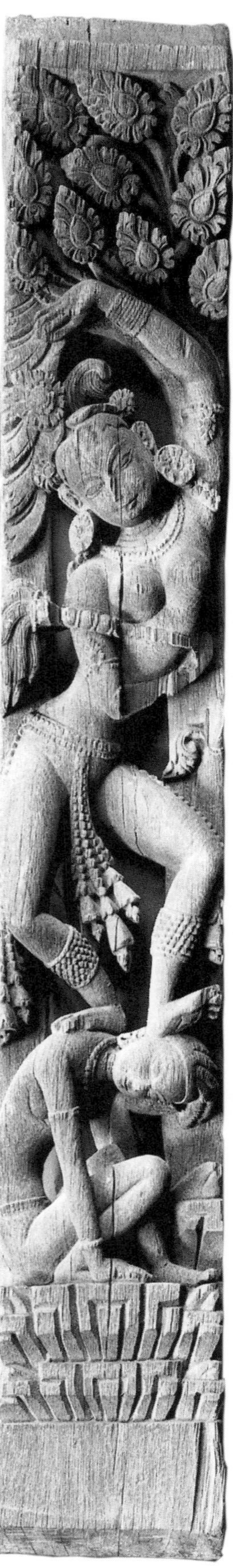

Two surviving historical struts from the upper roof; one strut was found in the temple's rubble. A neighbor brought the other to the project in 1996.



The Sulima Pagoda

# Iconography

Nutandhar Sharma

The Nepali *degah*, or temple, is fitted with icons and auspicious symbols on its struts, door frames, *torana*, niches, and windows. These religious representations, translated into architecture, elaborate, repeat, and complement the meaning of the principal deity housed in the temple. One basic pattern in conceiving a temple is the mandala, a cosmic diagram.[1] The main deity of the temple is always the central figure of the *mandala*, surrounded by other deities, *avarana devata*, at the periphery. This general formula accounts for the constellation of deities and images found in some sort of symmetrical relationship to the main deity in the center.

The *torana* of the main gate can be understood as a type of signboard for the temple, as the deity depicted in the *tympanum* is generally the principal deity of the temple. In the *tympanum* of the Sulima Temple, Nrityeshvar Shiva in dancing form represents the Ratneshvar Shiva *linga* of the temple. On the right and left sides of the dancing Shiva, there are Ganesha and Kumar, the two sons of Shiva, a near generic feature of all temples in Nepal. Flanking them are Nandi and Bhringi playing drums and two *gandharva* in half-human, and half-bird form. These are common features in many temple *torana*. Above the dancing Shiva, the *torana* depicts Lord Vishnu mounted on Garuda.

The use of Vishnu atop his mount Garuda as the crowning element of the composition differs from that of the earlier Licchavi period, in which the "face of glory" or *kirtimukha* motif is found. This use of Vishnu atop his mount Garuda and the constellation of gods around Nrtyesvara is an early example of its kind and was very popular during the Malla period.

An interesting original *torana* above the window of the upper level façade has survived at the Sulima Temple. In the middle of this *torana* three jewels (*triratna*) are carved, again a symbolic interpretation of Ratneshvar, the lord of jewels (*ratna*), who is in fact Shiva. The remaining iconography, now lost, may have included a *kirtimukha*. This *torana* can be compared with the stone *torana* of the sixteenth-century *caitya* temple of Hahkha.[2]

The entrance attracts a number of attendant deities. Surya and Chandra, the sun and moon gods, with two lotuses in each hand, are carved in the extended lintels of the main door. They are necessary witnesses to all ritual activity and are found on nearly every temple façade in the country. Similarly, the auspicious symbols and the holy river goddesses, Ganga and Yamuna, on the carved brackets, are incorporated into the temple entrance ensemble atop *makara* (crocodiles).

*Gandharva* are depicted on the projecting lintels (*lapu*), flying atop *vidhyadhara*, the bearers of secret knowledge. Small triads of figures are carved on the middle of the lintel of the four doors. Guardian figures and trios of gods and goddesses are also inscribed in the door jambs.

Several additional images in the door frames, windows and niches, otherwise full of decorative motifs, cannot be identified, but it is likely that the *mandala* design was followed here in designing this temple.

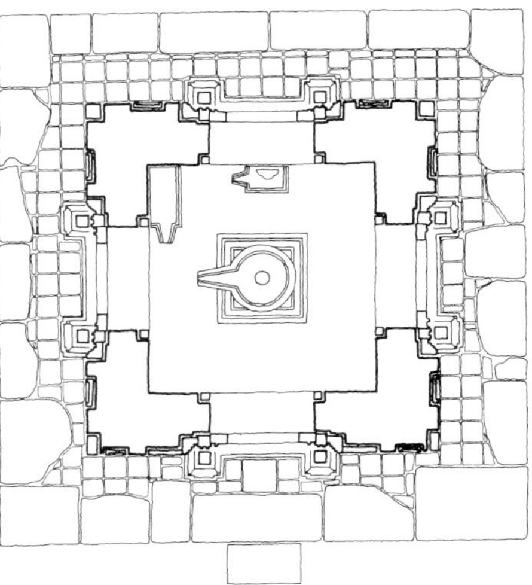

**Ground floor plan of Sulima temple
Drawing Sushil Rajbhandari**

We know about the virtuoso carvings of the struts from photographs. They depict some of the loveliest demi-goddesses ever carved in the Nepalin variety of dancing and standing positions. These female figures, *yaksini*, stand above miniature and grotesque figures, mostly male counterparts or *yaksa*, with the foliage of the sacred grove above. Six of the *yaksini* are dancing figures wearing *ghunghuru*, bells tied at the ankles, and four of them are *salabhanjika*, goddesses of the sacred grove whose extended arms grasp a tree branch. The other six figures stand still holding yak tails and musical instruments.

According to architectural historian Ulrich Wiesner, "the architectonic motif of the [Nepali] roof strut is related to a motif [the *salabhanjika*] that was used in India in many different artistic contexts."[3] Wiesner traces the motif from roof brackets to adaptations to other architectural features such as railing balusters. The motif of *salabhanjika* evokes the mood of goddesses in a sacred grove. The remaining struts follow the formula of the *salabhanjika* with different renderings, such as dancers, musicians, and attendants holding musical instruments, jewelry, and yak tails. Music and dance have always been a part of ritual worship in Nepal and India. The *torana* of the temple itself depicts Nrtyesvara as a dancing form of Shiva.

The *salabhanjika* figure is an ancient motif that goes back to the pre-Kushana and Kushana periods of India. Viennot gives an example of Sanchi, where the artists used the *salabhanjika* motif consisting of a standing female figure with crossed legs and holding the branch of a tree with one hand.[4] The *sal* (*shorea robusta*) is a South Asian tree that gives its name to this motif. Bhanjika refers to the bend of the branch as tugged by a yaksi, or demi-goddess. The yaksi has not been examined in detail by art historians. Until now only one researcher has been able to name any of these early *salabhanjika* demi-goddesses: an image on the struts of Ukubahal has been identified as Mahayaya Devi by Hemaraja Sakya.[5]

The iconography and composition of the struts is comparable to the *yaksi* of Ukubahal,[6] the struts of Indreshvar Temple of Panauti[7], and figures found on the *dharmasala* of Tyagal Tol, Patan.[8] According to Mary Slusser, the figures of Indreshvar and Tyagal Tol can be dated to the thirteenth century. Similarly, John Locke dates the struts of Ukubahal to the twelfth and thirteenth centuries.[9]

According to local belief, especially among the farmer castes, the Sulima Temple female strut figures are *dakinis* who were outwitted by Gayahbajya, a local Tantric. Coomaraswamy also suggests that the dakini must have originally been *yaksini*.[10]

The tradition of *yaksa* and *yaksini puja* in Nepal is an ancient one. One *thyasaphu*, a folded manuscript from the Malla Period, mentions them in the *kalasa puja* from the year Nepal Samvat 803 (CE 1682). It was held in the Sulima *agamchen*, the Tantric esoteric shrine connected to the temple.[11] *Yaksa* means "magical power" and this is what transforms these figures into demi-gods.[12] *Yaksa* are considered the subjects of Kuvera, a ruler and a devotee of Lord Shiva.[13]

*Yaksini* is the female form of *yaksa*. According to indologists Margaret and James Stutley, the Seven Mothers, the Sixty-four Yoginis, and some forms of Devi all appear to have been *yaksini* originally.[14] There are countless *yaksini* mentioned in the Tantric text, including Vichitra, Vibhrama, Hamsi, Bhishana, Janaranjika, Vishala, Madana, Kalakarani, Mahamaya, Mahendri, Shankhini, Samdika, Shmasana, Vatakaksini, Mekhala, Vikala, Laksmi, Manini, Satapatrika, Sulochana, Saubhagya, Kapila, Vilashini, Nayika, Bhaksini, Kaneshvari, Suvarnasurasundari, Manohara, Prabhavi, Ragini, Nakhakeshika, Padmini, Bhogini, Svarnavati, Davaratapriya, Karnapisaca, and Karakankani.[15]



**The Sulima Pagoda**

The subsidiary figure of the *salabhanjika* formula obviously corresponds to the artist's need to fill the elongated shape of the roof strut. It also reflects the typical association of deities with attendant figures and mounts. Here the figures amplify the special features of the *yaksi* above; a squatting female drummer, for example, keeps the beat for the dancing figure above. These dwarf, crouching figures also relate to be common theme of *yaksa*, the male counterparts often carved as pillar bases.

The *yaksini* as a strut motif may be a rule of the earliest temples of Nepal, and it is also found carrying the roofs of Buddhist quadrangles dating to the thirteenth or fourteenth century. In the later Malla period, the *yaksini* disappeared in this application, replaced by numerous other constellations of gods, including the eight mother goddesses and other Tantric deities. The compositional formula survives in the general registration of the elements, but the proportions of the later deities become more solid and are expanded with the addition of multiple arms.

On the basis of other, later strut schemes from the Malla period (1482-1768 CE), strut figures of the of Ratneshvara Temple might be understood as illustrating the concept of a directional *mandala*. Yet, based on our lack of knowledge of the specific identification of these *yaksini* and on the lack of documentation of a directional scheme using *yaksini*, this remark remains conjectural.

However, it makes little difference to the practitioner of the Newar Tantric traditions whether these figures are *yaksini* or *dakini*. For the Newars there is only one supreme deity to worship. She transforms herself into diverse forms with many aspects: male, female, good, fierce, and so on. All deities are considered to be her incarnations or creations. Thus, worshipping the *yaksini* of Ratneshvara is essentially worshipping the supreme female deity, a complement to the male deity, the *linga*, within the temple's sanctuary. This is the basic formula of Tantrism.

Comparative strut replacements —
plain versus carved

The project designed, produced, and
installed three strut replacement options:
an uncarved stut, a reproduction, and a
reduced  design.

top: a surviving historical corner strut
(center) is flanked on the left by copies of
the lost originals and plain struts on the
right
bottom: using a decorative strut instead of
a plain strut

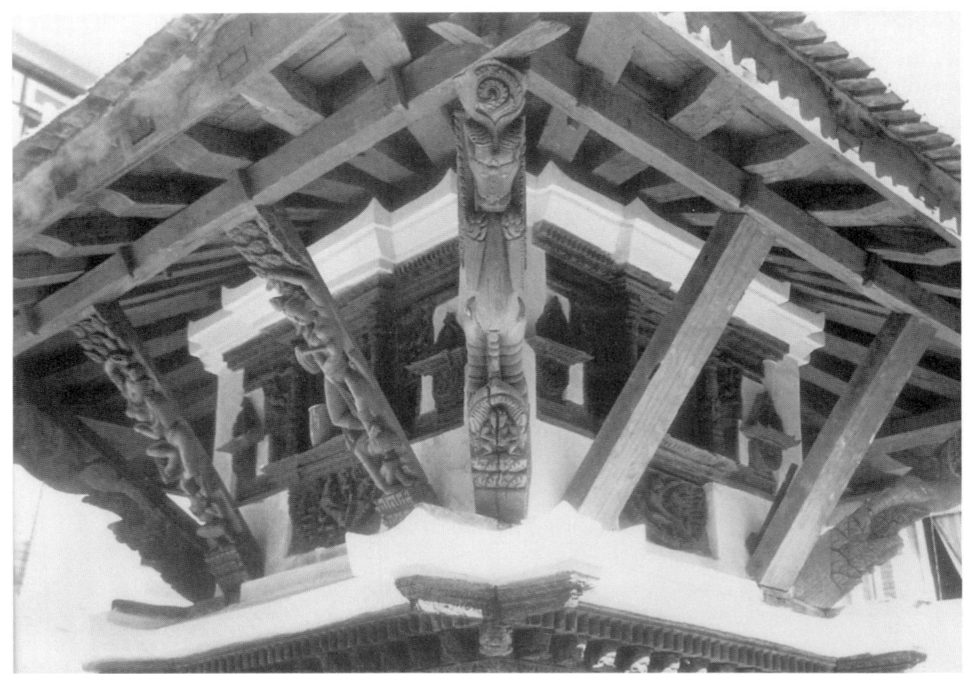

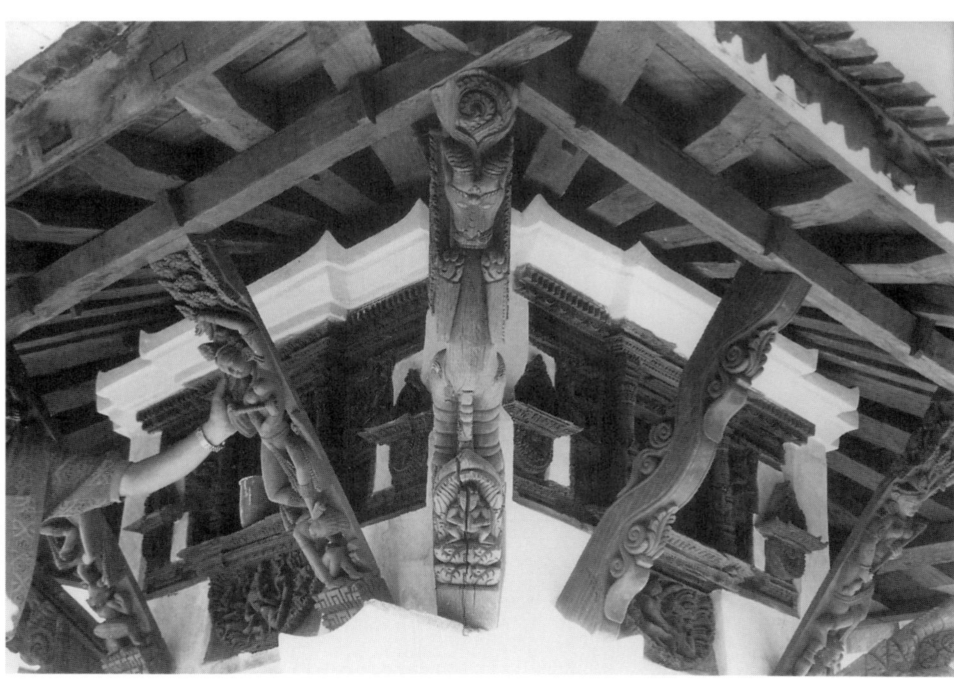

# The Sulima Strut
## A Conservation Design Problem Illustrating Global Issues

Erich Theophile and Rohit Ranjitkar

*Should lost carvings be reproduced based on historical documentation? Should new replacement carvings be reduced, left plain, or reflect a contemporary flavor? When records are unclear, should design by the local craftsmen, those traditionally responsible for this task, be encouraged? How do approaches to these questions reflect theories of authenticity in historic preservation and our understanding of the role of the contemporary restorer?*

## Introduction

The application of international historic preservation principles in the South Asian context has been much discussed in the last decade. Among other questions is a concern that the intellectual and modernist underpinnings of European approaches to historic buildings may not be appropriate to living cultures in which traditional values, building practices, and craftsmen survive. Clashes of "us" and "them" follow typical patterns. International practice advocates the ideal freezing of a building in time, whereas traditional societies—feeling no such distance from a building or its evolution—remain ever ready to add to, modify, or even replace buildings according to present needs or aspirations.

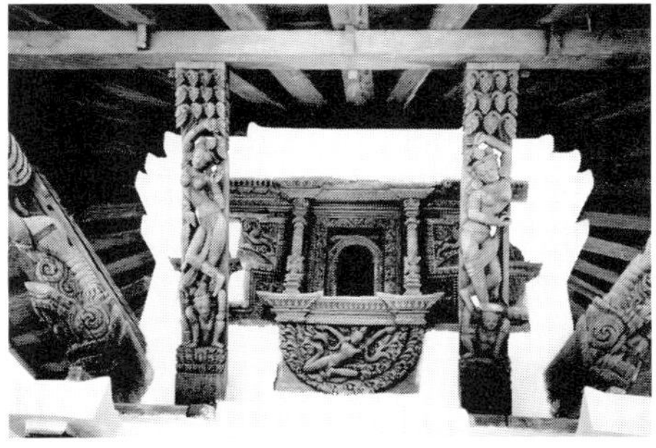

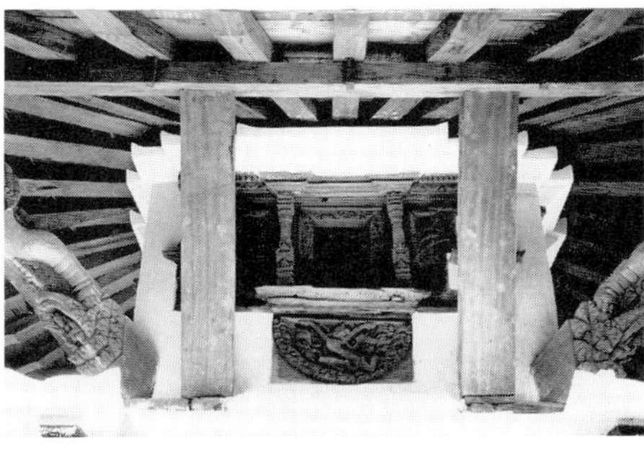

**The dramatic contrast between the use of carved and plain struts**

The most dramatic example of these differences of approach arose in the restoration planning for the Sulima Temple. The neighboring community's plans for renovation in 1994 began with a cost estimate specifying replacement of all the "time-worn" carvings of the temple by new ones. In 1996, from literally the other side of the planet, Harvard professor and Trust co-founder Eduard F. Sekler advised against any replacement carvings, especially of figurative sculpture, and most adamantly in cases for which there was no substantive historical evidence. Quality documentation and conservation of the surviving carvings were to be the project's highest priorities. In a simple but effective capsule of what most western architects believe, Sekler stated, "What's lost is lost and recreation will result in fakes..."

The proposal by locals to replace original carvings of exquisite quality, some of which survived in situ and showed clear signs of their 600-year-old age, is almost unbelievable to the western lover of historic buildings. The existence in Kathmandu of artists and woodcarvers capable of such a commission is equally remarkable.

Our contribution to the challenge of how to fill *lacunae*, or holes, in the historical fabric is the following documentation of the strut-replacement design process: the problem, the context, the issues, and the resolution. One advantage of this particular design problem was that something had to be designed and fabricated to carry the roof loads: non-intervention was not an option. And as the struts were already stolen, the restoration problem did not involve value judgements about conserving or reusing damaged historical elements. It became a concrete design exercise in which we would have to reconcile our own "western"

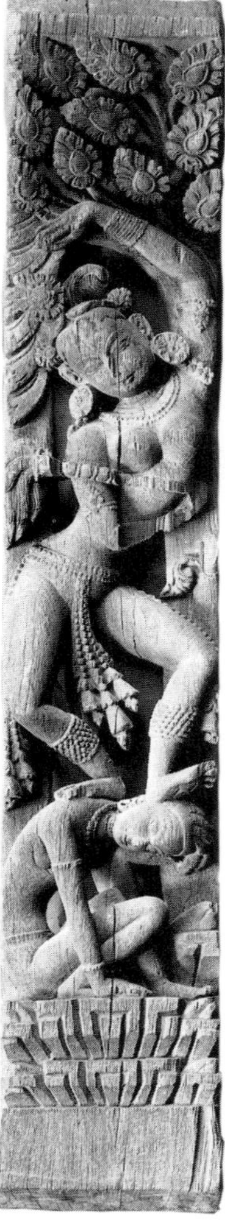
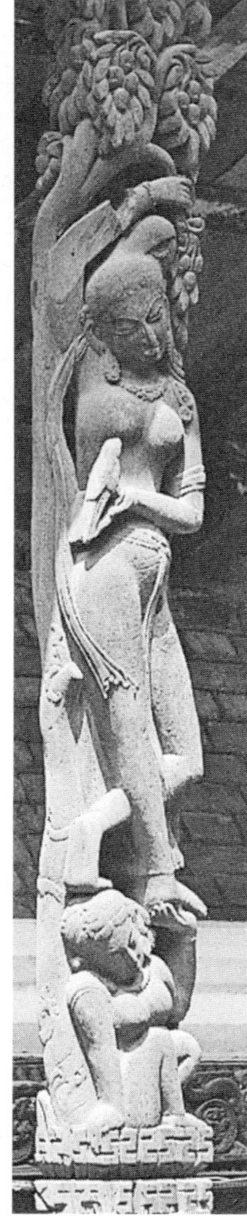

1        2

**above and opposite:**
**The struts on these two pages come from different locations: Itum Baha (1), Uku Baha (2), and Yetkha Baha (3). They are similar in age and composition to the Sulima struts. Each depicts a standing** *yaksi* **with one arm upstretched grasping the branch of a** *sal* **tree.**

notions of authenticity, scientific process, and presentation of historical fabric with local practice and ongoing traditions.

## Authenticity

For the western conservation architect considering producing a copy of a lost original, the amount of documentation is the critical determinant. Both the Charter of Venice and Burra, for example, specify that one should not go beyond the point where conjecture begins in the design of replacement elements. The conjectural design of well-known nineteenth-century restorations are generally frowned upon these days. The contemporary practitioner believes he would not make the same mistakes as his nineteenth-century predecessors.

The documentation for the lost Sulima temple struts was substantial, more than for just about any other temple in the country, having been photographed and published by two art historians. We nevertheless had varying amounts of information about these 16 lost elements, the eight figurative struts at each of the upper and lower roof levels. The four historical corner struts of a different design depicting mythical horses survived at both roof levels.

For the lost struts we could determine their overall size from site measurements, and we knew that they were similar in format and style, female demi-goddesses being the principal figures with subsidiary attendants below and foliage above. For four of the lower struts we had professional large-format photographs, taken head-on with the strut filling the frame. For the remaining four lower struts we had to rely on poorly published snapshots. Four of these eight lower roof struts could also be identified with specific locations on the temple; other locations were indeterminate.

For the eight upper roof struts we had only a written description describing them as diminutive renderings of the lower roof struts. Six months after project start-up, two of these lost upper struts were recovered. They only loosely matched the written descriptions.

For replication, we needed to determine specifics such as the subsidiary figures (for example, a dancer, a seated musician, a demi-god), the symbolic and decorative acoutrements of the goddesses, as well as the artistic qualities of their form and faces. We looked to comparables: if there was a complete set of similar struts that followed an identifiable program, we could extrapolate information about the Sulima struts. Although there are some artistic and historical comparables surviving in situ in the Kathmandu Valley, the specific proportions and details of the Sulima struts proved unique. And only two art historical articles deal with the woodcarvings and struts of this period in any depth. We had a lot of information, but certainly not enough to recreate the entire series with great accuracy.

The question of historical evidence is often presented in preservation literature as a simple yes or no question. The documentation here illustrates several challenging points along the continuum. What is enough? A photograph, a time-worn original, a bad photograph, a written description, a close comparable? Many of the above could be argued as sufficient or insufficient depending on circumstances, so we had to develop our own criteria.

A small group of interested professionals researching this square and the building for years—when would all this information and energy gather in one place again? We felt that a documentation on paper paled in comparison; it would be less convincing and less complete even if more "authentic." Interestingly, the amount of information we had about the lost struts, despite its limitations, made us feel obligated to carve new reproductions, a physical record of what we knew, even if



**The Sulima Pagoda**

imperfect. Designing replacements was actually a means to solidify and expand what we knew. From the beginning of the carving exercise we thus accepted that conjectural design was inevitable and were looking for the intellectual framework to justify it.

One possible approach would have been to reproduce only those struts for which we had the highest quality photographs, i.e. most of the lower struts, and leave the other ones plain. The fortunate presence of craftsmen able to achieve convincing artistic reproductions was critical. We decided to initiate the experiment by carving copies of the two upper roof struts that we had found, as well as of the struts for which we had excellent photographic evidence.

While supervising the carving of the new struts, there were dozens of instances in which lack of clarity in a photograph or subtle questions of artistic judgement came into play. Should we copy the slight asymmetry of the face that had resulted from the effects of rain and wind, or should we make it as if it were new? After months of close collaboration with the carvers, we learned a simple lesson about historical recreation: conjectural design and subjective decisions are unavoidable no matter how much historical evidence exists. It seemed important to document examples of this process because so much literature in the field of preservation treats only the scientific and objective design methods.

We noted that our carvers, working from the two upper roof originals, could produce results of great beauty—museum quality if you will. Those made from photographs were beautiful, but not of the same caliber in formal flow. They represented a greater artistic demand on the carver as he had to translate the image from two to three dimensions while creating. For the planning of future efforts we now knew to design and budget several rounds of carvings for new "experimental" carvings.

Based on what we judged to be successes with the first reproductions, we began carving the upper roof struts for which there were only written, iconographic descriptions. Even though we knew that these two- to three-sentence descriptions were insufficient and often even inconsistent, we trusted our carvers' abilities to design in the spirit of the monument.

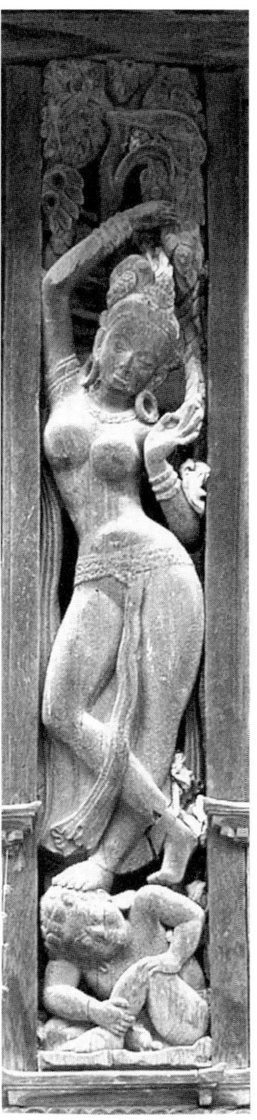

3

## Labeling and presentation

A general mandate among architectural preservation charters to distinguish new from old interestingly remains unquestioned despite the enormous philosophical and visual implications of this caveat. In the field of art restoration, "invisible" conservation of damaged areas in a painting is sometimes acceptable, so why not in buildings?

A visual indication of a replacement element's age actually represents two choices: first, to distinguish new from old, and second, how to do it. Stylistic reduction, visible or concealed labels, and project documentation are all ways to achieve the latter. One generally accepted criterion among conservation architects is that when new features blend in with the whole, they should at least be discernable as contemporary upon close inspection.

We had inhibitions about overt labeling, largely a reaction to our own recent restoration of the Kulima Temple in 1997. In that project, the absence of historical documentation about two lost roof struts had encouraged us to follow western norms and leave the replacement elements plain. The contrast of plain and carved elements on the restored façade turned out to be visually disturbing, an extreme example of labeling. One might say that only a modernist aesthetic could appreciate this juxtaposition.

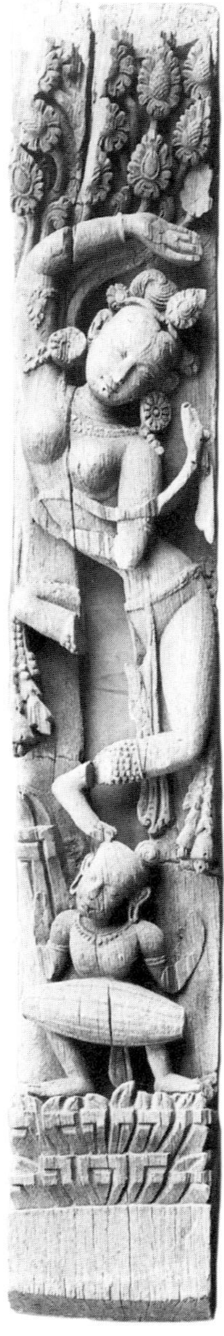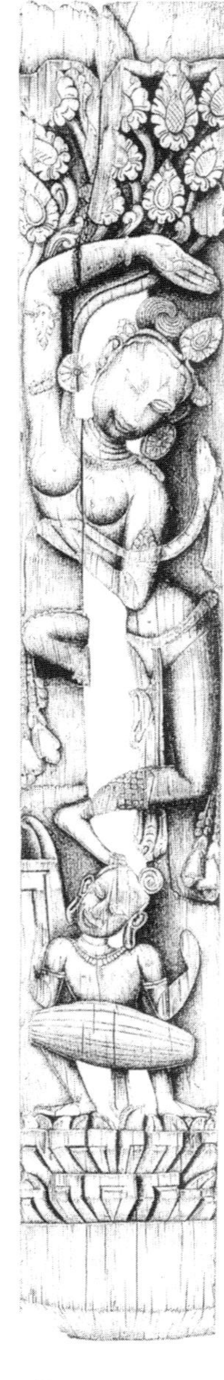

1                2

**The art of copying**
The original upper roof strut (1) was carefully documented by Bijay Basukala, who rendered a full size drawing (2). A line drawing (3) was then prepared and glued to the raw timber to guide the wood carver. Preparation of the drawings took as long as the carving of the reproduction (4).

Friends and local partners reacted negatively as well. Art historian Mary Slusser felt it was "harsh" and, given the living tradition of local carvers, "a shame" not to carve new pieces. At another nearby temple, where we had also left lost door carvings plain, neighborhood children repeatedly drew chalk figures on the panels. The Department of Archaeology was the only local discussion partner who seemed to understand our philosophical position, having been initiated into the line of reasoning through numerous discussions with visiting UNESCO experts. In several but not all of the Department's projects, indeterminate elements had been left plain.

For the temple at Sulima, we felt that visible labels would be an imposition of our western thinking. Our "labeling" was thus conceived on a less visible, but more ambitious scale. We undertook extensive historic documentation, a historic structure report, the development of an archive to house the materials, and the publication of this book. We asked the carvers to date each new carved component on the back—they went even further and signed each piece as well.

## Designing in the spirit of our times

Many have discussed the tautology of the Charter of Venice's mandate to brand modern interventions with the "spirit of our times." The term is so vague that anything from an antique reproduction or revival to a modernist juxtaposition could be construed as suggesting the spirit of our times. In conservation circles, the mandate has often been interpreted to mean that modern interventions, while remaining compatible, should "look modern."

In this light, we explored the possibility of designing a "modern" strut, perhaps even executing it in another material such as steel. Several inspirational modern examples stand nearby, such as the elegant steel and timber pillars designed for the Patan Palace restoration by architect Götz Hagmüller. There are also intriguing, early twentieth-century struts in sheet metal installed on another Patan Palace façade: non-traditional and original sculptures by a local artist coping with shortages of timber after the 1934 earthquake. At Daubaha, a Buddhist monastery in Patan, we documented examples of strut figures crudely painted on flat boards in 1968 to simulate lost iconography.

We decided early on against the introduction of steel. For steel we would actually need an industrial designer capable of creating a new member elegant enough to complement this temple. We also felt that it was disrespectful to introduce a steel element on this temple façade. Given the significance of the surviving carvings in the walls, something more respectful and less aggressive seemed appropriate. We love Carlo Scarpa's modern and contrasting interventions at Castelvecchio in Verona, Italy, but to emulate this level of stylistic contrast on a temple seemed inappropriate. Besides, we thought that the amount of time we would spend designing a new member would be better spent refining a reproduction of one of the lost originals.

## Presentation of historical fabric

Given the artistic and historical importance of the surviving windows (which would be framed by the struts), another consideration was how replacements would compete with, complement, or detract from these original features. As discussed above, we knew that the juxtaposition of plain and carved could be distracting: the advancing surfaces of the plain elements draw the eye away from the historical carvings, the opposite of the intended effect. Eduard Sekler's suggestion in the context of "avoiding fakes" was to design something in reduced form, "in outline, but without detail."

This design challenge started us looking for comparables, our most practiced approach to design questions. In the local residential architecture we found examples of nineteenth-century struts whose geometric modeling recalled the form of the figurative temple struts. We decided to design and commission such a geometrically reduced strut for comparative study, although we knew that installing a non-figurative carving on a temple was certainly artificial. Ideally, this exercise could produce a more neutral addition whose curvilinear forms would not detract from the historical carvings.

During the test installations we found this reduced element promising. Unlike new plain members, it did not "block" one's viewing of the adjacent carved windows. It blended in, but still looked different. The carved alternatives were, nevertheless, so convincing that the reduced alternative would remain an academic exercise. The new and old carvings "sang" together—both looked more beautiful when juxtaposed, making our conclusion quite simple. In sum, these new sculptures were the most artistic way to present the historical windows. The reduced strut with historical flavor was a useful alternative for future projects in which there was less historical evidence or a more limited budget that could not support replacement master carvings.

## Living cultures and votive offerings

A tradition of votive donations to temples, gifts made in a charitable way to achieve religious merit, is relevant and takes place on many scales in Nepal, ranging from small gift offerings to buildings and substantial additions and reconstructions. The amount of religious merit earned by such an act naturally varies in relation to the magnitude of the gift.

In this context one can understand why the community's original restoration plan proposed replacement of all the "worn" carvings of the wall elements and the surviving corner struts with new ones. Their value as historical art objects played no role in this decision, nor did the age of the iconographic images increase their religious value. The community believed that the act of recreating was a gift of greater magnitude and constituted greater good, a moral position ironically comparable to how preservationists feel about retaining the same objects.

At Sulima, our principal discussion partners for the design process were community members, who were donating 25 percent of the construction costs. They fully supported the plan to reproduce carved struts, but the retention of old woodcarvings on the façades required considerable convincing. We thought it was critical to demonstrate both. As fortune would have it, a mixture of new and retained historical carvings was a middle path, an illustration of thoughtful diversity.

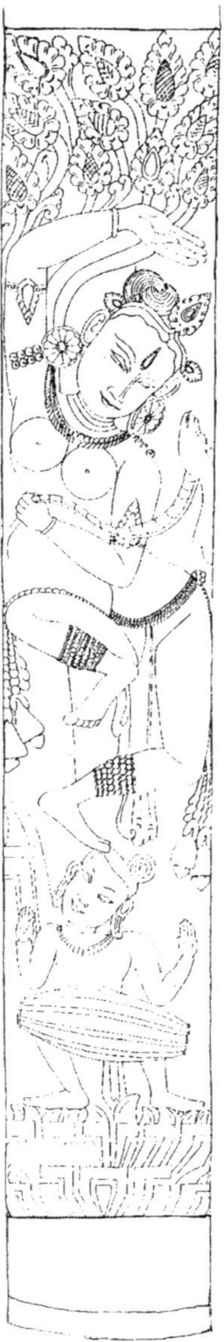

3

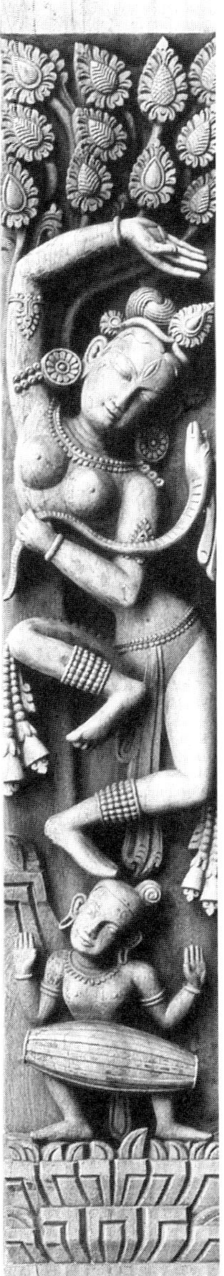

4

West                North

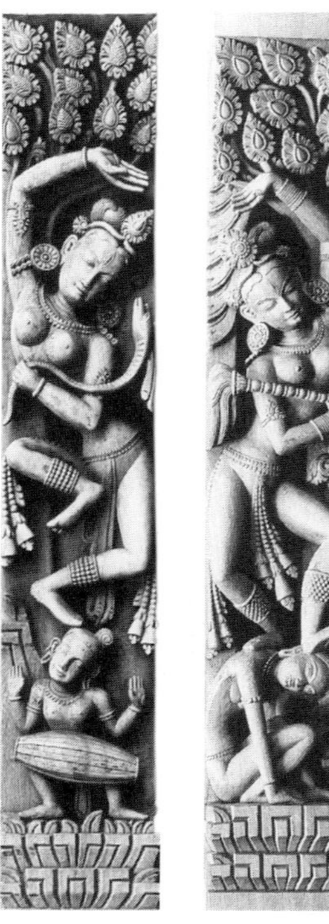

1, 2

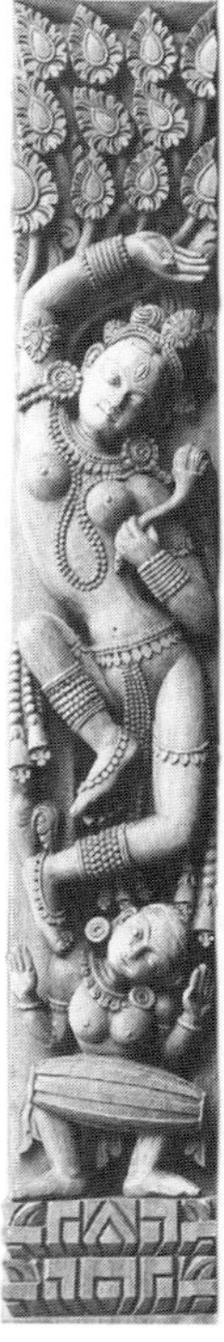

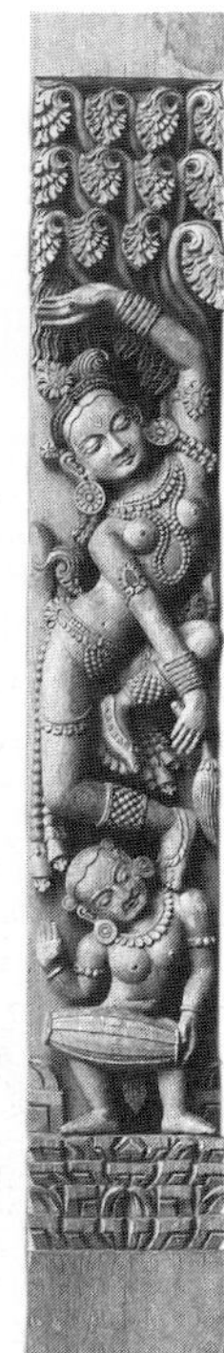

3, 4

The new upper roof struts
1, 2  Reproductions of struts copied
      from the two surviving struts
3, 4  Designs based on short
      written descriptions
The new lower roof struts
5, 6  Designs based on Mary Slusser's
      photographs
7, 8  Designs based on snapshots
      and short written descriptions

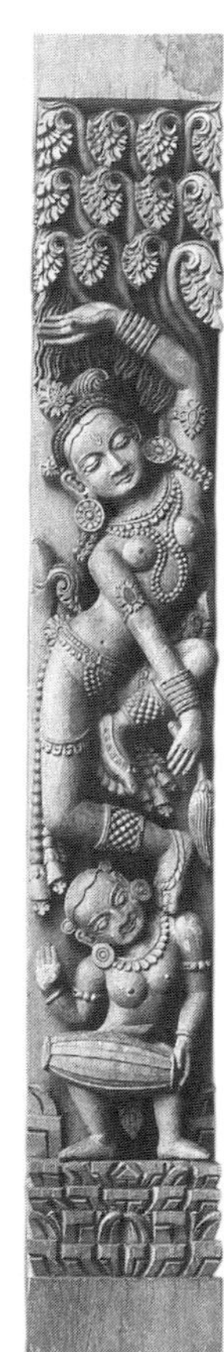

5, 6

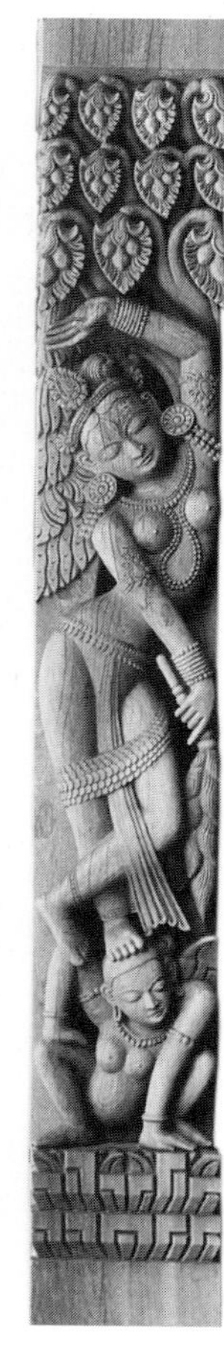

7, 8

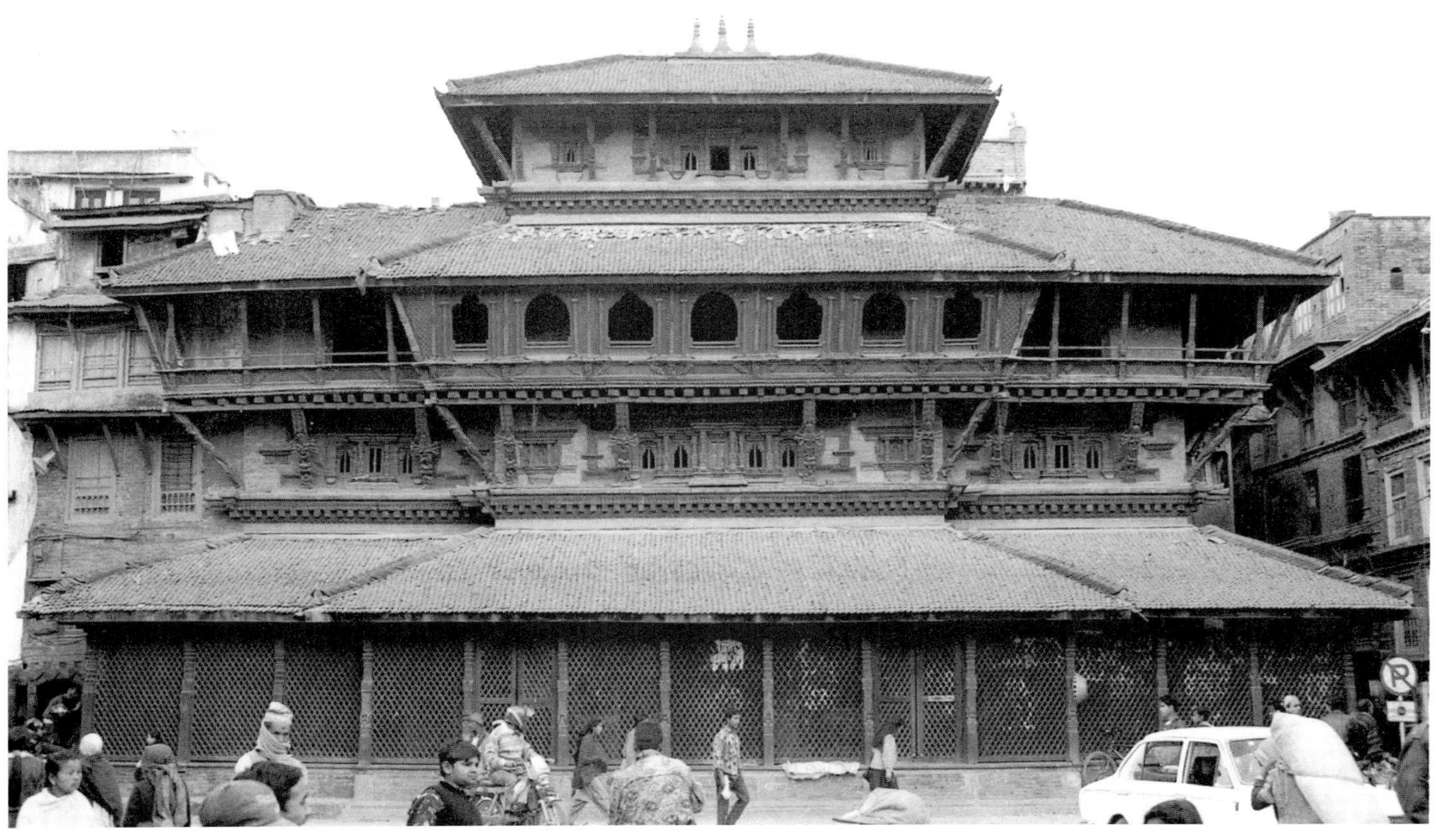



## Religious significance

As the Sulima Temple is still actively used for worship, a key consideration was how the new elements would enhance or detract from the religious meaning of the temple. A survey of the philosophy of strut and carving replacements in local projects was undertaken as part of the design research.

Local initiatives by the *guthi* or neighborhood leaders universally prefer new decorative and figurative elements of religious significance, but with variable relationships to the lost or historical elements. In a recent restoration of the popular Lunchu Lu Ajima Shrine at Indrachok, Kathmandu, historical elements were even over-carved to achieve the sharpness of features lost in the original's 300-year-old patina. New replacements in concrete, and crude but more durable polychromed substitutes, are also popular.

At Maruhiti, Kathmandu, the restoration of an important eighteenth-century temple to Santaneshvara, led by the priestly family, thoughtfully commissioned strut copies of the "closest Shiva shrine." This turned out to be a nearby temple rebuilt in 1969 by the Guthi Sansthan. Thirty-year-old struts were thus dutifully copied and installed at Santaneshvara, religiously appropriate, but artistically unrelated to the restoration.

To complete our restoration of the Radha Krishna Temple, in 1992 we interviewed numerous priests, carvers, and religious historians in an effort to determine what figure would be appropriate. Opinions varied considerably. The most suggestive proposal, made by a local priest, was to redesign all of the

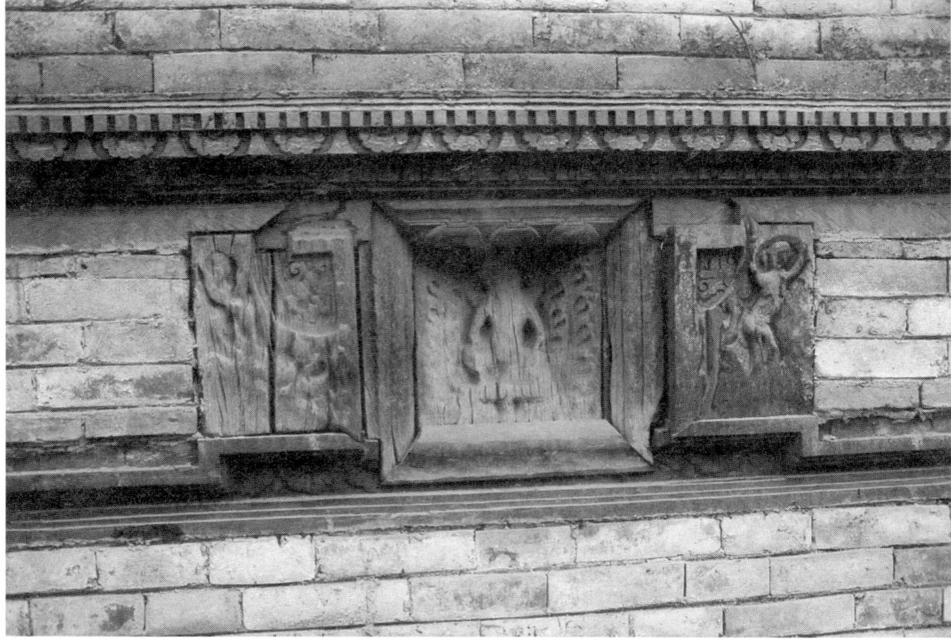

historical struts because the extant cycle, in his mind, was incorrect for the enshrined deity.

Individuals, priests, and woodcarvers thus continue to have strong feelings about which deities should be installed to fill gaps or replace the historical fabric. These considerations are notably independent from questions of artistic continuity and faithfulness to the original.

## Conclusions

In general, our western perspective is well practiced and sophisticated in its approach to a monument's physical remains. However, many of the philosophical underpinnings of preservation are not at odds with living culture but have not been stretched to address such design challenges.

The experiment at Sulima and the rich complex world of the Kathmandu Valley provide valuable testing grounds to explore this meeting of worlds. International or bilateral projects emphasize "educating the locals." The recent wave of interest in autochthonous cultures emphasizes "doing it like the local." But the story of the Sulima Strut is the story of a middle and hybrid path. Sensitive approaches will involve expanding our goals and working methods, not limiting them. We will accept diversity and relish it. We contribute design research methods, a multi-disciplinary team, and a love of documentation. Our Nepali partners provide artistic talent, a will to adorn, and, most importantly, a historical and authentic living human connection to the buildings and their gods.

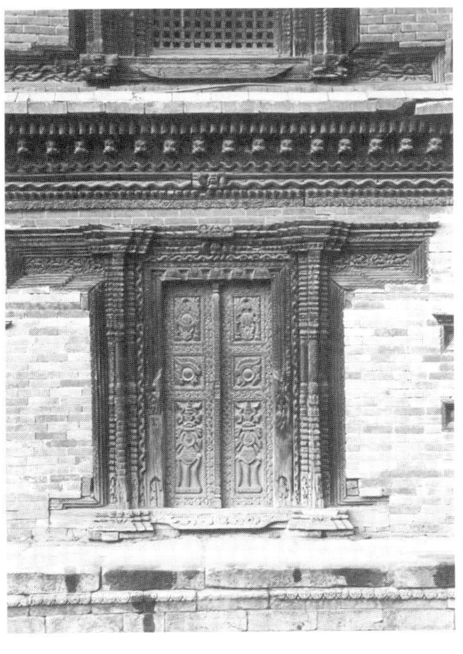

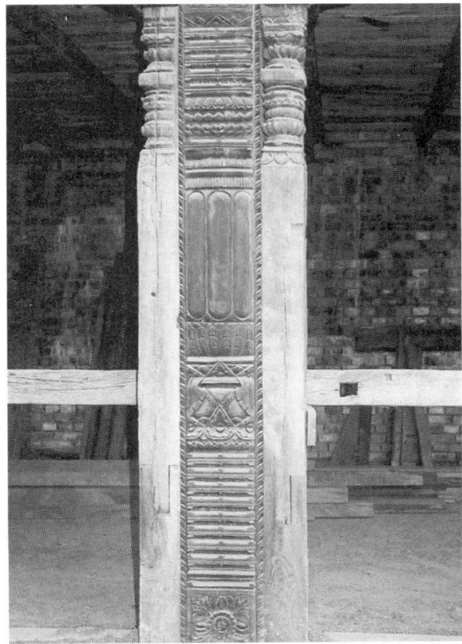

**Creative solutions**
far left: Plain door panels were replaced with contemporary carvings in the seventeenth-century Palace of 55 Windows, Bhaktapur. This elaboration coincided with the King's coronation in 1975.

left: The rebuilding of a historic resthouse at Pashupatinath mixed a new concrete frame with historical elements.
Here the two historical timber columns are artfully attached to a concrete pier.

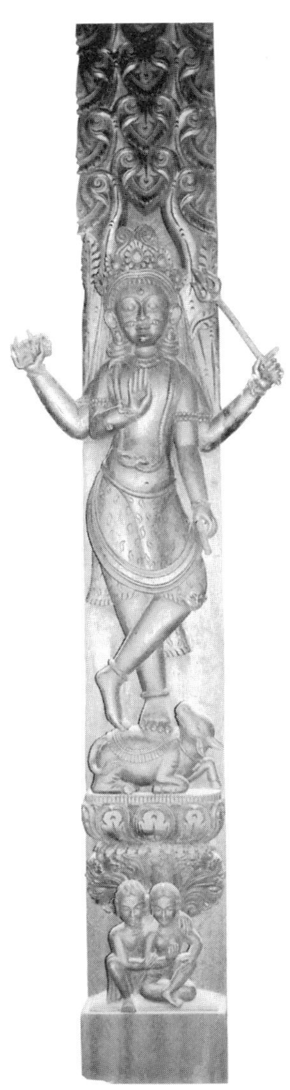

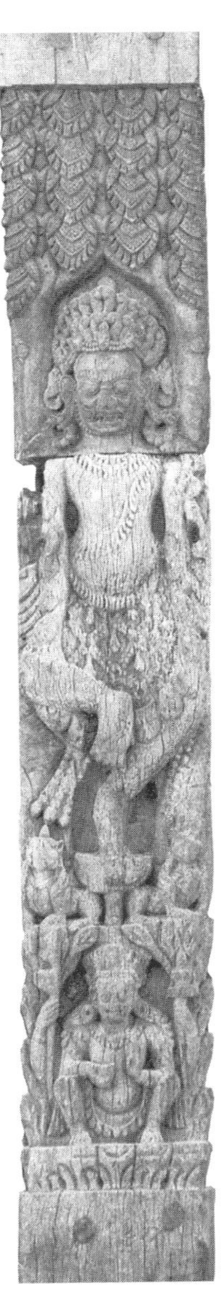

**Appropriate replacement?**
far left: This new strut was commissioned by the priest of Santaneshvara, an eighteenth-century Shiva temple in Kathmandu. He instructed the carver to "copy those [struts] of the nearest Shiva shrine." This turned out to be a nearby temple rebuilt in 1969 with contemporary carvings. Carver Indrakaji Silpakar dutifully reproduced the modern elements, but says he is not proud of the commission.

**Reconstruction of historical fragments**
left: This seventeenth-century strut depicting Bhairav was recovered from the debris during the Trust's restoration of the Radha Krishna Temple in Patan. The lost upper third of the strut, including the deity's head, was replaced. This attempt to retain the historical fabric seems artificial in retrospect. A more sensitive intervention, especially given the willingness of patrons and craftsmen to recreate, would have been to make a new strut and document the surviving portion of the strut.

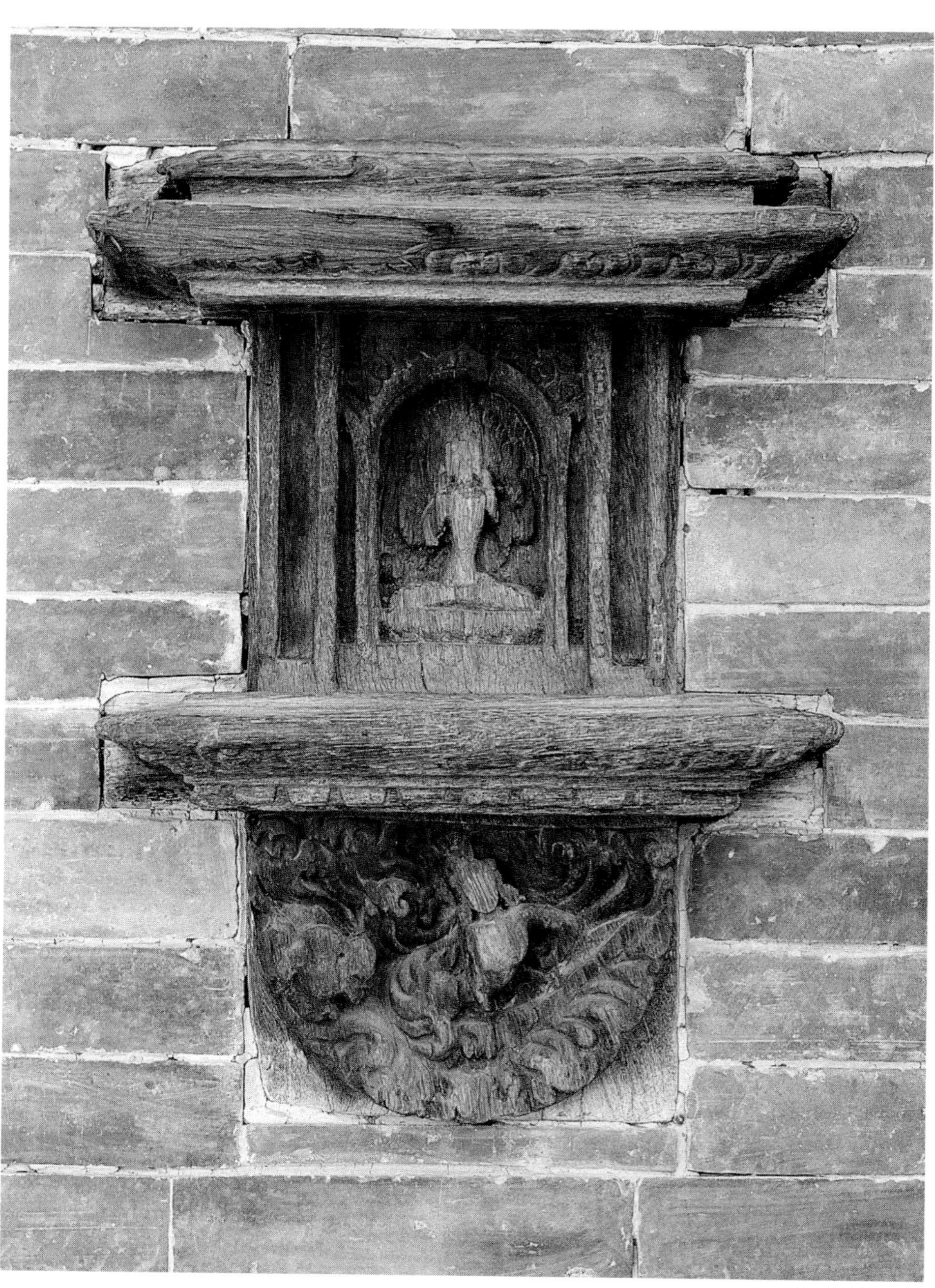

Sulima Temple blind window
The ground floor blind window on
the northeast side after restoration

# Recapturing Lost Elements

Niels Gutschow

The great historical importance of the Sulima Temple became clearer during the course of the project, partly as a result of parallel documentation and analysis of other comparable early Newar woodcarvings. These included detailed drawings of the Manjushri Degah at Sasunani and Gayahbajya's house at Sulima Square. The blind windows of the Sasunani structure are among Nepal's oldest extant wooden building components, dated stylistically to the eleventh or twelfth centuries. Comparing them with the carvings of the Ratneshvara Temple, we also felt more comfortable about Mary Slusser's dating of the Sulima carvings to the fourteenth century.

We felt confident that our original hypothesis was sound, that is, that all the carved elements of the temple had survived earlier reconstructions and documented an unusually rare unity of style. We took stock again of uncarved elements, all features either lost or replaced that we had decided not to recreate at an earlier planning stage. The blind windows or niches of the ground floor survived in a deplorable condition, missing their architectural frame of colonnettes, but had gone unnoticed as long as the entire temple was without roof and struts. We also reconsidered recreating the *tympanum*, discussed in the next chapter. The reinstatement of the colonnettes could be justified as a way to achieve the characteristic framing of Newar wall openings, achieved through multiple layers of timber mouldings and elements.

## Process

We were aware that fashioning the replacements of lost elements to look like originals was, and still is, widely branded as a falsification of the historical fabric. Nonetheless, we decided to consider what a local craftsperson would do if faced with this task of repairing the temple. This question served as a tool for analyzing which repairs and replacements would be appropriate. As our local carpenters would not hesitate to replace an element like a lost colonnette, we decided to proceed. At the same time, and out of respect for the more hands-off western approach, we replaced only the colonnettes on one side of the temple (in two of the six niches). The others were left as they were, as was the threshold of the principal entrance, whose fragmentary figurative sculpture was indeterminate.

The design process relied on the identification, study, and measured drawings of comparables. The replacement colonnettes would be fashioned by our lead carver based on measured and "designed" drawings. The process of making the drawings would afford the opportunity to clarify certain details that could be missed if the carver simply worked from a photograph, the typical working method.

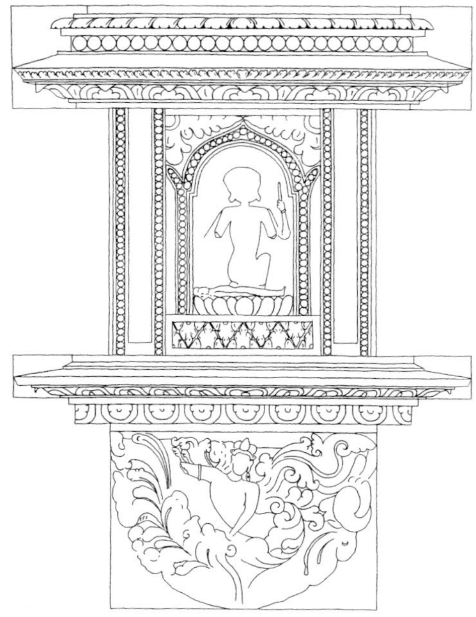

The process of designing these replacement colonnettes can be compared to the German trend *Schöpferische Denkmalpflege*, or creative conservation, describing a synthetic approach to conservation design in Germany's 1948-1958 post-war reconstruction period. It is perhaps not surprising to find this parallel, as the ravages of war are not so different from the very dilapidated states of temples here. Both situations necessitate hundreds of design decisions to complete or present what are fragmentary monuments. Interestingly, this attitude, which represents a significant part of ongoing practice throughout the world, rarely surfaces in official statements. Instead, "scientific" or pseudo-rational presentations either ignore or downplay the creative process.[1]

The forward-standing posts or colonnettes of the ground floor blind window were designed on the basis of several conscious choices by Bijay Basukala, draftsman and designer. Bijay has drawn more square feet of historical buildings than anyone in Nepal. The lost elements being smaller than any comparables we studied, he favored the details of the diminutive window from the house of Gayahbajya. He also introduced a half-round profile (*nagvah*) above the *amalaka* motif that echoes a design found on the temple's top story blind windows.

The relationship between the column components, i.e. top-middle-bottom, similarly reflects the proportions of the Gayahbajya window. We were pleasantly surprised when the completed sample was installed—it not only fit, but looked like it had always been there despite the difference in patina. Our partner architect, Rohit Ranjitkar, inadvertently ordered enough of the colonnettes for all the niches. We decided his instinct to repair all of the niches was deserving of mention even if we didn't install the other pieces.

## Assessment

In developing this article we reflected upon the question of what a local carpenter would have done. Our belief that a local would replace the colonnette with an exact copy was merely wishful thinking. A local artisan would fully replace such a worn-out looking carved component with a new one. (In fact, this is what the Municipal Government had proposed doing years earlier.) He would also not hesitate to "improve" the design of the new component, making a new one only loosely based on the historical one. And finally, the new piece would definitely be as ornate as possible, a universal trend in contemporary carving.

We do admit an inconsistency in these decisions about replacements, achieving completeness in some places and maintaining *lacunae* in others. We probably want to consider these new forward-standing posts for a while before we propose more replacements on the basis of comparative design. This exercise was a small step, an experiment to build confidence and inform future decision-making.

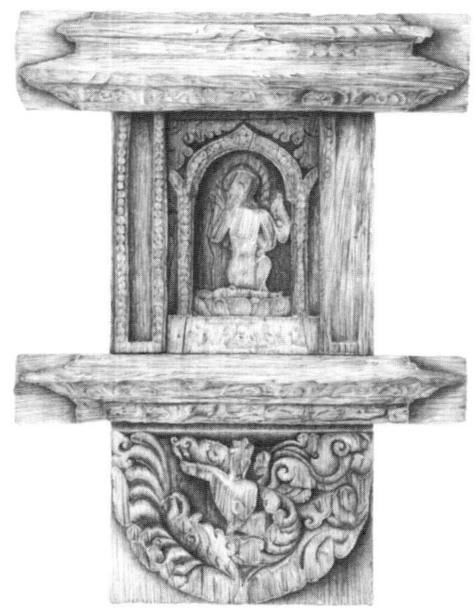

**Sulima Temple blind window
above: line drawing of the ground-floor
blind window on the northwest side
Drawing by Anil Basukala, 1999
left: detailed rendering of
the same window
Drawing by Bijay Basukala, 1999**



**The Sulima Pagoda**

So if our solution was not local, what was it? Ultimately it was a hybrid process through which our western obsession with historical fabric was tempered by an eastern willingness to modify, and through which our western ideas about rigorous study, documentation, and testing were complemented by an eastern inclination and ability to simply act. The ultimate lesson of this exercise may be that the interesection of different worlds offers new opportunities for building conservation.

## Dignity versus authenticity

Repeated discussions about what to do helped us identify one concept that is generally missing in conservation policy statements: dignity. Historic buildings have the right to emerge from the process of conservation in dignity. In Nepal, this dignity often rules out stabilizing a building as it is found, as this would mean freezing ruins. It also rules out erasing all signs of age, or "scars," which is the preference of our Nepali clients and partners. They always prefer the impression of a new building, in which the leaning wall or old carving is replaced by a new one.

By dignity we also mean that a building can recapture, sometimes to a significant extent, its original shape. History produces patina, and fortunately new elements attain patina rapidly in Nepal's monsoon climate. With this consideration, we advocate that new carved elements be "compatible" without imposing any guidelines or rules. We aim for a sense of harmony for each structure, a balance between creation and heritage preservation. We also acknowledge that as an architect works on a building his inclination to create and embellish only increases. In this process the responsible architect requires discussion partners who encourage a balance between heritage and creation, between love and respect.

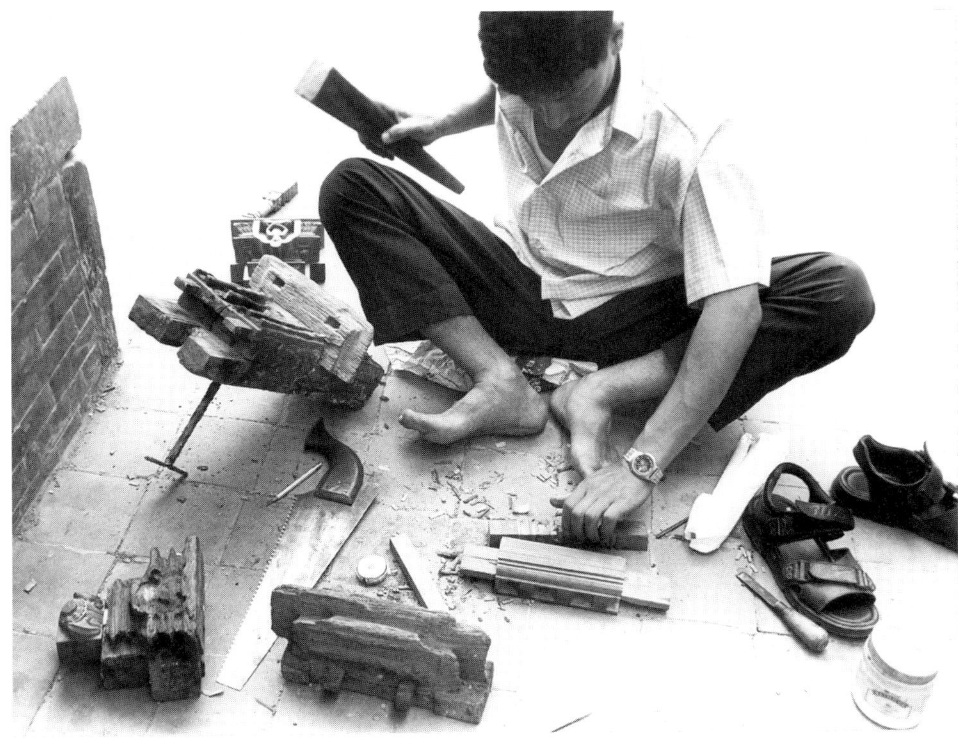

**Hari Silpakar repairing a blind window**

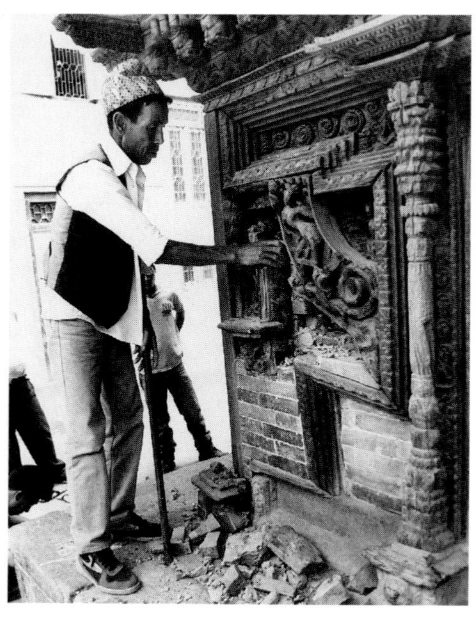

Installation of the colonnettes on the
principal façade of the Sulima Temple



Ratneshvara *torana*
The design for the replacement colonnette
follows a canonic formula: capital with
*amalaka* motif above an octagonal
transition, a principal circular shaft, and
at the base, the auspicious *kalasha*, or
vessel, with flowers. The square base block
is incised with the abstract lotus leaf
motif, *palasicvah*.
Drawing by Bijay Basukala, March, 1999

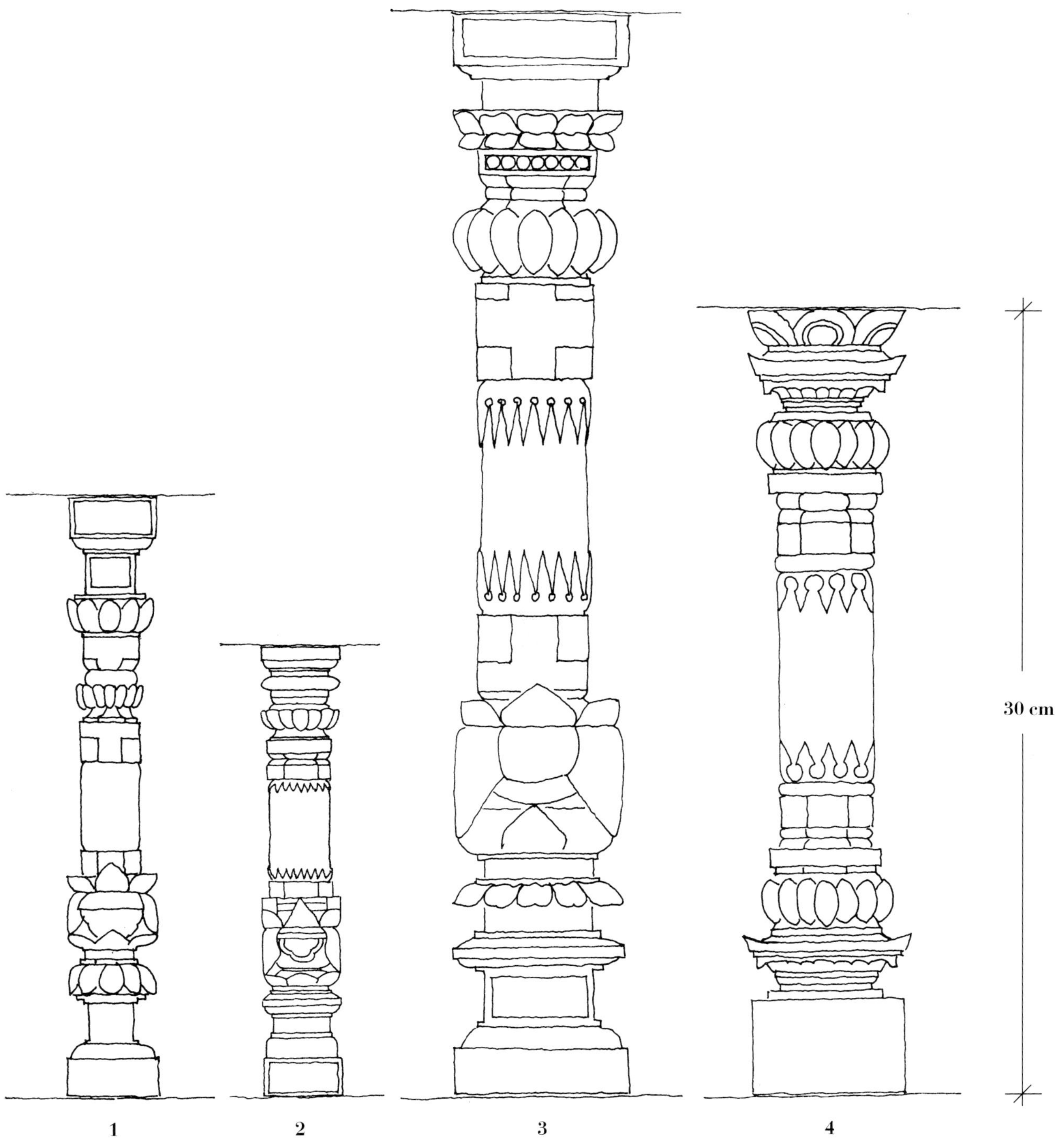



**A study of comparables**
Moldings of comparable early colonnettes reveal a prescribed formula: square blocks at the top and bottom, a round central shaft, and the symbolic ring of *amalaka* fruit representing the celestial world above and hinting at the primordial tree that bears fruit of that shape.

A *kalasha* is always found below, filled with water and overflowing with vegetation it is the vase of plenty on which the pillar rests. An octagonal cross section makes a formal transition between the square above and round forms below.

1  Twelfth-century colonnette, Sasunani Manjushri Degah, in Kvalakhu, Patan

2  Design for ground floor blind window, Ratneshvara Temple, Sulima

3  Colonnette from auxiliary window flanking a larger window with five openings (pasukajhyah) on the first floor, Gayahbajya's house, Sulima, Patan

4  Seventeenth-century auxiliary window colonnette flanking another *pasukajhyah*, Malachuka, Taumadhi, Bhaktapur

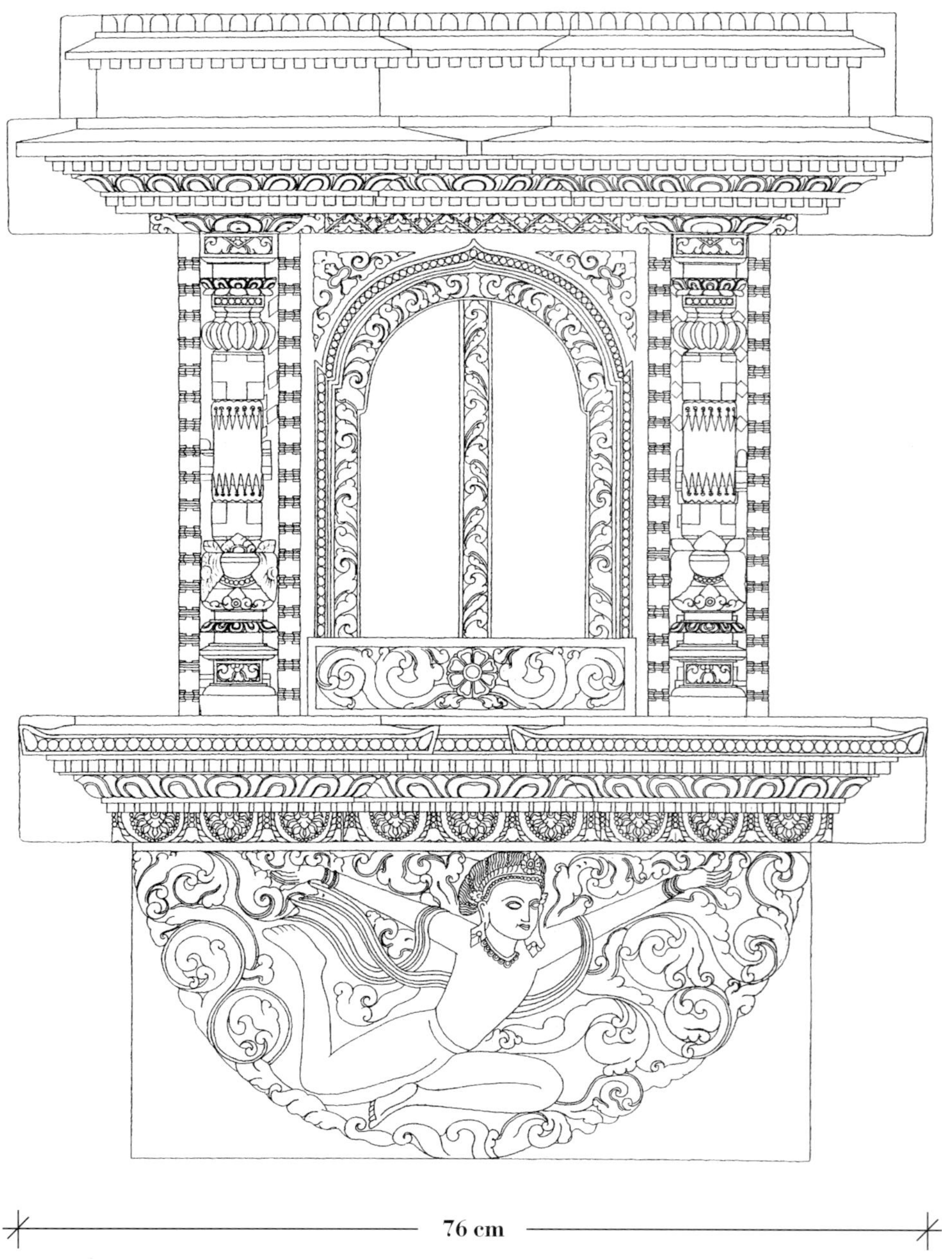

— 76 cm —

**Window at Gayahbajya's house**
This first-floor miniature window (*gahjhyah*) flanks a window with five small openings or *pasukajhyah*. This type of window usually indicates the location of an esoteric shrine. In this case, the house shelters the spirit of the famous Tantric, Gayahbajya. This fourteenth-century window is more than double the size of the Sulima Temple examples. It also displays more elaborate and refined figurative and ornamental details: the two cornices are elaborately carved; dentils punctuate horizontal projections. The colonnettes are treated as real "orders" with projections suggesting base and capital. Probably the composition carried a *tympanum* or *torana* above, now lost. The figure at the base, a *vidhyadhara*, does not bear offerings as was the convention in the early Indian prototypes from which it was copied.
Drawing by Bijay Basukala, 1998

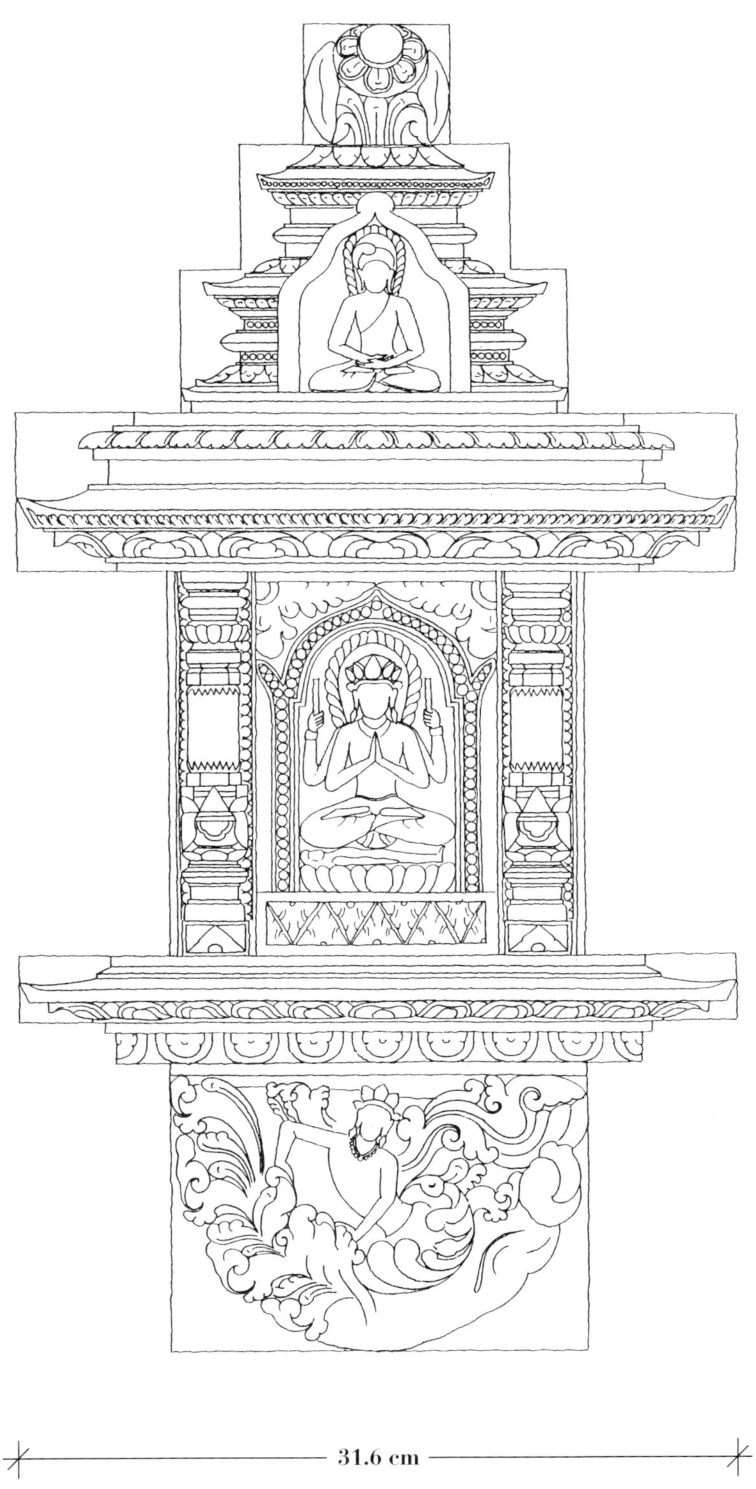

— 31.6 cm —

Blind window design
for Sulima Temple
The colonnettes, which translates
literally from the Newari as
"forward standing posts," carry
a cornice. Above, a stepping
architectural feature frames a
niche in which Shiva meditates.
An elaborate lotus flower crowns
the composition.
Drawing by Bijay Basukala, 1999

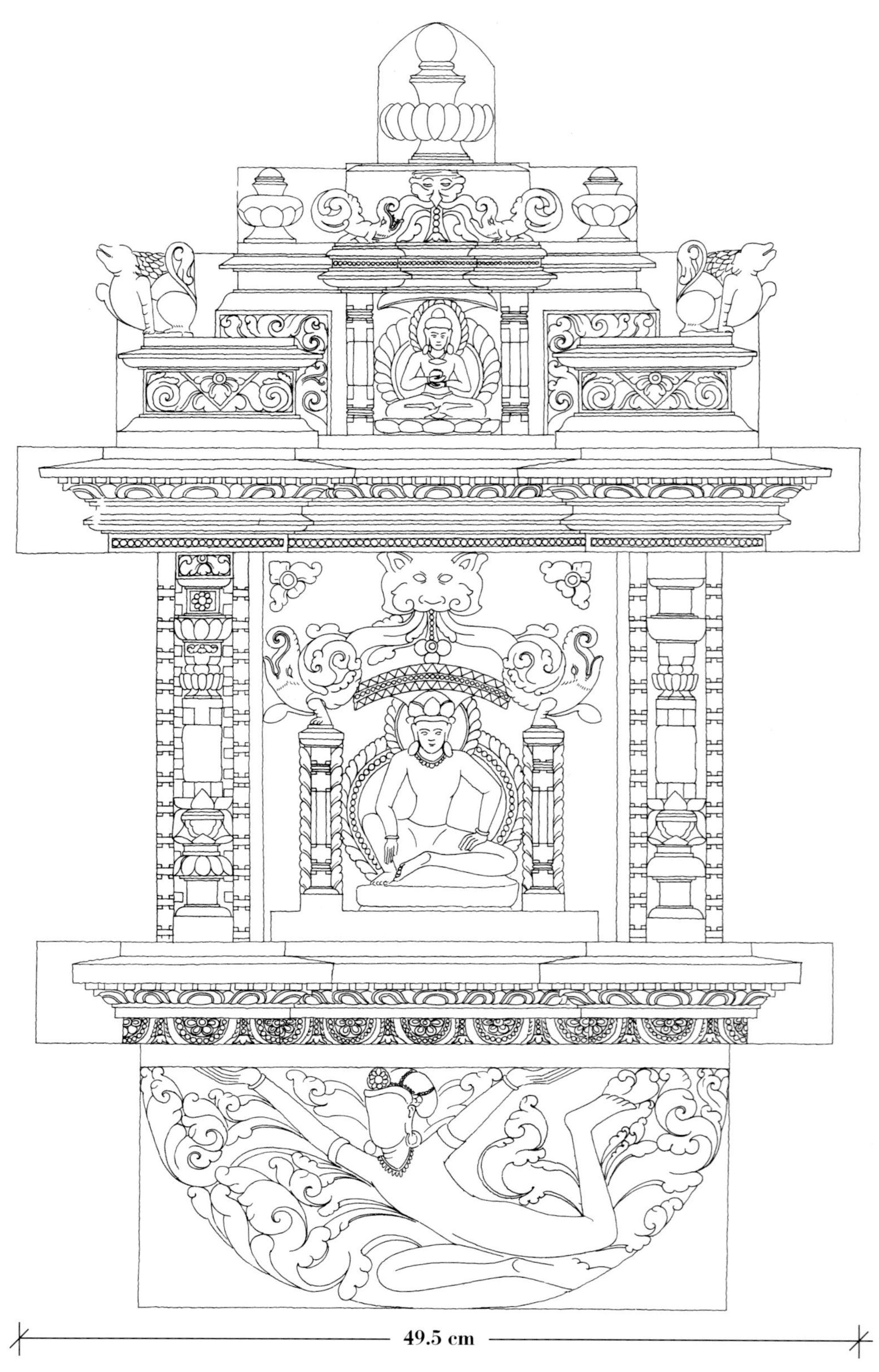

Blind niche at Manjushri Degah,
Sasunani, Patan
Drawing by Bijay Basukala, 1998





The Sulima Pagoda

# Gahjyah at Sasunani

## Notes on an Early Blind Window

Niels Gutschow

A carved timber niche, or *gahjyah* (literally, "blind window" in Newari), at Sasunani, Patan, is an important comparable to the Sulima Temple façade elements. It is a rare and significant survivor of Nepal's Transitional Period (950-1200 CE). The few examples that survive *in situ* in Patan are models for the many later derivations of the Malla period (1482-1768 CE). Their close resemblance to Gupta architecture in North India (320-840 CE) documents an early stylistic import.

The accompanying documentation drawings are the result of many months of study of an individual architectural element that included cleaning, tactile investigation, and disassembly/reassembly. Only in this way (e.g. by studying the backs of the component pieces and the textures) were we able to reconstruct certain faint, time-worn details.

The overall composition of this window suggests a miniature building of sorts, a universal theme in the architecture of the Subcontinent. In Nepal, many windows frame images of gods rather than providing openings for light and ventilation. The principal frame is a complex and ambitious composition, more aggregate than synthetic in effect. It supports a heavy, stepping superstructure that is roof-like with its heraldic vases and lions. This composition is carried by a semi-circular base block inscribed with a *vidyadhara*, a flying mythical being who is the "bearer of wisdom." It closely follows Gupta prototypes of the fifth and sixth centuries and is one of the most common motifs in Indian art and architecture. Other examples are found at the ninth-century Buddhist center of Orissa and the seventeenth-century temples at Vishnupur, Bengal. In later developments, the *vidyadhara* are often joined by groups of celestial musicians, *gandharva*, and *kinnara*, mythical bird figures with human heads.

The Sasunani niche's combination of elements is unique. We find many examples of the base block and niche composition in later buildings, but the superstructure is a rare form found in only one other extant example, the Sulima Temple niches. In later Nepali examples, this superstructure is reduced to a rectangular block, like an entablature, or reinterpreted as the common half-round *tympanum*, or *torana* in Newari.

The niche achieves a deep layered effect through its repetitition of architectural frames, which is typical of the Newar canon. Two pairs of miniature columns also flank the Buddhist icon within and above the principal *trabeate* composition. The main icon, an unidentified seated *boddhisattva*, is flanked by rather basic columns bearing a *kalamakara* motif.

This motif, found throughout all ages of Indian art, consists of a central mythical animal whose "face of glory" or *kirtimukha* spews foliate serpent bodies. The serpents curl up in reverse symmetry and are rendered as fanciful mythical crocodiles, or *makara*. The silhouette of the *kalamakara* is bold and shapely like

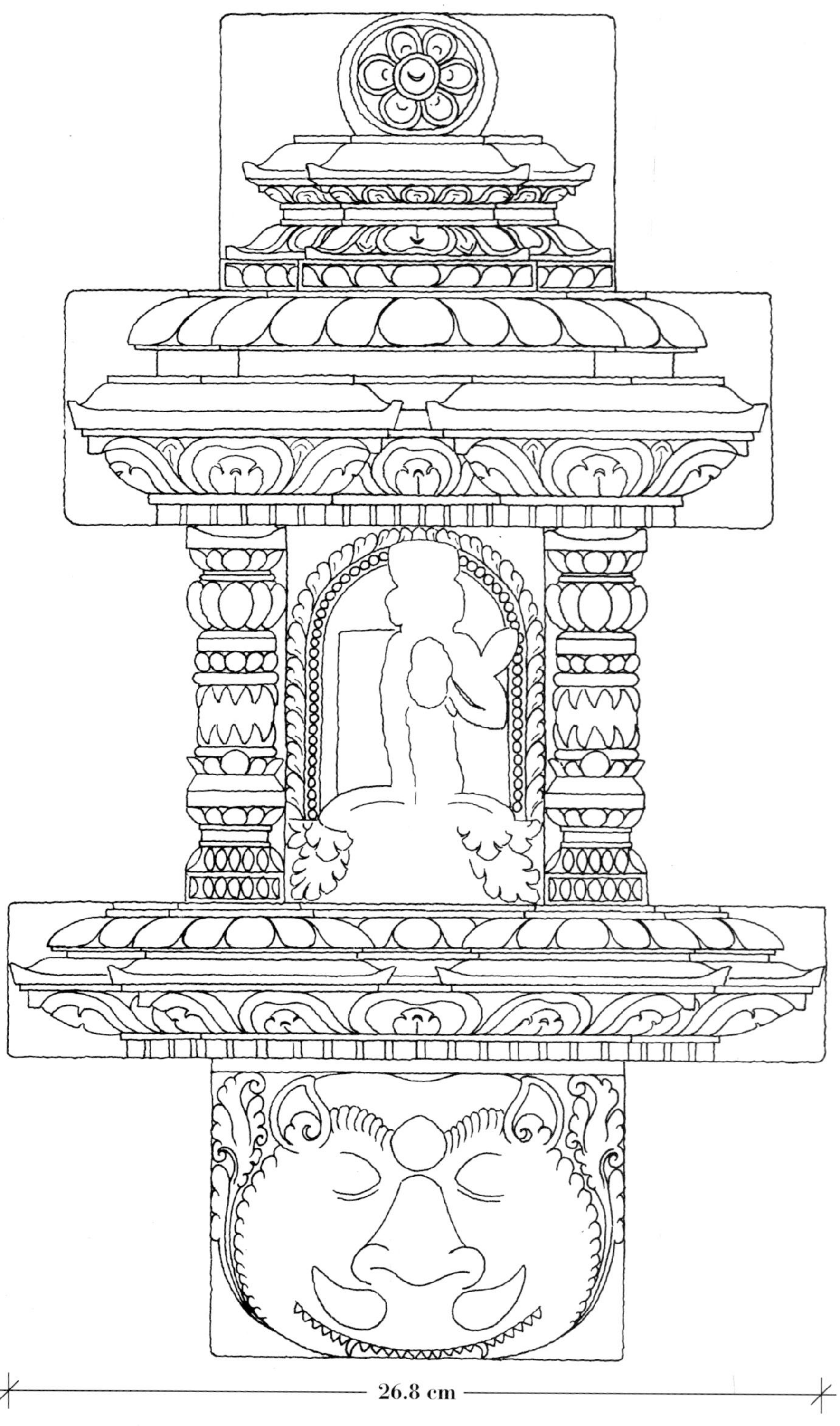

— 26.8 cm —

Blind window (fourteenth century)
Ground floor of Mahadeva Temple, Panauti
Only a little smaller than the Sulima Temple blind window, this example employs a similar design with a *kirtimukha*, or face of glory, below.

A crowning flower is inscribed in a circle far above. The forward standing posts, probably the smallest found in Nepal, are unusual for their lack of such figurative motifs as the *kalasha*.
Drawing by Anil Basukala, 1999



The Sulima Pagoda

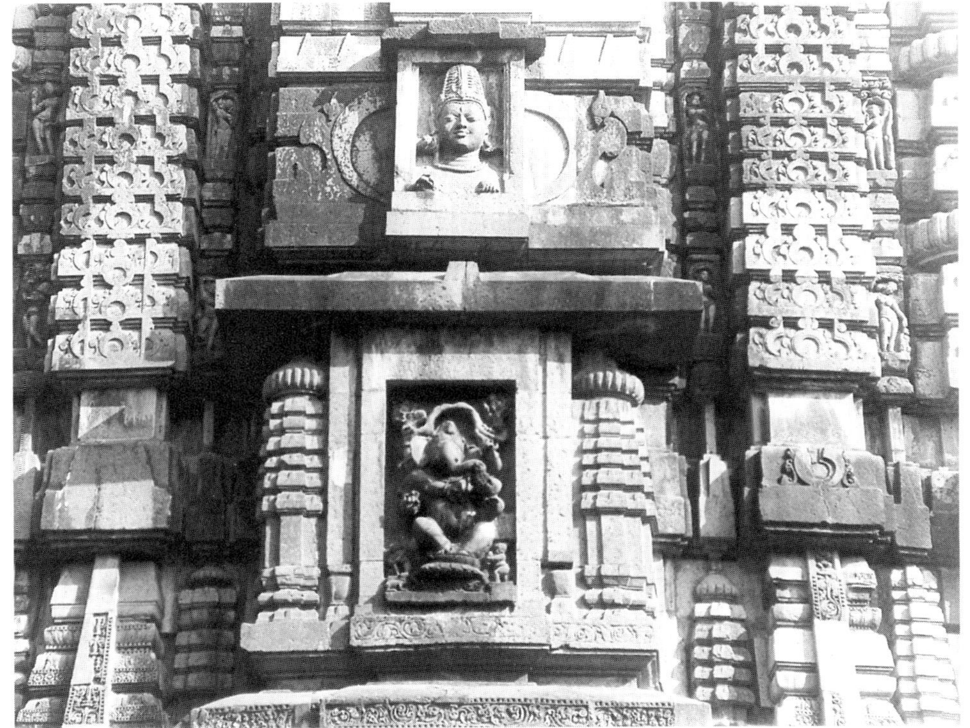

Blind window (tenth century)
Detail of Kichakeshvari Temple,
Kitching, North Orissa, India
Shiva emerges from a boxy frame similar
to the blind window frames of the Sulima
Temple. Behind is the shapely *gavaksha*
(ox-eye), a prominent architectural
motif. This motif has occurred on almost
every temple in Nepal (and on stupas)
since the fourth century, making the
blind window a key architectural
prototype.

the superstructure above, and recalls the shape of the ox-eye or *gavaksha* motifs of Gupta rock-cut architecture. In this early example, the heads of the *makara* extend beyond the architectural frames, but in later Nepali examples less robust compositions are bound by the architectural frame.

The great richness of the architectural tradition of the Subcontinent lies in an ability to conceive of architecture as sculptural form, composed of myriad symbolic elements and beings that simultaneously inhabit and create their own architectural spaces. The antithesis of abstract art, this local canon exults in formal metaphors and the cunning rendering of one thing as another.

The transformation of serpent bodies into lotus leaves and crocodiles is just one example of this predilection. The local craftsmen similarly delight in the opportunity to render a motif in different scales or patterns. For example, the many permutations of the lotus leaf in this example emphasize aquatic associations recalling that creation starts with water. This delight in iconographic and decorative details is part of a long, evolutionary history in Nepal deserving of further study.

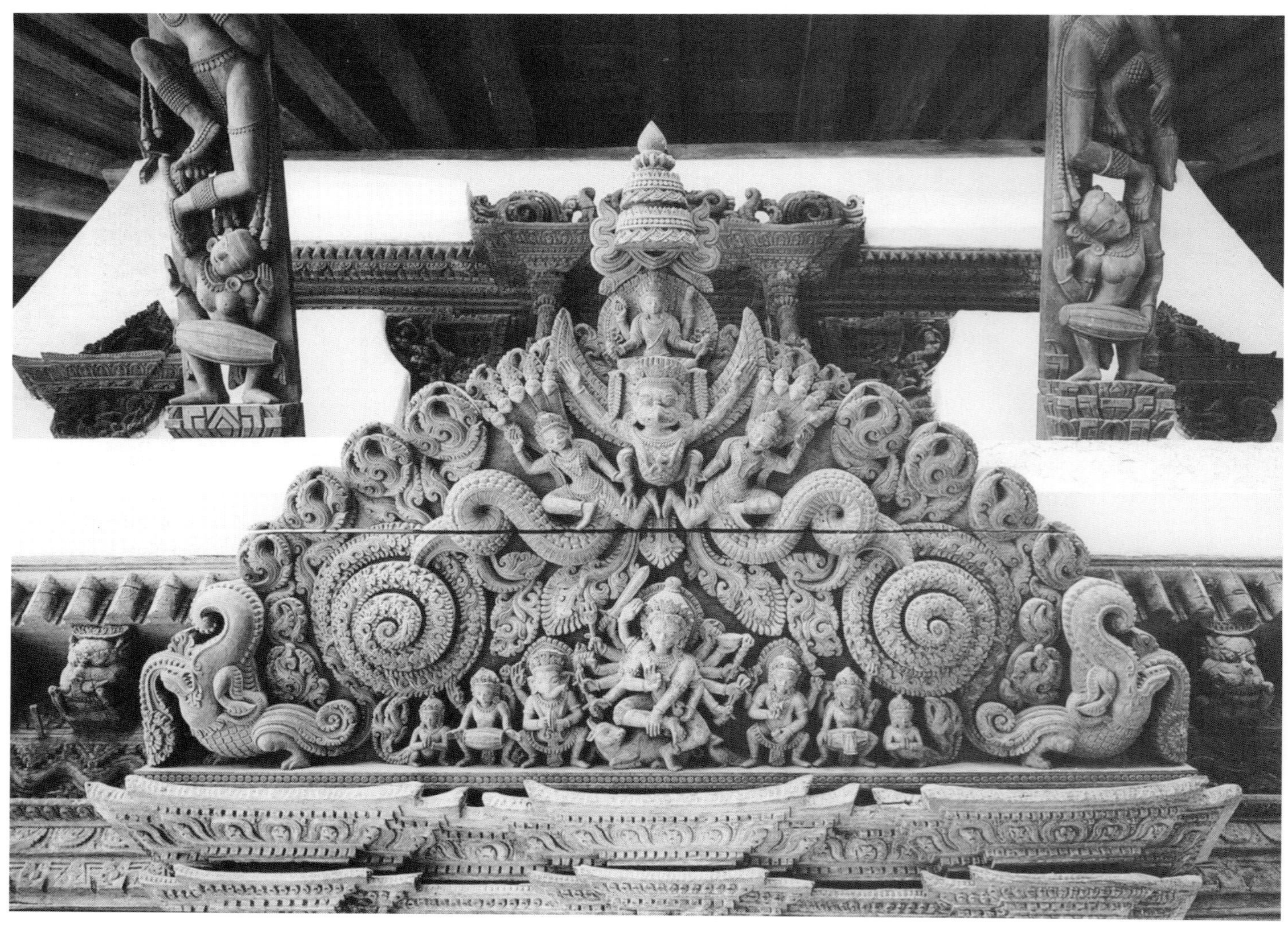

The new torana



The Sulima Pagoda

# The Torana
## Designing Beyond the Point Where Conjecture Begins

Erich Theophile and Rohit Ranjitkar

The discussion about recreating the lost *tympanum* or *torana* above the temple's entrance came very late in the project, in May 1999. New roof struts were necessary for the structural consolidation of the building and had helped force a decision to recarve, but in the case of the *tympanum* stolen in the 1970s, we had implicitly accepted the loss of this virtuoso piece of carving. Given the extent of art theft in the Kathmandu Valley, we had become used to seeing the entrance ensemble without this religious "signboard." At the beginning of the project we were uncertain as well that our craftsmen could pull off such an ambitious artistic assignment. Based on the strut experiment, however, we had more confidence, and with the addition of the new carved struts the partially restored façade looked bare without the *tympanum*.

The recreation of the *torana* would be another exercise in carving detail and iconography of the temple. The *torana* always depicts the temple deity along with a constellation of complementary and auxiliary gods, attendants, and mystical figures. In this case, Mary Slusser's 1968 photograph gave us the primary information; the recreation would then be a matter of detail, refinement, and artistic skills. Meanwhile, the exercise would also allow us to document the micro-scale conjectural design discussions involved.

Slusser's photograph was the only evidence of the lost *torana*. From enlargements the iconography was clear: the dancing form of Shiva represented the *linga* within and was flanked by the typical figures of Ganesh and Kumar, attendant musicians, and snake goddesses. The mystical crocodiles and Garuda framed the overall composition although the crowning figure, Vishnu (determinable by his mount Garuda) was cut off in the photo. Although the overall form and principal deities were determinate, numerous details of the symbolic hand-held attributes of the deities, patterns of dress and foliage, and artistic resolution remained puzzles.

## Design process

The goal of the first round of design was to produce a full-size line drawing of the lost *torana* to serve as a basis for the actual carving. To determine the overall shape of the composition (which is foreshortened in the photograph) we experimented with computer graphics to stretch the vertical dimension. Later we mocked up the *torana* in cardboard, fixing its height and curve from the same point of view as the historical photograph. The length of the element was determinable from its relationship to carvings below.

The team, including the architects, two woodcarvers, an iconographic painter, two draftsmen, and a historian, made scouting trips to find comparable *torana* to help solve the formal and iconographic problems. It took draftsman Sushil Rajbhandari two weeks to produce an initial line drawing.

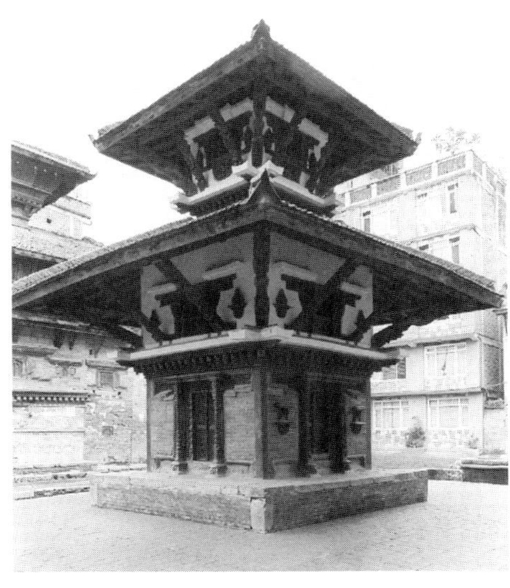

**The temple restoration completed but without the torana in May 1999**

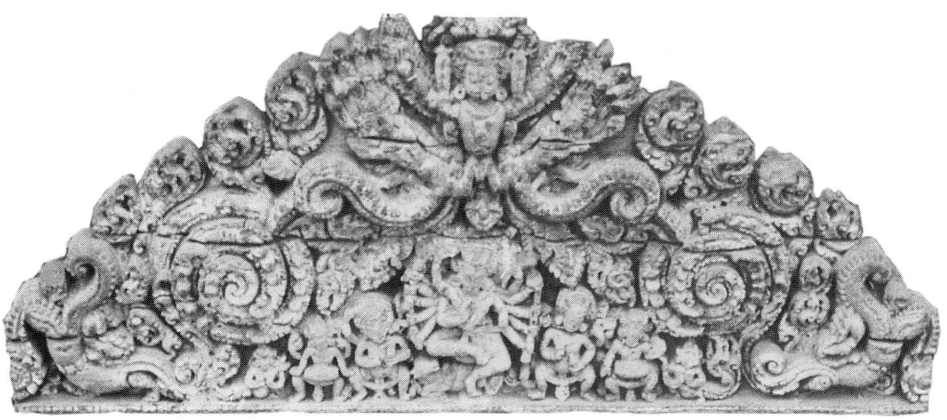

An enlarged image of the lost *torana*,
partially corrected by computer graphics

After several afternoons surveying some 25 comparables, the team decided on several pieces of the larger composition that would be pre-carved as a discrete experiment for the final production. The final *torana* would be carved from several large blocks, which would discourage experiments. We also knew from the strut exercise that it would take several attempts to get a formal resolution of new details.

The field trips confirmed an initial hunch that there was no exact comparable from which to copy. We would instead borrow individual solutions from ten different historical examples to solve the puzzles—a testament to the artistic inventiveness of Kathmandu Valley carvers. Another two weeks of drawing by two draftsmen produced the final base drawing for the carving. Accompanying photographs document several of these detailed design decisions.

## Patronage and craftsmanship

In an effort to realize the almost cliché goal of most conservation projects to train local craftsmen, we continue to analyze the goals, working processes, and artistic results of various conservation projects, both local and international. The role of the conservation architect, for example, is not to tell the master carvers how to hold the chisel, but rather to act as a generous and challenging patron.

Our inputs to the design process, the paid study tours, and the production of full-size detailed drawings, are luxuries for the typical carver, whose similar layout sketch would be a two-day effort at most. He could not afford to spend weeks refining the design, given the limited amount he could charge for the finished product. We encouraged quality by paying carvers on a time basis without fixing the final price of the artistic creation. Intellectually, the project redefined criteria, bringing the carvers closer to western notions of accuracy and authenticity. Before the arrival of modern conservation projects in Nepal, a carver would never have felt obligated to produce a close copy; free variations made without layout sketches would have been the norm.

The ambitiousness of the *torana* design assignment forced us to develop a step-by-step methodology for the interactive development of the final carvings in conjunction with field studies and detailed drawings. The final documentation drawing of the completed *torana*, for example, took almost as long as the four-month carving process.

We certainly would not have attempted the task had we not had one of the best woodcarvers in Nepal, Indrakaji Silpakar, on the project team. Silpakar is one of three carvers (out of 25 with whom we have worked over the years) who has the talent and skill required for a project such as this. We were able to take advantage of his three years' experience working with Niels Gutschow and Götz Hagmüller on the recarving of the elements of Cyasilin Mandap in Bhaktapur. Silpakar was one of the first Nepali wood carvers invited to exhibit his work in Delhi, and he toured Germany in 1994 to study contemporary European woodcarvings. He embodies the Japanese notion of a human monument deserving of honor.

When it was finished in the workshop the replacement *torana* looked convincing, but painfully new. We discussed the possibility of distressing the wood, but the carvers were opposed to the artificial scarring of their masterpiece. We were all happy when, upon installation, the juxtaposition of the old and new was softened by the artistic continuity of the craftsmanship, most specifically the depth and detail of the carvings.

## Assessment

While reviewing the project with foreign and local professionals, Silpakar related his insights. He said he had never realized that the process of making a carving could involve so many inputs, "in a good way," he added with a smile. He listed the architects' technical knowledge, the draftsmen's interpretations of lines, the iconographers' identifications, and the study of other old carvings, drawings, and photographs as essential components of the process. "Normally local people just pick some carving they like and ask me to copy it. They'd rather talk about the price than the details."

In retrospect, we were able to produce a masterpiece through this team effort, although we acknowledge many decisions and details that we'd change if given the chance to start over. Design is never perfect. We might even have thought twice if we had known the assignment would turn out to be a six-month job. But the design process was a rich learning experience for all and suggested that such conjectural design was actually the point at which human engagement begins. Was this human, non-materialistic goal more important than mistakes in our final product?

A telling episode took place one summer afternoon when the five-man team had just returned from a field trip and was sitting at the conference table pouring over the full-size preliminary drawings. The conversations in Newari were heated, and photographs and field notes were pulled out as each man argued for a different solution. The words of a German conservation scholar of Japan's cyclical rebuilding came to mind:

"Not a molecule of the former building is retained. That is, in fact, landmarks preservation in its highest degree: all action expended on the new construction originates in the heads and hands of living humans who are compelled every time to clarify for themselves how forms are precisely determined, how material and technology must be implemented to serve a function conceived for eternity."

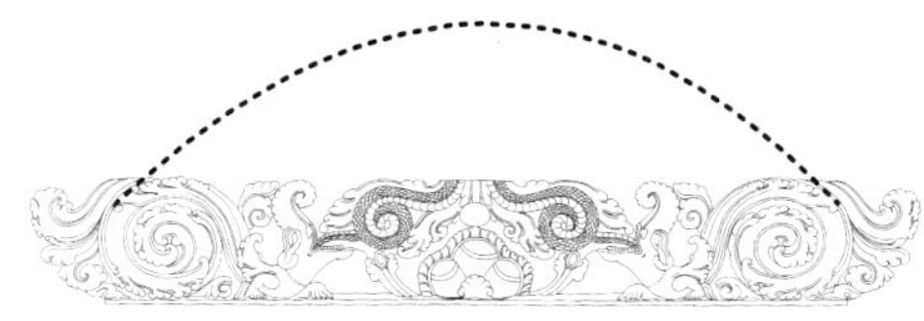

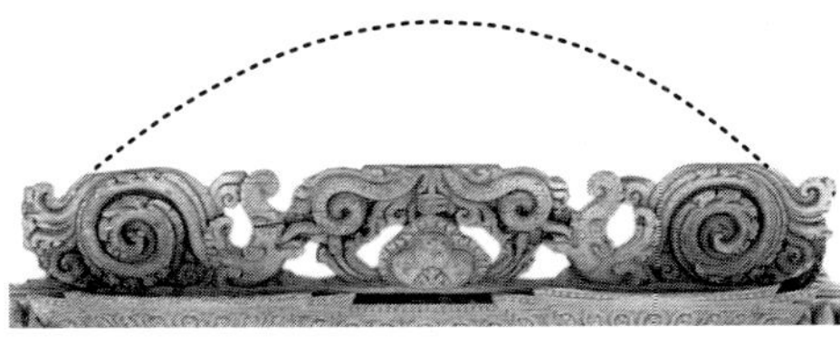

**Documentation of upper *torana* fragment**
The architects decided not to recreate the lost portion of this rare historical fragment. Instead, the torana was reinstalled in the same condition as it was found, above the upper floor window.

Indeterminate details and comparables

Unable to find any examples to help us recreate the implements of the central 14-handed dancing Shiva, we turned to a 16-handed Shiva at Harishankar Temple, Cikamugul, Kathmandu (top) as it most closely approximated the Sulima Shiva.

The *torana* from the sixteenth-century Char Narayan Temple in Patan (center) provided the detail of the irregular foliage silhouette. Its outline stands in contrast to the typically smoother shapes seen in the upper and lower photos.

The *torana* at Uma Maheshvar Temple, Patan (bottom) provided the model for Nandi, for the garland of snakes on Garuda's chest plate, and for the uplifted position of Garuda's hand.

We were unable to find any comparables for the hanging ornament of Garuda's headdress or for the precise patterns of the swirling foliage: these designs were left to the carver's inventiveness. Most significantly, the crowning figure of the composition was cut off in the photo. It was clear from iconographic conventions that it was most likely a four-handed Narayan, but hand and leg positions were indeterminate. The carvers improvised the design after looking at a dozen comparables.

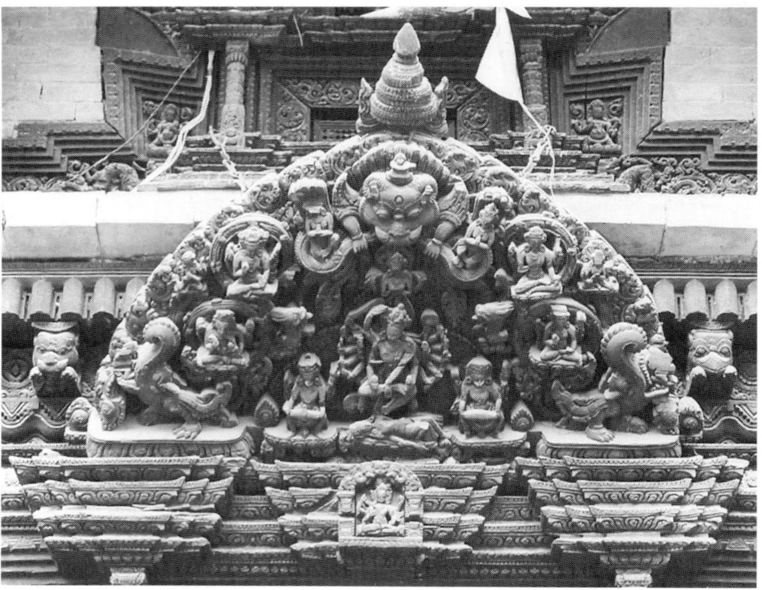

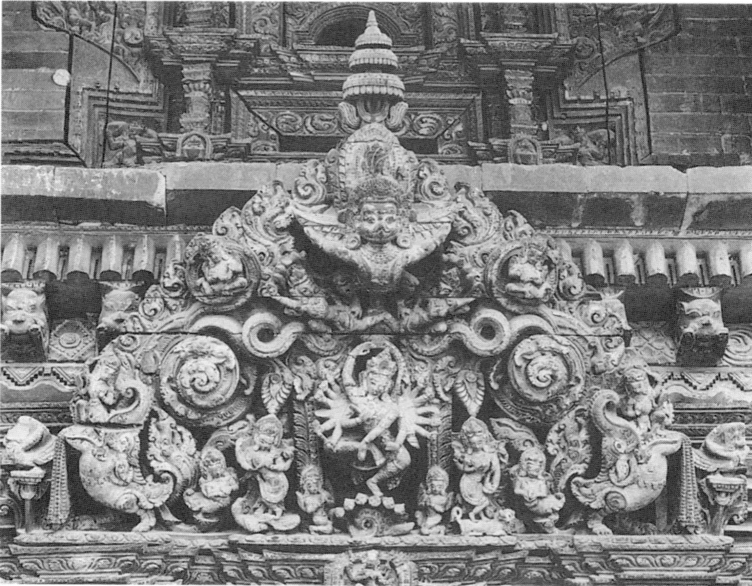

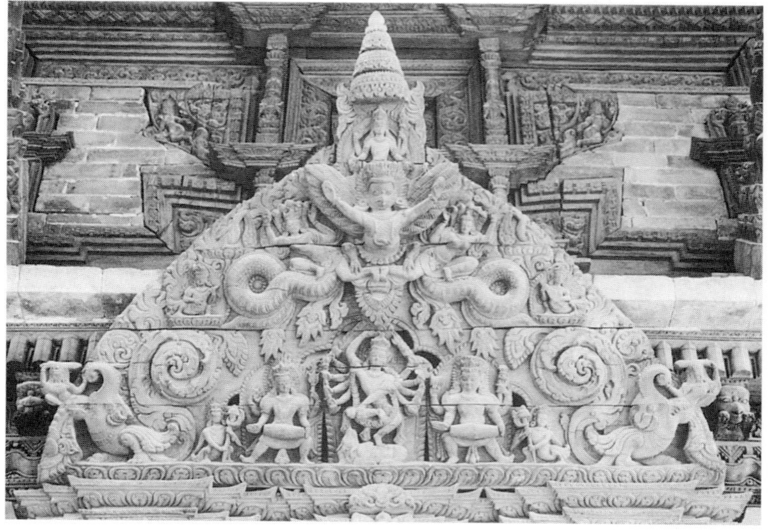



The Sulima Pagoda

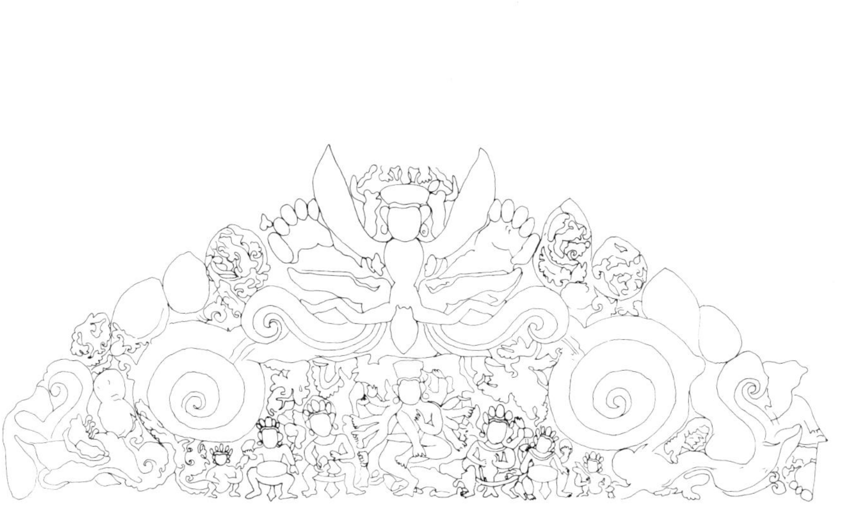

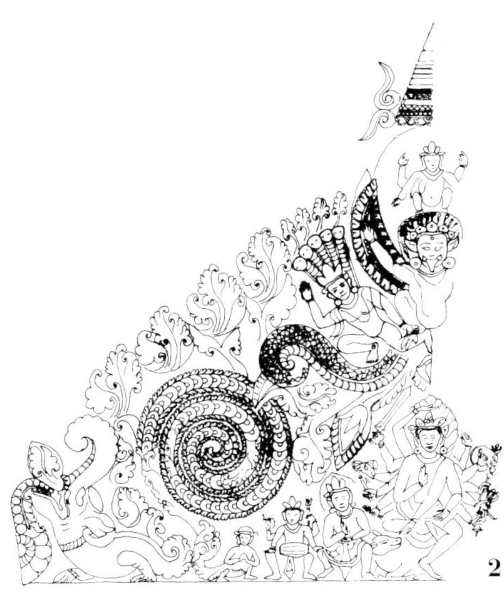

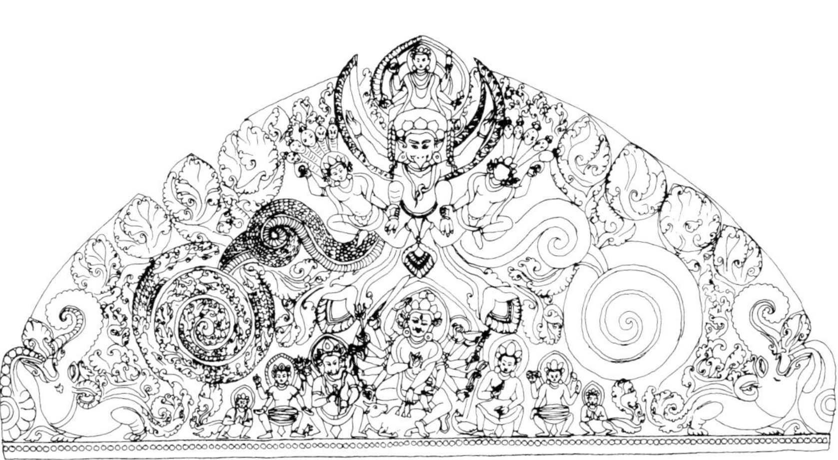

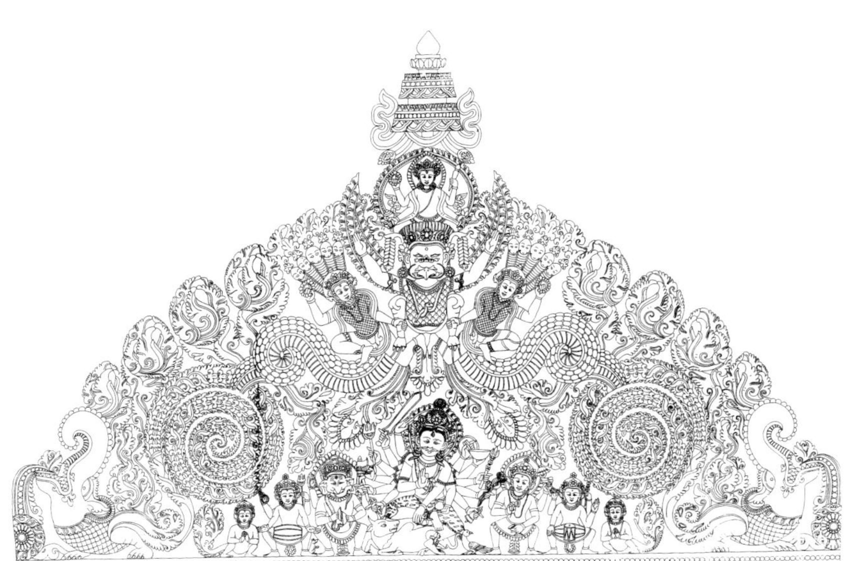

Documentation of the design process

1  This is Sushil Ranjbhandari's first attempt at laying out the overall shape and composition.
2  Bijay Basukala then refined the postures, hand positions, and foliage detail.
3  In the third round, Sushil Ranjbhandari and Krishna Ram Chitrakar incorporatedBijay's figures in a new layout; its overall proportions were corrected by superimposing a grid on the historical photo.
4  The final pencil drawing adds enough detail for the final inking to be done.

**The Sulima Temple**

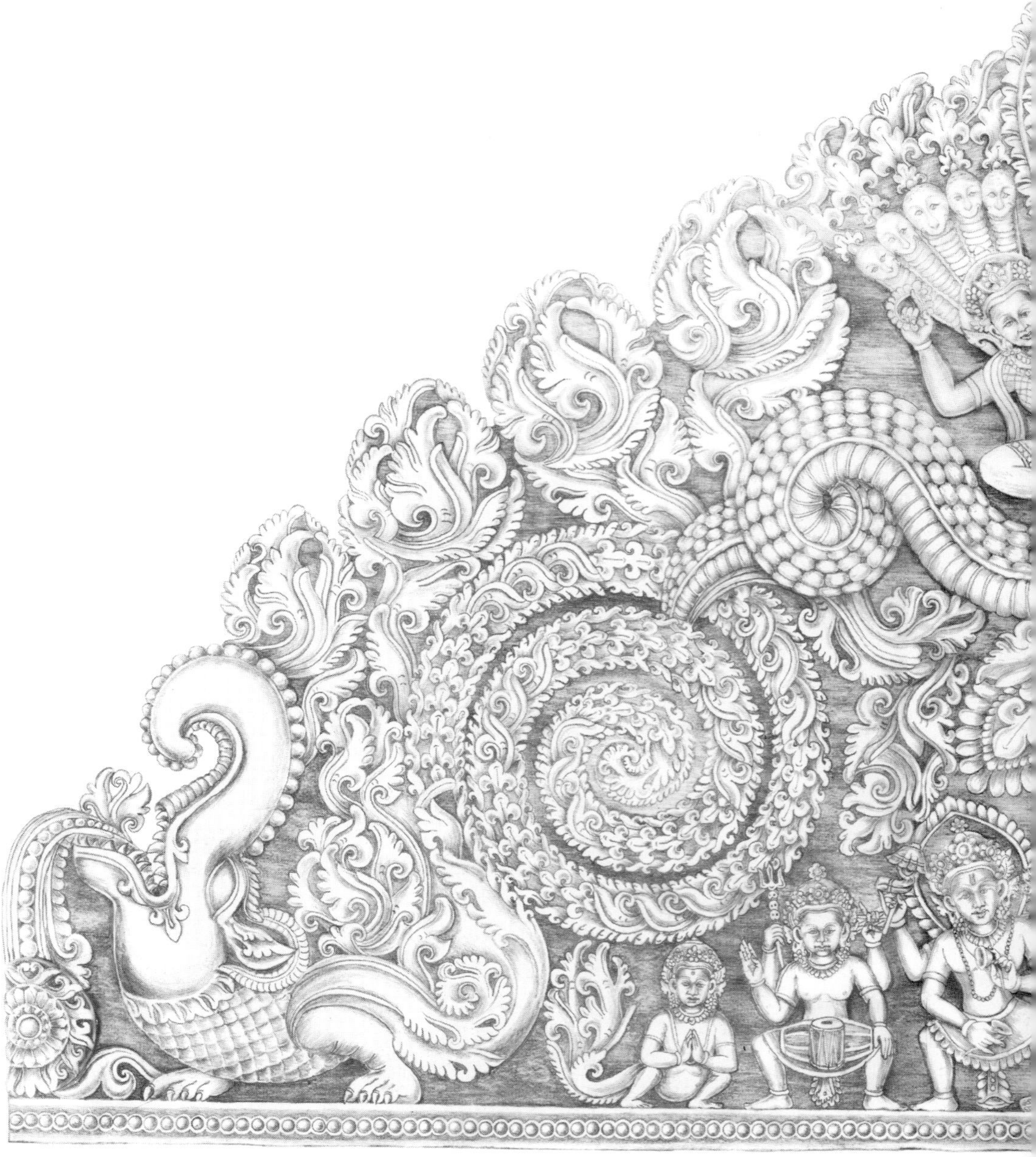

Rendered drawing of the
new *torana*, Sushil
Rajbhandari and Rajan
Shrestha, 2000

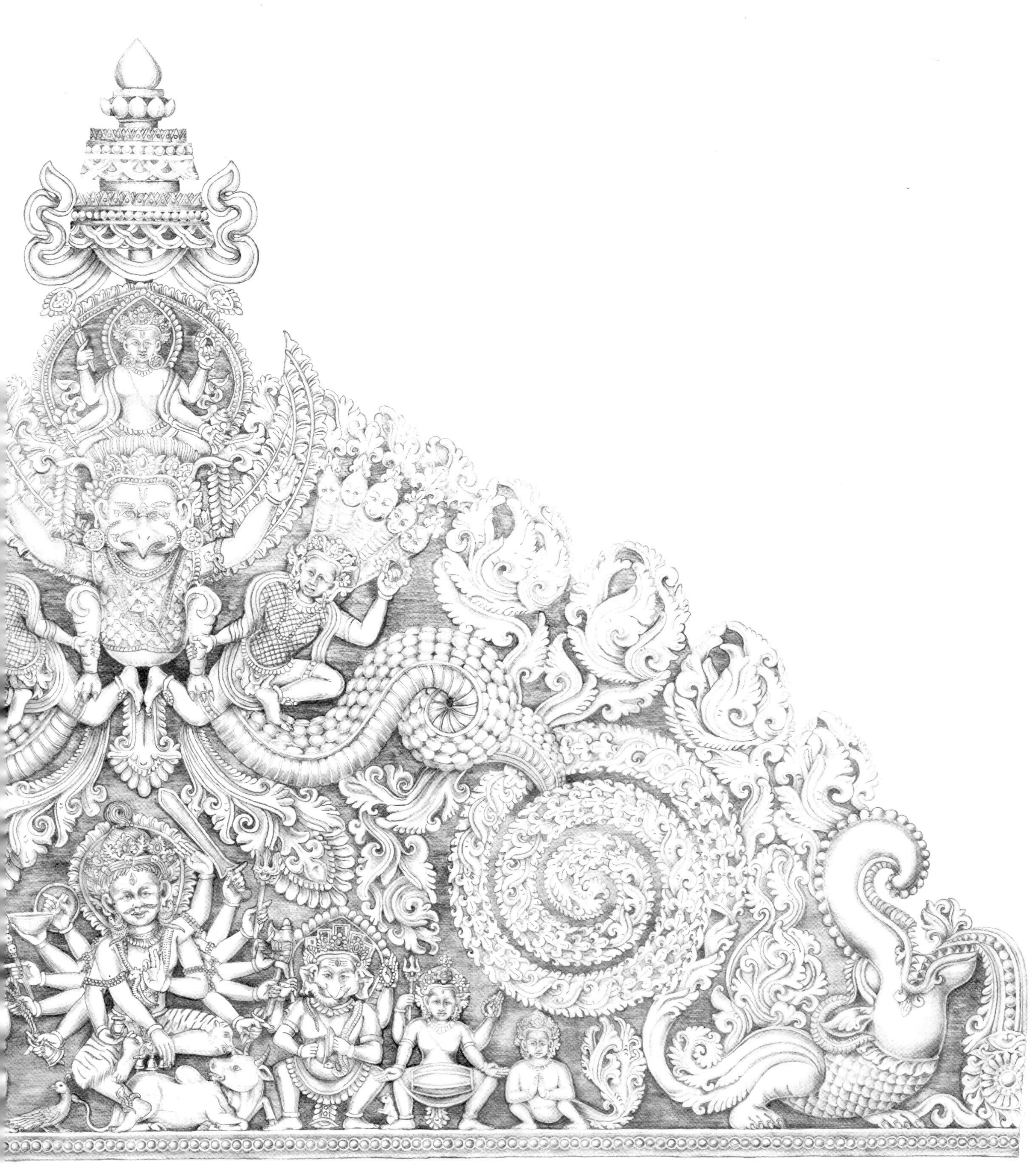

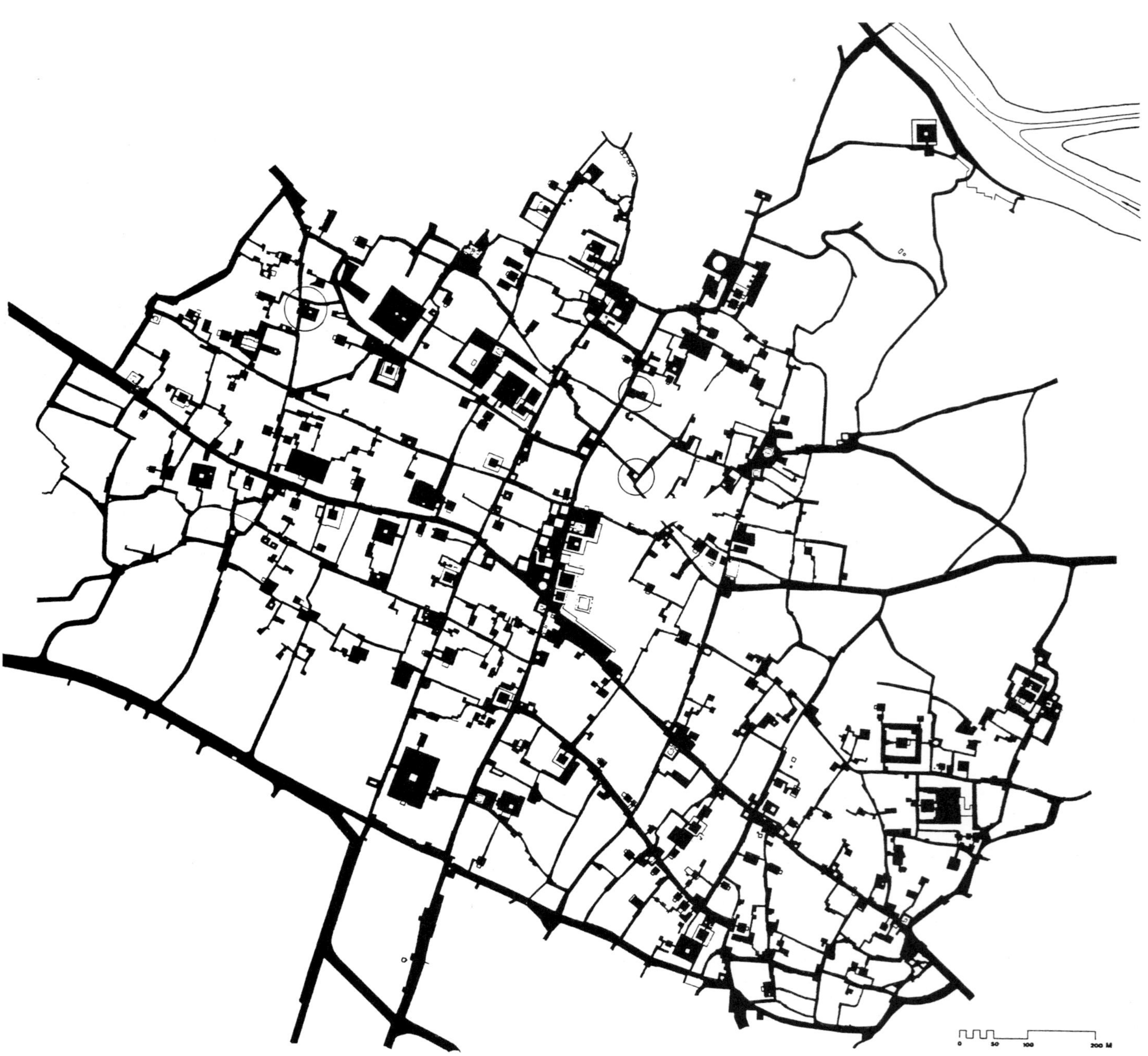


Map of Patan



The Sulima Pagoda

# THE SULIMA SQUARE

## Urban Patterns in Patan

Niels Gutschow

The map of Patan (opposite) shows streets, lanes, squares and monasterial courtyards, revealing a prominent network of large semi-public courtyards. The more important layer of urban organization, a street grid in the form of a double cross, may be the result of efforts before the fourth century to link numerous, smaller settlements into a unifying pattern of cosmic dimensions, an example of Indian planning principles realized on Nepali soil.

In addition to these hundreds of courtyards, each of which houses Buddhist shrines, many small squares characterize the urban fabric. These squares provide a type of infrastructure corresponding to the needs of those in the neighborhood, and vary according to the status of the people. The eastern quarters, for example, are dominated by farmers and invariably include a meeting house whose focus is a shrine dedicated to the god of music. Upper-caste quarters are organized around esoteric shrines dedicated to the deities of their clans, while the temples on the squares, constructed and endowed by affluent families, are mostly dedicated to the gods of the Brahmanic tradition, such as Shiva or Vishnu-Narayana. Almost all of these private temples fell into ruin over the past three decades as the nationalization of temple trusts left original local endowments penniless.

The Ratneshvara Temple in Sulima is such a case. The *guthi*, or trust, of 12 Brahman families living around the square was not willing to support the temple with private funds, and the government rarely funds individual monuments outside of World Heritage Sites. The Kathmandu Valley Preservation Trust stepped in to fill the gap, as it had with the Uma Maheshvar Temple on Kvalakhu Square (1993), the Narayana Temple on Kulima Square (1997), and the ongoing restoration of the Narayana Temple on Tum Baha Square. These are all examples of private temples threatened by reduced endowments whose destruction has been forestalled by the Trust.

Sulima Square is in the Pimbaha quarter, one of 24 neighborhoods of Patan historically entitled to send representatives to select a new king. Pimbaha contains a focal pond and five squares of religious significance. Although Sulima Square is not the center of Pimbaha, it lies on the *pradakshinapath*, the main processional route along which important deities are transported in palanquins. The Ratneshvara Temple *dabu* (platform) serves as one of 24 platforms in Patan used for music and dance performances on special occasions.

The temple is part of a rich ensemble of local religious significance but, like the two Narayana temples at Sulima (which collapsed in 1934 and 1970 and were not rebuilt), draws little attention during such processions today. Interestingly, only the small Ganesh shrine at the Square's northern edge attracts much attention, serving as the neighborhood's guardian. The importance of this small shrine is acknowledged by its inclusion as a stopping point during a procession to 41 Ganesh shrines held annually, four days after the great *Mataya* Buddhist procession crosses Sulima Square.

Detail of a symbolic eye flanking the door of the *agamchen* (esoteric shrine house) south of the Sulima Temple, carved in stone
**Drawing by Bijay Basukala, 1992**

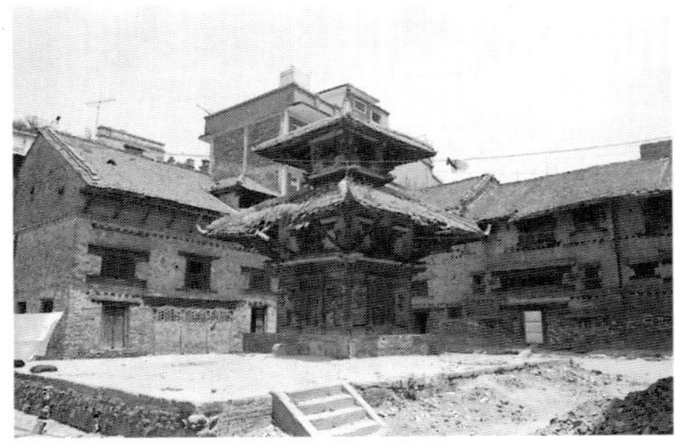

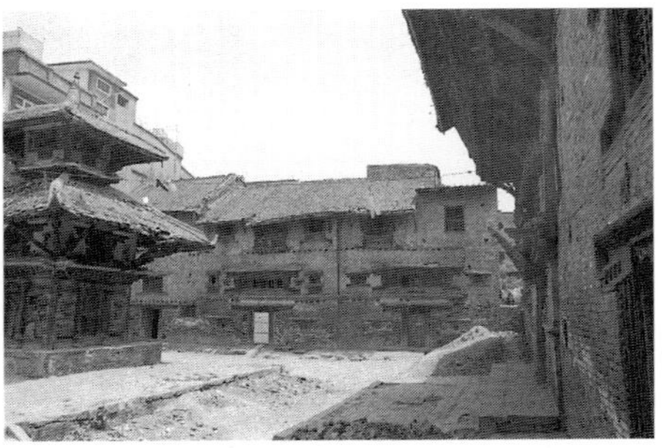

**Sulima Square in 1992**
**The Maharjan house (above, top) to the left of the temple, and Gayahbajya's house (above) to the right of temple, were subsequently demolished.**

In May 1991, in the context of the Patan Conservation and Development Program (German Technical Cooperation, or GTZ), the editors of this publication identified Sulima Square as a Secondary Monument Zone. The *Guideline Plan* (July 1992) announced the restoration of the Sulima Temple and the neighboring Gayahbajya house. It envisioned the designation of five structures as National Monuments in an effort to prevent their demolition and attract public and international support. While the plan was being drafted, the important Maharjan house, north of the temple, was demolished, along with two houses on the western side. Our designation and subsequent compilation of a gazette of monument zones seemed futile, nothing more than an expatriate dream. To make matters worse, part of the *agamchen* structure was demolished in 1996, and in 1997 half of the Gayahbajya house, whose unique windows are documented elsewhere in this volume, was destroyed. No official listing of monuments has been undertaken thus far, although the Department of Archaeology undertook an extensive inventory between 1995 and 1998, with assistance from the editors.

Such developments demonstrate how difficult, if not impossible, townscape preservation in Nepal can be. By identifying and repairing key landmark structures, the Kathmandu Valley Preservation Trust makes significant and realistic contributions to the preservation effort. But these restored temples will survive only as isolated structures in a changing urban landscape. Further, material efforts such as temple restoration are only part of the equation. These efforts must be informed and complemented by the research and documentation of oral history, rituals, music, dance, and other non-material aspects of the fast disappearing heritage, as discussed in later chapters.

**Area proposed in 1992 for the Sulima Secondary Monument Zone, prepared for the *Patan Conservation and Development Program***

**Monuments of architectural and historical merit:**

1. **Sulima Rajupadhya (Brahman)**
   *Agamchen*
2. **Ratneshvara Temple**
3. **Candesvari Temple**
4. **Gayahbajya's house**
5. **Maharjan house**

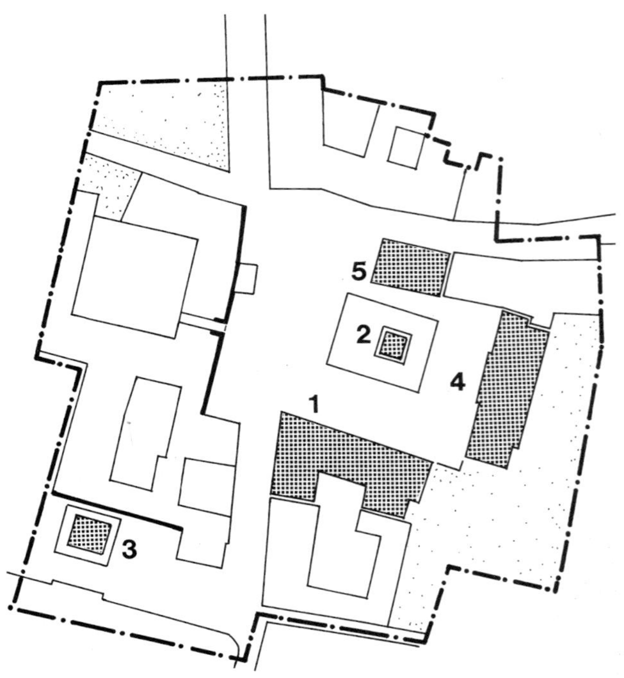

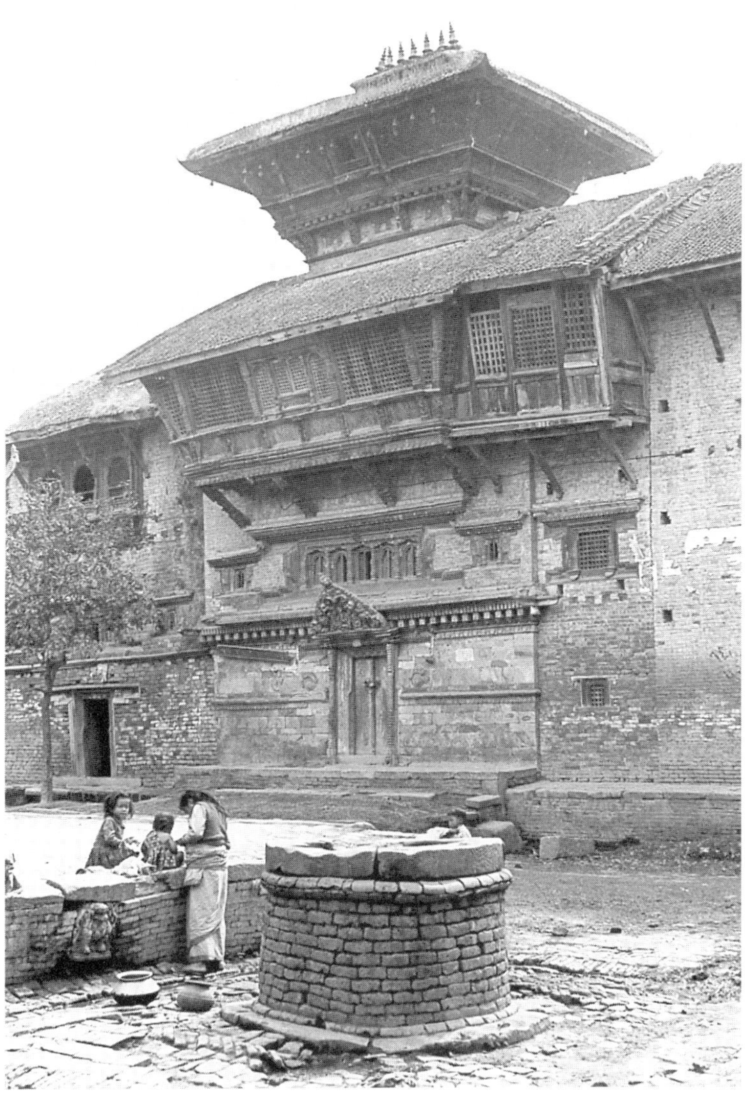

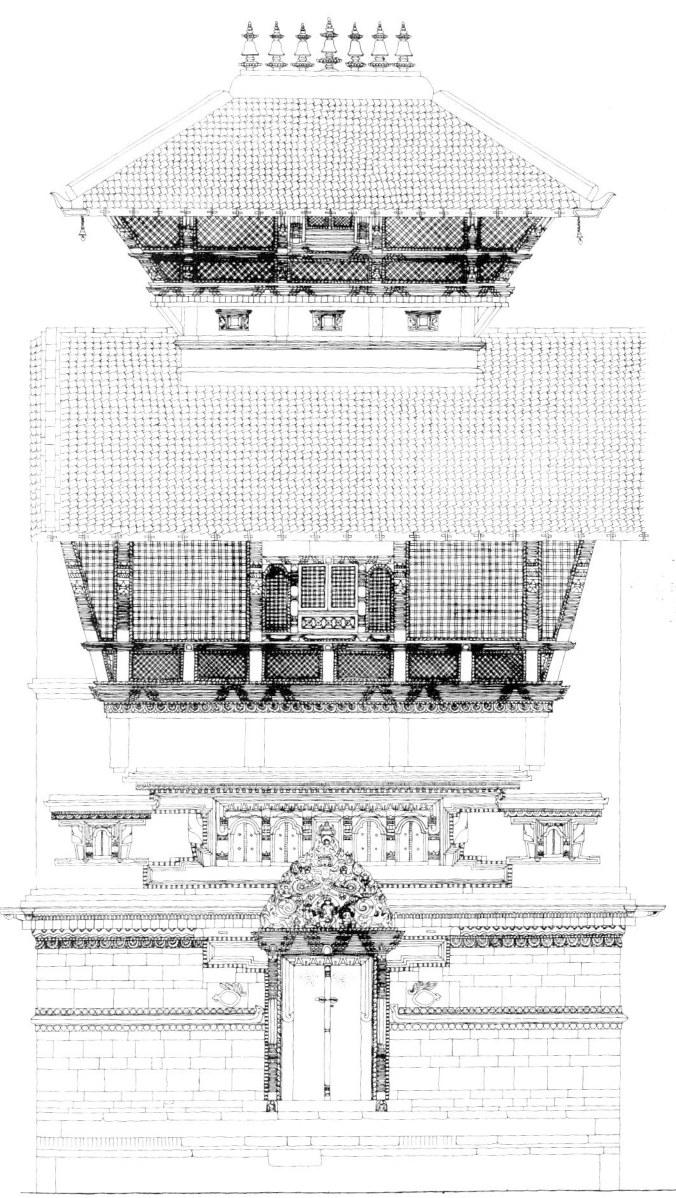

Rajupadhya Agamchen
Sulima Square, principal elevation

This fifteenth-century structure is the
earliest surviving example of the
*agamchen* building type in the
Kathmandu Valley. Its massive
proportions and stone facing are unique.
Drawing by Gyanendra Joshi, 1992

**Inventory of Sulima Square**

During the second half of the seventeenth century, most probably under the rule of King Shrinivasa Malla (1661-1684), one branch of the Rajupadhya, the Newar Brahmans to the Court, established its *agamchen* at Sulima. They built this structure next to the house of Gayahbajya, their ancestor and famous Tantric. Here, Gayahbajya had tried in vain to become a *siddha*, a person in a state of spiritual perfection whose "perfect body death cannot touch."

Closely connected to the *agamchen* were nearby temples dedicated to Ratneshvara (3) and Candesvari (10), as well as shrines to the guardian gods Ganesh and Hanuman. Ganesh was installed in a small existing shrine.

A new shrine to Hanuman was established in the neighboring courtyard.

Five *phalca* (Newari) or *pati* (Nepali), public buildings with open arcades on the ground floor, once enriched the public space and provided shelter and the locus for feasts. The ritual function of these *phalca* is not to be underestimated: specific programs of religious activity were associated with each one. For example, Yamadyah or Bhairava icons were displayed in the *phalca* during Indrajatra. *Samay*, a ritual food, was distributed from them on special occasions. At Amliphalca (16) *samay* consisting of five symbolic varieties of food was regularly given to children and *Pode* (untouchables) by those who first established the *phalca*.

Only three *phalca* remain. Two collapsed in the 1934 earthquake and were never reconstructed. Another was demolished in 1990 to make room for a new private building. The remains of a temple once dedicated to Narayana (6) were removed in 1970. The platform and a small shrine of another lost temple dedicated to Santana Gopal (5) survive.

A deep well, or *tun* in Newari (15), and (10) a drinking water fountain (Newari *jahrun)*, once provided what today we would call public infrastructure. Since the introduction of piped water at the beginning of the twentieth century, this fountain, like some hundred others in Patan, remains dry. The well continues to be used, particularly for the washing of laundry when water is scarce, a regular feature of life in Patan.

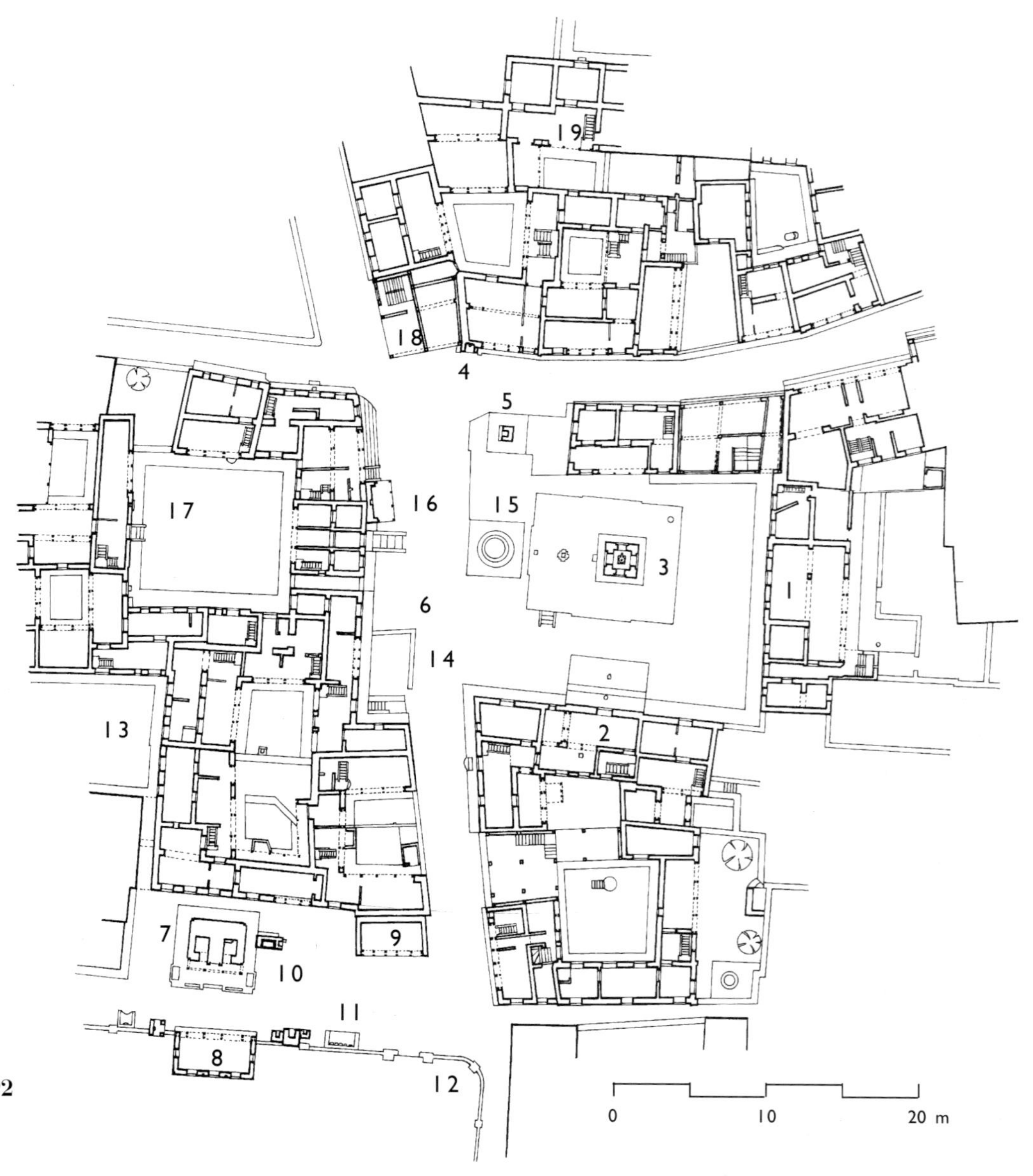

Sulima Square: site plan
drawing by Gyanendra Joshi, 1992

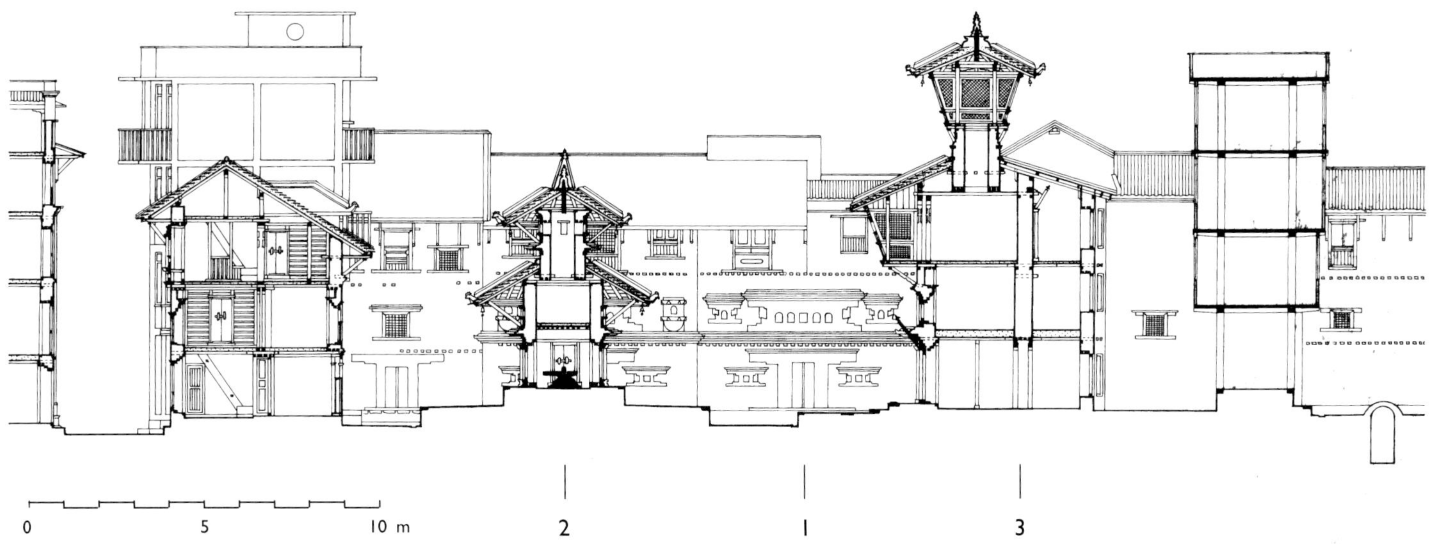

Sulima Square: north-south section
drawing by Gyanendra Joshi, 1992

1 Gayahbajya's house, residence of his descendant, Surjenath Rajupadhya, and largely rebuilt since this survey.

2 *Agamchen* housing the esoteric shrine of the Sulima Rajupadhyas, one of six branches *(kavah)* of Brahmans in Patan.

3 Ratneshvara Temple with *linga*, a thirteenth- or fourteenth-century two-story pagoda.

4 Shrine to Ganesh, the guardian *(dvarpala)* of the square.

5 Remains of a seventeenth-century Narayana temple called Santana Gopal, not rebuilt after it collapsed in the 1934 earthquake.

6 Site of the former Narayana Temple that collapsed in the 1934 earthquake. Its remains were cleared in 1970.

7 Candesvari Temple, a three-story pagoda erected in 1663. One of the ground floor chambers is dedicated to Ganesh. The other is empty, a *dyah maru* (no god) because Gayahbajya did not become a *siddha*. Between the two chambers are three holes, the triangular one representing Candesvari or Nasadyah, the others representing Bhairava and Bhairavi.

8 *Phalca* used as a *bhajanghar* for music performance. Renovated in 1975, the anniversary ritual of the *phalca* is performed on the occasion of *balacaturdashi* in December.

9 *Phalca*, a three-story *sattal* for public use. This *phalca* collapsed in 1952, but a neighbor renovated the ground floor arcade (now occupied by *Kusle*-tailors) in order to use the roof as his *kausi* (terrace).

10 *Jadhun*, a drinking water fountain.

11 *Digyudyah* (ancestral shrine) of farmer castes from Tahnani and Konti. An annual ritual is performed three days before the full moon in November *(Yahmaripunhi)*.

12 Site of the former *phalca* where *samay* (ritual meal of five different foods) was offered to Lakhe Shrestha from Patukva by the Rajupadhya.

13 *Akhadanani*, the courtyard where Gayahbajya is said to have brought the *Astamatrika* from Harasiddhi.

14 Site of former *phalca* that collapsed in 1934 earthquake. During Indrajatra, Yamadyah was displayed here.

15 Well *(tun)*, which is still in use.

16 *Phalca* of *amaliguthi*, established by the *Jyapu* (a Newar caste) of neighboring Mikhabaha. Annually, during the month of *Mangsir*, *amala* fruit and beer were offered to the untouchable *Pode* caste here.

17 Hanuman, or Hamva, Shrine at Hamvachok.

18 Site of former *sattal* established by the Maskey clan, demolished in 1990.

19 *Agamchen* housing the esoteric god of the Maskey clan.

# The Ritual Life of Sulima Square

Nutandhar Sharma

Although ritual life at Ratneshvara has decreased over the last century, there is still sufficient activity to enable us to understand the importance of the site and to help us extrapolate its historical context. Unlike contemporary Indian sites where ritual life shows less continuity with the past, Sulima typifies the Kathmandu Valley's richness of contemporary life, one of the reasons such documentation is critical.

According to a fundamental Hindu belief, countless numbers of repetitions of the ritual work in a temple maintain its sacredness. Because these make the it a "living" temple, continuation of the ritual work is essential.

The Lord of the temple, in the form of a *linga*, is worshipped twice a day: the regular morning *nitya puja* and the evening *arati puja*, or light offering. For the *nitya*, worshippers perform *sodasopacarapuja* with an offering of "sixteen required articles" such as *asana* (a seat), *svagata* (a welcome gesture), *padhya* (respect shown to the feet), *argha* (respectful reception by offering water, rice and flower), *achamaniya* (vessel used for sipping water), *madhuparka* (a mixture of honey and milk), *punarachamaniya* (sipping water again), *snaniya* (anything used for bathing), *bhushana* (an ornament), *gandha* (something fragrant), *pushpa* (flowers), *dhupa* (incense), *dipa* (a lamp), *naivedya* (ritual food), and *vandana* (prayers).[1] The *arati puja* in the evening is performed in a simple fashion by offering a lamp and incense sticks. These formulae for *nitya* and *arati puja* are historical norms throughout a large part of the Subcontinent.

Terms of priestship of the temple are divided among the initiated members of the Sulima Rajupadhya clan, each lasting a month for each member.[2]

Two special types of *puja* are to be performed each year. The first, *varsavandhana puja*, a form of worship common to almost all temples, is performed on the fourth day of the bright half of the lunar month of *Phalguna*. During this *puja* an additional *rudri*, a *puja* to Lord Rudra (Shiva), and *homa*, a fire sacrifice called *visvadeva*, are performed.

During this anniversary a secret Tantric *puja* is also performed in honor of the living goddess, *Kumari*, from the Dangol clan of *Mikhabahal*. She is worshipped by the most senior members of the Rajupadhya clan. In 1998 the Kumari appeared in person, but in 1999 only her ornaments were sent. The *Bhairav Stone*, a guardian deity on the southern side of the temple, is propitiated as well. The aniconic image is painted with vermilion and annointed with oil. Normally Bhairav demands animal sacrifices, but that is not the case here.

While searching for documents about the rituals of the Ratneshvara Temple, a *thyasaphu* (folded manuscript) from the Malla period was found, mentioning the anniversary *puja* performed on the fourth day of bright half of Lunar month of *Phalguna* in N.S. 802 (CE 1681).[3] The document testifies to the age of the ongoing traditions at the Sulima Temple.

The second annual *puja*, the *Grita-kamvala* of the Ratneshvara *linga*, is performed on the first day of the month of Magha. On this day *ghee* (clarified butter) and sesame seeds are mixed together and applied to the Ratnesvara *linga*, as if to blanket it for the cold season. This mixture is left on the *linga* for four days and removed during daily worship by the priest. The three senior-most members of the clan are responsible for performing these two annual *puja*, typical for Shaivite shrines in the Kathmandu Valley.

*Shivaratri*, the night-long festival in honor of Lord Shiva that falls on the fourteenth day of the dark half of the lunar month of Phalguna, is also celebrated at Sulima Temple. On Shivaratri, devotees light a big bonfire on the temple plinth's fire sanctuary, or *yajnakunda*. Wheat, soybeans, sweets, and fruits are distributed as the *prasada* (blessed offerings) of Lord Shiva. The wedding anniversary of Lord Shiva and his consort Parvati is celebrated on this day as well.

Unlike other important temples, the Ratneshvara Temple is not used for the *pavitrarohana puja* (sacred thread offering) or the *damanarohana puja* (offering of the fragrant *damana* flower), except when performed in the adjacent esoteric Tantric shrine, the Sulima Agamchen.

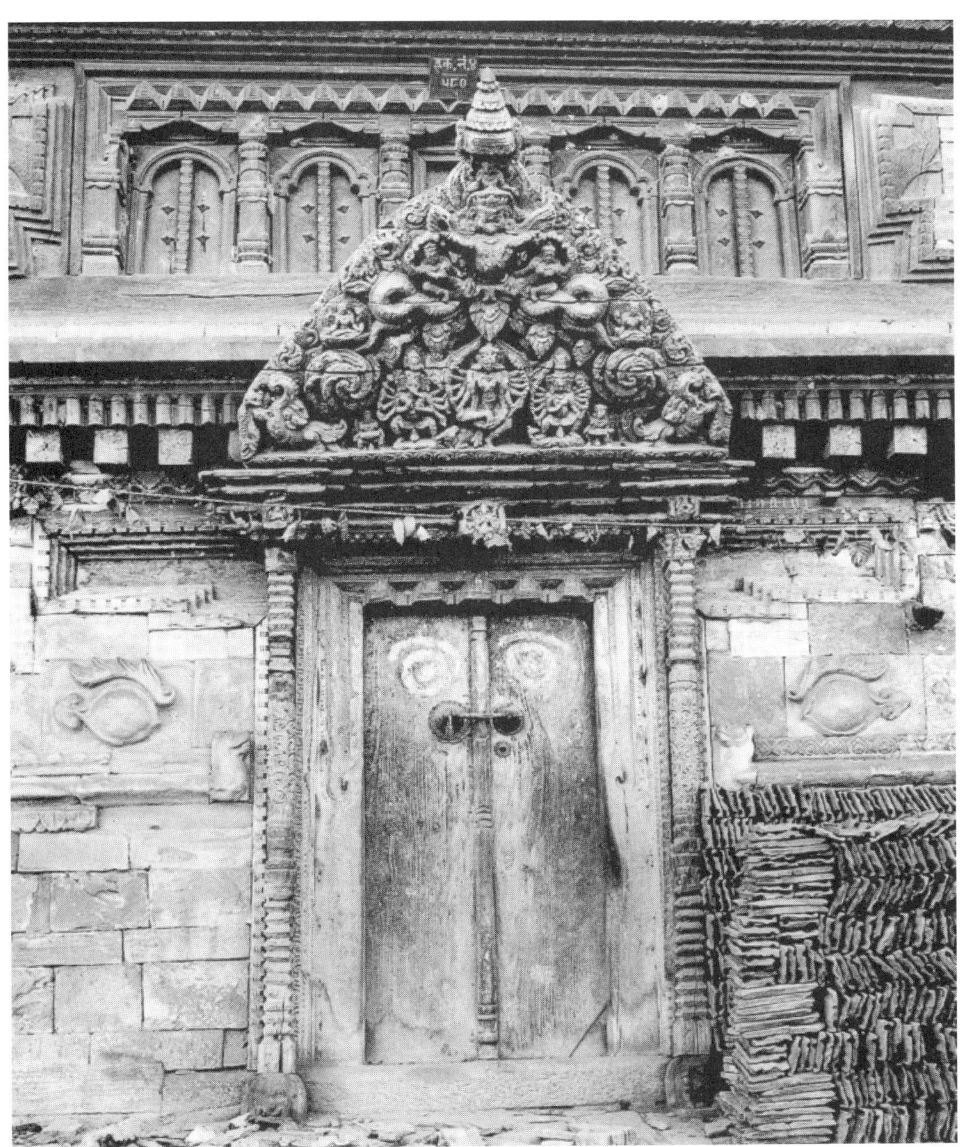

The Sulima Agamchen: doorway with *torana*
The rituals of this esoteric shrine are linked with those of the adjacent temple. When special offerings of the sacred thread are made at this *agamchen* as part of the Hindu life-cycle rituals, the worshippers and priests also perform *puja* at the temple.

# The Legends of Gayahbajya

Nutandhar Sharma

## The Social Topography of Gayahbajya's World

While collecting oral history in Patan in 1991, my attention was drawn to the legends of Gayahbajya, literally a "Brahman named Gaya" in Newari. These legends suggest that a remarkable figure named Gayahbajya once lived in Sulima, near Patan Dhoka. According to these legends he performed many miracles in his day comparable to those performed by the famous Jamana Gubhaju of Kathmandu[4] and Gunu Jha of Mithila.[5] Each of the three medieval kingdoms of the Kathmandu Valley had such Tantric heroes: Gayahbajya of Patan, Jamana Gubhaju in Kathmandu, and Siddhivanta Josi[6] in Bhaktapur. This article documents the most intriguing of the Gayahbajya legends, while additional evidence is correlated to establish the existence of this legendary figure, who lived ten meters from the Sulima Temple.

The Gayahbajya legends incorporate Tantric ideas and depict life and death, magical spells, interactions between high and low castes, and relations between the teacher and his disciples.[7] Presented in the simple language of children's stories and evocative of the manner in which locals relate such tales, they provide a clear picture of medieval Newar society in Patan.

Even today the Gayahbajya myth lives on, and the places where he worked his wonders can still be visited. In the Gayahbajya house at Sulima, where his descendant Surjenath Rajupadhya resides, Gayahbajya's room remains locked. Beside the house stands an *agamchen* housing the esoteric shrine of Gayahbajya. The Sulima Rajupadhyas, one of the six branches of Brahmans in Patan, worship in this *agamchen*.

Southwest of Sulima Square, near Pimbahal *pukhu* (pond) is a three-story pagoda, the Candesvari Temple. One of the ground floor chambers is dedicated to Ganesh. The other chamber, *dyah maru*, (literally "no god") remains empty because Gayahbajya did not become a siddha. Between the two chambers are three holes. The triangular one represents Candesvari or Nasahdya, the others represent Bhairava and Bhairavi.

The Sulima Temple is connected to the esoteric shrine of Gayahbajya. Until recently there was a *phalca*, or rest house, in front of the Sulima Temple. This Amaliguthi was established by the Jyapu caste of neighboring Mikhabahal. Here, once a year during the month of Mangsir, *amalaka* fruit (Indian gooseberry) and beer were offered to the untouchable Pode and their children.

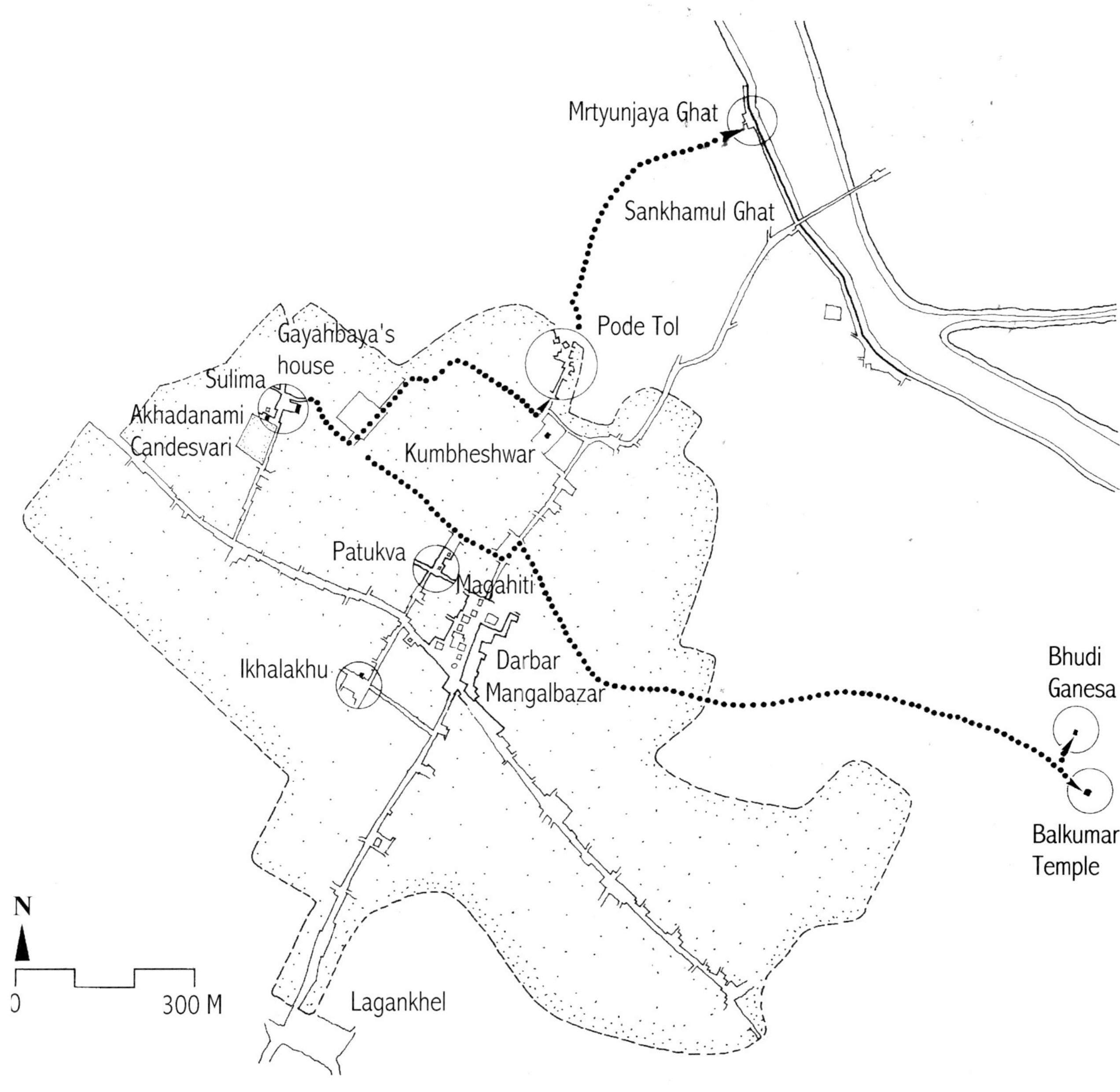


**Patan: Traces of Gayahbajya's activities
Drawing by Niels Gutschow, 1992**

Gayahbajya's legends touch many parts of Patan: the Mrtyunjaya *ghat* at Samkhamul where Gayahbajya bathed; the Lagankhel woods where he tended his cows; Pode Tol of Kumbhesvara, the location of his guru's house; the Bhudi Ganesa shrine where he observed penance; and the shrine of the mother goddess Balkumari, where he worshipped and where he outsmarted the frightening *dakini* in order to acquire magical powers. Gayahbajya imprisoned the goddess Candesvari at the temple of the same name. Vaisradeva, Gayahbajya's younger brother, once lived at Gujibaha. And, a stone marker at Phulchowki Mountain marks the location from where Gayahbajya brought the Harasiddhi dance.

# The Story of Gayahbajya

As told by Sri Bhaktilal Shrestha of Pimbaha, Patan

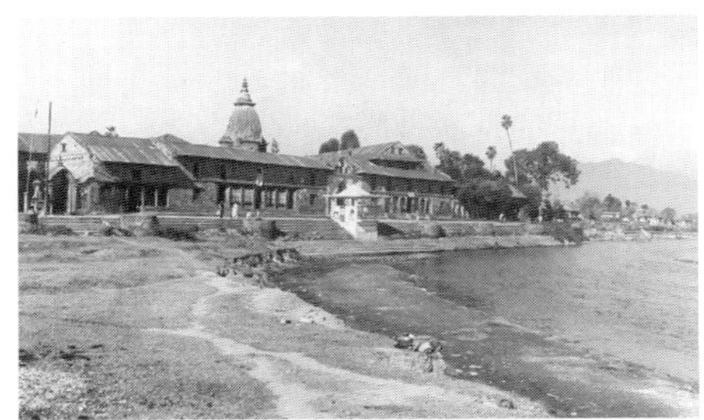

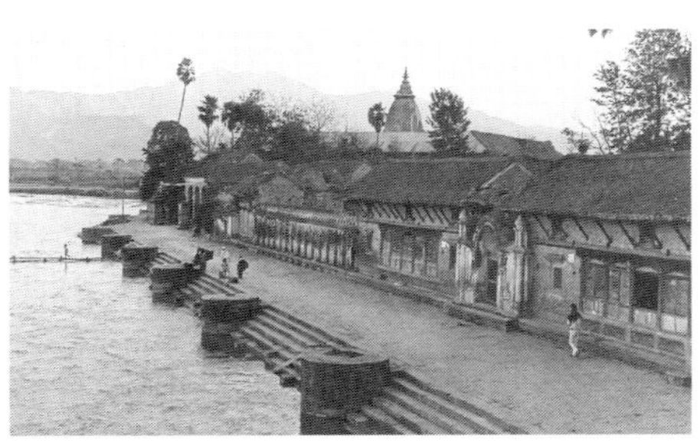

**Two views of Shankhamul ghat, where Gayahbajya bathed**

*This tale suggests that Gayahbajya was not just a legendary figure, but a historical one as well. Although Gayahbajya was a Brahman, his guru belonged to the untouchable Pode caste. This untouchable taught him Tantra, and Gayahbajya became the great Tantric of his time. Parts of his house, including the chamber where he finally gained siddhi, or enlightenment, still stand just ten meters from the Sulima Ratneshvara Temple.*

His name was not Gayahbajya. Actually, his name had been Gayapati. Gayahbajya had no one but his mother. He was a Brahman and went for a daily bath at Mrtyunjaya Ghat in Shankhamul at the confluence of the Bagmati and Manohara rivers. One day, as he was crossing Kumbheshvar on his way to Mrtyunjaya Ghat, it suddenly started raining hard. He looked for shelter but found only one house belonging to an untouchable (Pode). As a Brahman he could not enter a Pode's house, so he stood outside in the rain.

Inside the house one child was vexing his mother. She became very angry and stabbed her son with a kitchen knife. The child died immediately. Then the mother began to cry. After some time the child's father came home. When he learned what had happened, he told his wife not to cry about it. The father took the child into a separate room and brought him back to life. Naturally, this surprised Gayahbajya very much. He began to wonder what sort of knowledge this Pode had that could make his dead son live again. He became very curious about this secret knowledge.

The Pode was a Tantric. Many people visited him to discuss their problems. Gayahbajya also began to go there, but he never went inside. He just stayed outside. Whenever the Pode looked at him, he would leave and go for his bath. This was his routine for a long time.

One day, while Gayahbajya was standing outside the house, the Pode came to him and asked, "Why do you come here everyday? Why are you spying on me?" Gayahbajya immediately asked the Pode for the secret training, saying "What you have, give me."

"You are a Brahman and I am of low caste, so how can I give you anything?" replied the Pode.

"You must give me that training," said the Brahman.

"If you insist I will help you. Please come back after four days and bring one bunch of *belpatra* (leaf of the wood apple tree)," the Pode replied.

After four days Gayahbajya went to the Pode with a bunch of *belpatra*. Then they went to the Mrtyunjaya Ghat. The Pode asked Gayahbajya to take his bath first. When he finished his bath Gayahbajya wanted to get out of the river but the Pode stopped him. The Pode went and sat on the *tungah* (platform) used for *sraddha* (the death ritual). He wrote a *mantra* (an incantation or a magical spell) on each of the *belpatra* leaves, threw them into the river, and told Gayahbajya to catch and swallow each one. It was a miracle: after Gayahbajya had caught and swallowed *belpatra* leaf he knew every single mantra the guru had written.

"You brought this many *belpatra*, so the *mantras* are also this many," the Pode said. He told Gayahbajya to go back home. But Gayahbajya said, "Well, I know every *mantra*, but I don't yet have every *siddhi* (spiritual power). You must give me these powers as well."

The Pode said, "I can give you only the *mantras*, not the powers. If you want these powers, go to Bhudi Ganesh (a shrine in the eastern part of Patan honoring a deity believed to grant perfection) and worship him." Gayahbajya followed this advice. One day, after Gayahbajya finished reciting his *mantras* there, the god appeared and asked, "What do you want?" Gayahbajya replied, "I need *siddhi*."

"If you want to achieve *siddhi* go to the Balkumari shrine on the night of the fourteenth day of the dark fortnight in *Pacahre* (March). The *dakini* (witches) will come there on that night to prepare *mohani* (lamp black used for ritual purposes) for their Tantric *puja*. You must capture the *mohani* at once," said Ganesh.

Gayahbajya went to the Balkumari shrine as he'd been told to do. He hid and waited. The *dakini* came to perform their *puja*. They placed three human skulls on the ground to make a fireplace and then put a big *la bhegah* (earthen pot) on top of it. After lighting a fire in the middle of the skulls they began collecting the black soot that formed on the bowl. This Tantric *puja* pleased the goddess Balkumari, who suddenly appeared before them. Just as the *dakini* bowed down to Balkumari's feet, Gayahbajya snatched the soot-covered pot and ran to his house.

When Gayahbajya reached his house his mother was outside waiting for him. As soon as Gayahbajya entered the house she closed the door and fastened it with a *sikri* (iron lock). Because it was made of iron, the lock had the power to prevent witches and evil spirits from entering the house. The *dakini* had followed Gayahbajya but could not enter the house. They waited and waited outside hoping to get back the soot-covered pot. When morning came they were still outside, pleading with Gayahbajya for just one piece of the pot covered with soot. Gayahbajya agreed, gave them a piece of the pot, and sent them away. After putting the black soot on his forehead Gayahbajya attained *siddhi*, as well as several other kinds of powers and fulfillments. He became a great Tantric.

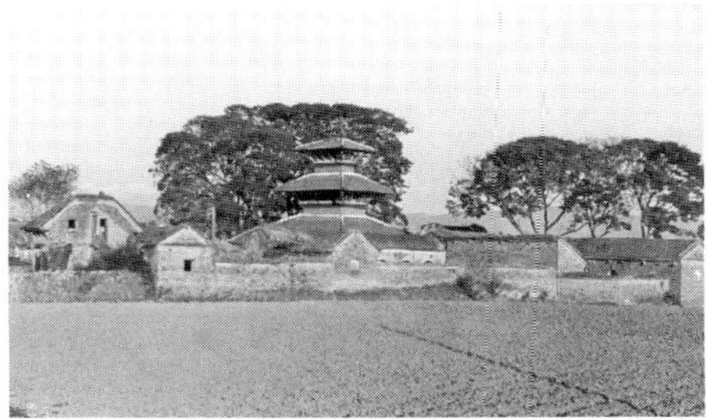

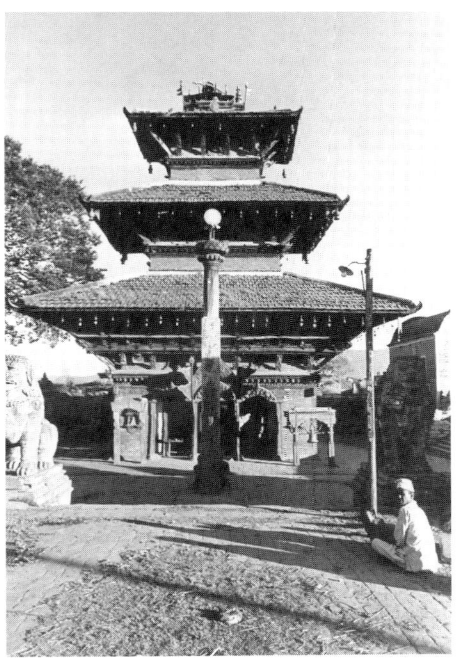

Two views of the shrine to Balkumari, the Mother Goddess. It was here that Gayahbajya outsmarted several dakini and snatched the soot-covered pot he needed to help him obtain special powers.

# Gayahbajya and the Magician

As told by Sri Bhaktilal Shrestha

Once Gayahbajya was sitting in the Amaliguthi Phalca, a rest house at Sulima, smoking "hubble bubble." Many people were running towards Mangalbazar. He was surprised and asked one of them why they were running. One of the men said, "One foreign magician is showing very interesting magic. We are going to see that magical show." The magician's trick was to kill a boy, take out his heart and lungs, and bring him back to life.

Gayahbajya then sent some of his students to Mangahiti fountain in Mangalbazar to fetch water in a *dokoca*, a basket made of bamboo. A *dokoca* has a lot of big holes, so it is not possible to carry water in it. But because of the power of Gayahbajya's *mantra*, it became possible. This surprised the people, and many of them started gathering around the students to watch them carry water in the *dokoca*.

The magician thought that if this continued there would be no charm to his magic, so he cast a spell and threw a small stone into the *dokoca*. This caused all the water to spill out, and it was no longer possible to keep water in the *dokoca*. Gayahbajya's students returned and told him what had happened to them.

Then, a buzzard flew into Mangalbazar and snatched the heart of the boy from the foreign magician's hands. Now, this was a big problem for the magician. He wept because he could not bring back the boy's life without the heart.

Someone suggested that the magician consult Gayahbajya about his problem. The magician went to Sulima to meet him, but he was not there. Only Gayahbajya's wife was present. She was cooking rice, using her own leg as wood for the fire.

After introducing himself, the magician asked to meet Gayahbajya. The wife told the foreign magician to go to Lagankhel forest, where he would find Gayahbajya tending his cows.

So the magician went to Lagankhel. Gayahbajya was there feeding his cows, bending the branches of the trees with his toe so that the cows could eat the leaves. When he saw Gayahbajya the magician apologized for throwing the stone in the *dokoca*. He asked Gayahbajya to forgive him and to give back the boy's heart.

Gayahbajya smiled and then gave back the heart, which, while disguised as a buzzard, he had taken. Later, the foreign magician decided not to show his magic in Nepal ever again.

# The Dyahmaru Phalca of Candesvari

As told by Sri Bhaktilal Shrestha

Inside the Candesvari Temple is an empty niche where an icon of a god would normally be. This story tells us why the niche is empty. According to the legend, Gayahbajya wanted to be a *siddha*, an immortal being, and stay inside the temple with Candesvari, in his own separate chamber, forever. But, as happens with impossible dreamers, he failed.

Gayahbajya wanted to attain *samadhi*, or enlightenment, by taking refuge in his house in Sulima. He told his family he was not to be disturbed for six months. He went into an underground room in the house, had his family cover him up, and told them to wait for six months before exposing him. He said that if during this time he received spiritual powers and fulfillment, *siddhi*, an icon of him should be placed in the empty niche of the Candesvari Temple.

Unfortunately, however, one of his daughters went to see him on exactly the last day of the six-month period. Because the full six months were not completed, she saw Gayahbajya in a half-stone and half-human form. Above the stomach his body was pure human flesh, but the lower part was stone. Gayahbajya cried out to her to cover his body immediately. He condemned her and her descendants. As a result, the niche in the Candesvari temple has always remained empty.

# Gayahbajya and His Untouchable Guru

As told by Sri Ananta Jvalanada Rajupadhya of Patukva, Patan

Once Gayahbajya, a Brahman, was walking near the Patan Palace when he saw his untouchable Pode guru coming towards him. According to the social customs in those days, a pupil must bow down to his guru by touching his feet with his forehead as a mark of respect. But as Pode are untouchable for the Brahman caste, for a person like Gayahbajya to bow down to a Pode's feet would certainly be considered a social offense. As the street was full of people, Gayahbajya cleverly acted as if he had slipped on cow dung and fell down at his Pode guru's feet, a trick to enable him to bow down to his guru's feet without offending anyone. The guru understood the situation and was pleased with Gayahbajya. Afterwards, the guru told him that it would not be necessary to bow down to his feet in front of other people as it was breaking social custom.

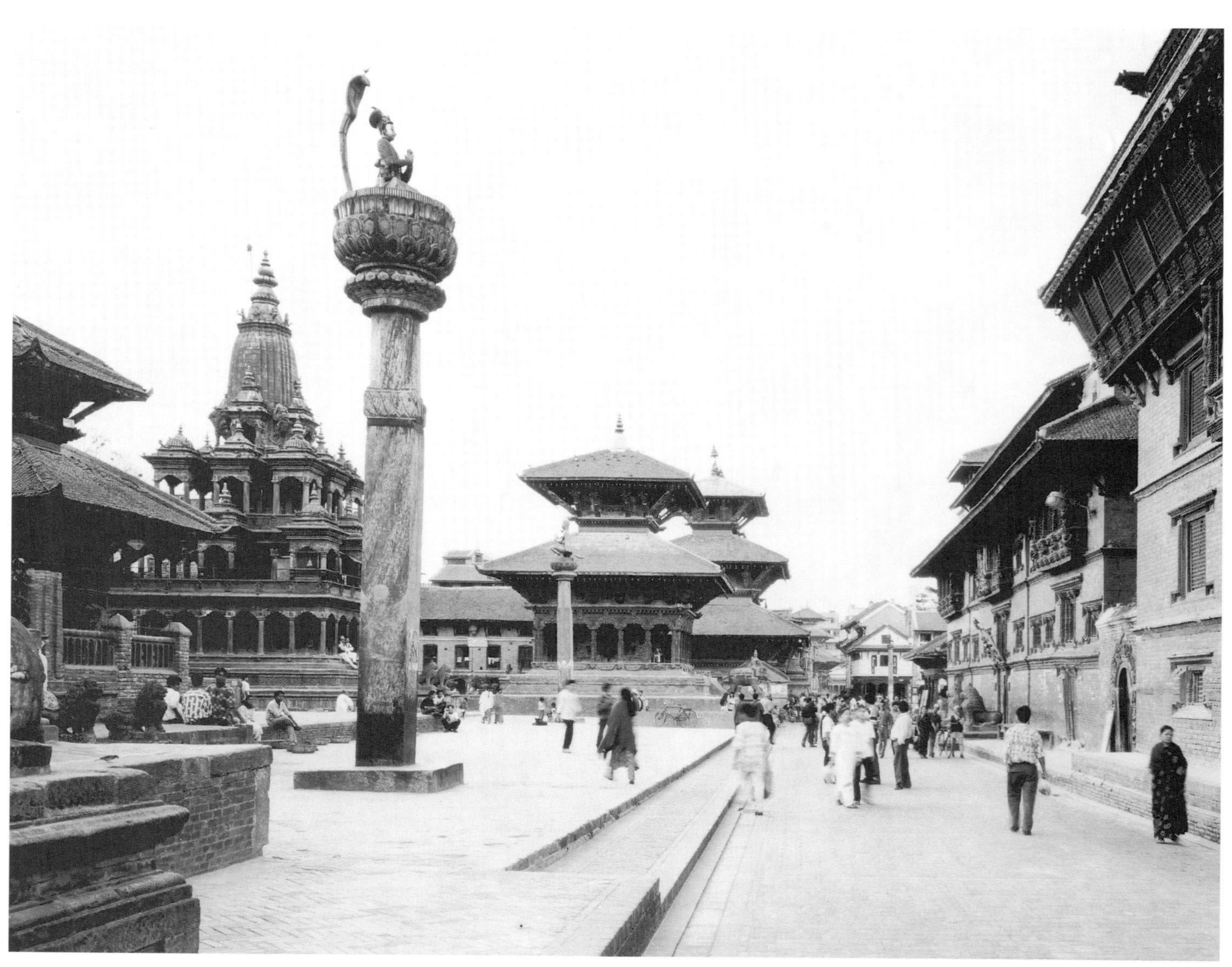

Patan Darbar Square, looking north
Keshav Narayan Chok, home of the
Patan Museum since 1997, is on the right.



The Sulima Pagoda

# CONTRIBUTIONS

## The Artificial Life of Heritage

Wim Denslagen

Walking into Darbar Square in Patan for the first time is like entering a fairy tale, a theater where the visitor is confronted with an undisturbed scene from the eastern Middle Ages. Patan is one of three ancient royal cities in the Kathmandu Valley in Nepal. Even if one tries not to see them, many tourists—modern intruders—have discovered these cities. The modern world seems far away from Patan's Royal Square.

The fairy tale loses a bit of its enchantment, however, when we read in the guidebook that none of the buildings in the square is older than the seventeenth century. As if to console the reader, the guidebook says that the building traditions on which the square's architecture is based are age-old. A few pages later the dream is once again disturbed when we learn that much of what we are looking at was actually reconstructed after the earthquake of 1934.

This newly acquired knowledge may disrupt our first impressions of the square, but the strange and overwhelming architecture of the place continues to enchant. And besides, nobody likes to have his dreams shattered.

### Living culture

The tourist visiting Patan's Darbar Square turns to the royal palace and enters through a golden door. There he notices that the fairy tale is suddenly being told in another language. The enchanting story has been taken up by someone who speaks differently: this different voice is that of the architect who restored the palace, turning it into a museum over the years from 1983 to 1997.

In the Patan Museum, we see the East as most tourists would like to see it. It is a picturesque scene from the past, polished and refined, without the visual noise of everyday life, which one can barely escape when outside the museum. In the quiet atmosphere of the museum, sculptures are displayed as works of art, not in the way they function in everyday religious practice. Every museum creates such distance between the present and the past, between everyday life and the sophisticated corridors of taste and culture.

In the temples the statues represent gods, and worshippers rouse them from their dreams with the sounds of bells hung in front of their shrines. In these temples the past is not yet detached from the present, it is still subservient to the needs of daily worship. The historical value of the statues is of secondary importance to the worshippers.

For the tourist the historical value comes first, unless he or she takes an anthropological interest in living religious practices and their actual visual expressions. The educated tourist deplores expressions of living culture because they diminish the historical significance of the monuments. In his eyes historical temples that have been modernized, *i.e.* with modern materials and forms, have suffered from a lack of effective professional monitoring that responsible

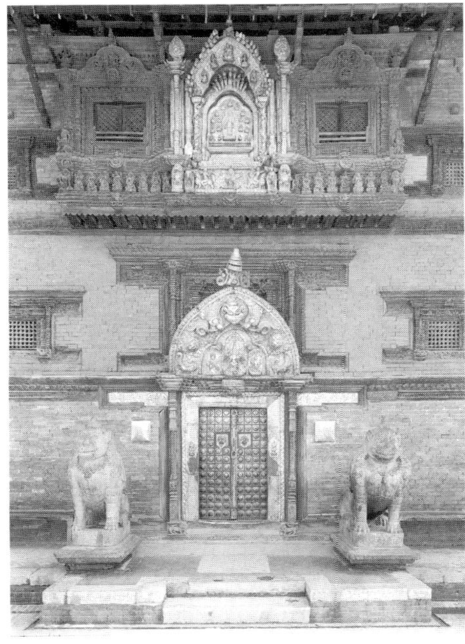

**Keshav Narayan Chok
The Golden Door, entrance
to the Patan Museum**

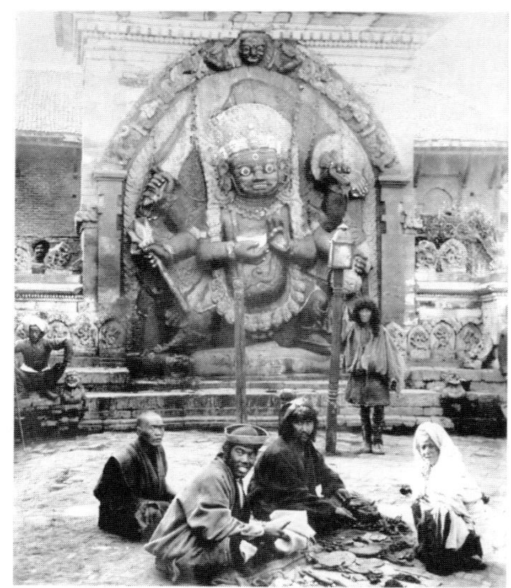

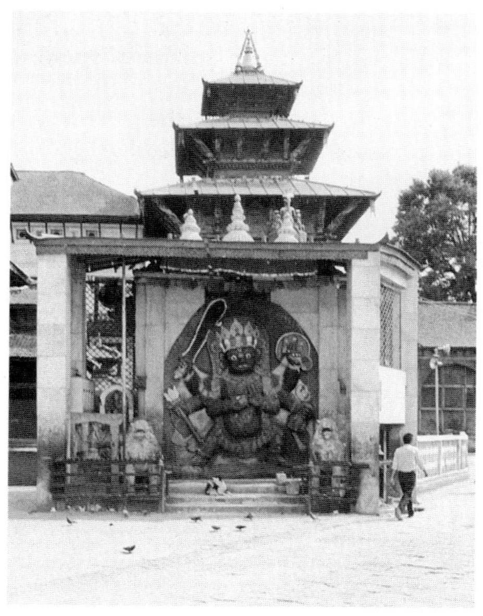

**Kal Bhairav Shrine,
Kathmandu Darbar Square**
Constructed by King Pratap Malla in 1660.
Additional roofs, to produce contemporary
layers of votive offerings, were added in
1934 and in 1980.

institutions should provide. Modern deviations from building traditions are a slap in the face to our tourist as well as to professional institutions. In 1980 the Shrine of Kal Bhairav, built in 1660 on the Darbar Square in Kathmandu, was embellished by a marble facing, much to the disappointment of UNESCO and ICOMOS specialists. The use of this material was condemned by them because it "disrupted the architectural fabric of the Darbar Square."[1]

The opposition of the educated tourist and foreign specialists to modern manifestations of affection toward the gods of the temple is the inescapable consequence of a wish to protect historical values. It is the same old story: protection means obstructing development, or at least slowing down the rate of change, something not readily acceptable to the people who want to modernize their environment. Only tourists and specialists deplore modern additions to historical architecture—their dreams get shattered.

The fact that a small group of specialists tries to protect historical architecture against the wishes of a majority is not very strange. This has been the normal situation in most European countries, where protective measures have met with more resistance than support by the general public. The care of monuments has never been a generally accepted cultural phenomenon. It has always been forced upon a majority by a cultural elite, which had the power to get support from government. Even now, contemporary architecture is much more valued in most European cities than historical architecture, for new architecture expresses flourishing entrepreneurship and old buildings only nostalgic feelings.[2]

The famous architect Rem Koolhaas claims that people do not need history or identity. "Regret about history's absence is a tiresome reflex," he writes. And he explains that historic cities are turned into caricatures of themselves by the tourist industry. More and more people visit the old centers like "an avalanche that, in a perpetual quest for 'character', grinds successful identities down to meaningless dust."[3] This complaint is often voiced by people who think that tourists destroy the reality of the site, which they do to a certain extent, but how could it be otherwise? Koolhaas prefers to reject the artificial life of old cities and many follow him in this view.

Patan's Darbar Square is a beautiful and enchanting place in which the architecture will hopefully not change significantly anymore. The picture is more or less frozen. If the tourist wants to see the living culture of Nepal, he has to leave the protected area and enter the ordinary world, where a living culture is allowed to change in a process that will eventually annihilate a substantial part of the historical value.

## Imported knowledge

The care of old buildings is and has always been something artificial, restorations or reconstructions always revealing the spirit of the restorers. And that is what you immediately feel when you enter the Patan Museum. The interior and the garden behind the museum represent western ideas. When one climbs the stairs to the exposition rooms on the first floor, one hears the soft tones of a chime, these tones evoking the mystical atmosphere the tourist associates with the East. Chimes are not common in Nepal, as the architect told me, but they nevertheless convey the spirit of the old works of art that one is about to admire.

The restoration of the buildings themselves is a paragon of responsible architectural behavior, but the newly designed interior has more in common with the refined taste of Italy than with Nepali traditions. The architect, Götz Hagmüller,



**The Sulima Pagoda**

is an Austrian, and the restoration reflects his European background, not only in his designs, but also and perhaps even more so in his professional attitude. He has, for instance, abstained from coloring the façades of the old palace because there is no proof that the brickwork and the woodwork of this eighteenth century building were originally painted. The trouble is that the adjacent building, which is not yet restored, shows red paint on the brickwork and black paint on the woodwork. He would have used paint in the same way, he told me, if there had been proof that the paint was original. But there is no proof and he refused to do something irresponsible.

This kind of responsible behavior betrays the influence of western attitudes. During and after the restoration, he had to be on his guard against criticism from experts who might accuse him of violating the Charter of Venice. This is understandable as the museum is part of the UNESCO World Heritage Site. Götz Hagmüller had good reasons for not following international guidelines in every respect, but he was extremely aware of his reasons and he even explained them in the periodical *Architektur Aktuell*.

John Sanday, the architect who restored the royal palace of Kathmandu, Hanuman Dhoka, relates that during the restoration more than fifty women were given the task of removing sometimes more than eight layers of paint on the woodcarvings. The restoration was supervised by the Department of Archaeology of Nepal in collaboration with UNESCO, whose experts had discovered some original carvings bearing no traces of paint. That discovery determined the course of the work. Writing about one of the towers of the palace, the Basantapur Tower, John Sanday declares, "It is hard now to believe that every square centimeter of it was once covered in paint."[4]

Removing paint in order to reveal the original appearance of a building most likely reflects a professional approach. The conviction that the original appearance should be the ultimate goal at the expense of later alterations has been developed in a world where the study of architectural history has produced specialists capable of making historically correct reconstructions. These kinds of specialists have nearly always been influenced by western or Japanese attitudes. Especially in the West, the desire to recreate the original appearance became a threat to the authenticity of historic architecture, that is to say, a threat to the state of the building before restoration, as it came down to us through the course of history.

This threat provoked the charters of ICOMOS (International Council on Monuments and Sites). Take for instance Article 11 of the Charter of Venice of 1964: "The valid contributions of all periods to the building of a monument must be respected, since unity of style is not the aim of a restoration." The statement was necessary at the time, and it still has its value within the bounds of sound reasoning. The article contains a general principle, no legal judgement: it asks simply that the visible traces of the past not be destroyed by a merciless reconstruction of the original appearance. The statement was necessary in Europe and it still is.[5]

There is no reason to reject the influence of the West on the culture of Nepal. To do that would be absurd in today's world. The influence of UNESCO on the management of its World Heritage Sites in the Kathmandu Valley is a fact of everyday international life. The international community wants monument areas to be protected, giving these areas a special position, isolated in a way from ordinary life. The gap between this special position, which was invented in the West, and local traditions is already considerable, but it may have become too wide in the case of the removal of the paint at the Hanuman Dhoka Palace. Many old temples in the Kathmandu Valley are still covered with colors and no one knows how old

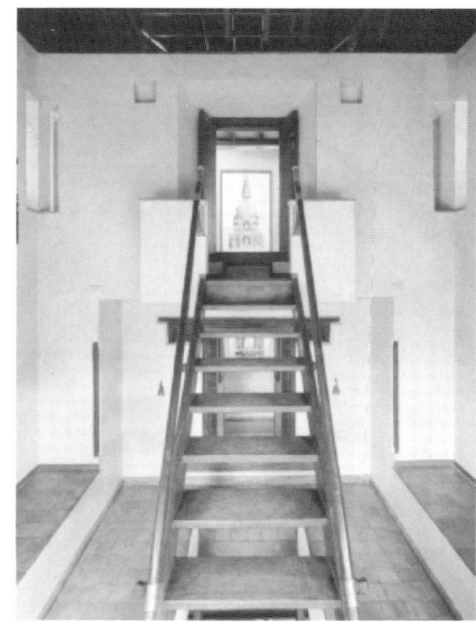

**The first floor staircase in the reconstructed east wing of Keshav Narayan Chok**

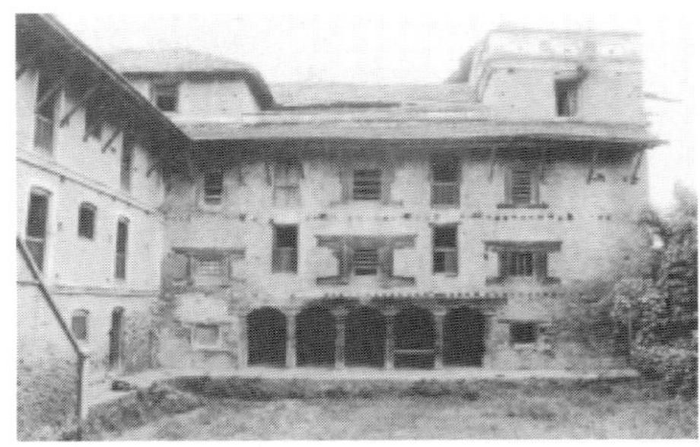

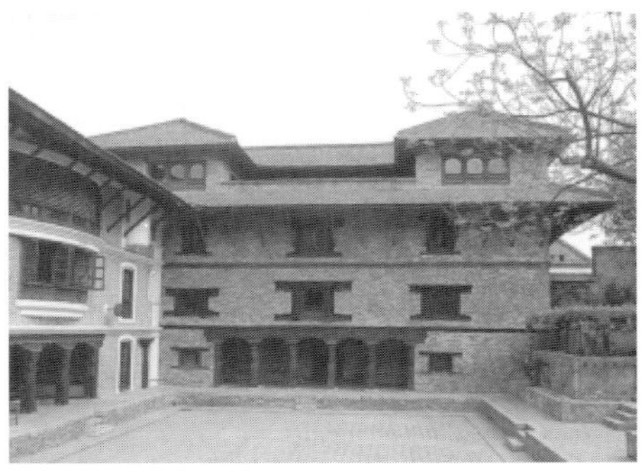

**The east (left) and northeast wings of Keshav Narayan Chok before dismantling in 1988 (top) and after restoration in 1997**

**Both wings of the palace were devastated in the 1934 earthquake and subsequently redesigned, reconstructed, and used for government offices and a school.**

**During the 1990s restoration, four windows of upright proportions in the northeast wing, which had been added by the school in the 1950s, were eliminated. The upper level was redesigned, partly in analogy to similar seventeenth-century roofs. New cornices above the ground and first floors were added, and historic bricks were used to the fullest extent possible.**

**The east wing was completely rebuilt, with new features such as the bay window (left) added.**

these are. What could have been the reason to destroy the layers of paint other than the imported and contestable assumption that the original represents a higher value than the authentic?

## Artificial culture

All efforts to reduce the speed of change are artificial, and it is obvious that historic architecture will hardly survive without such efforts. But who directs these efforts makes a difference. Restorations in Nepal seem, to a certain extent, projections of western ideas about the East. Perhaps this cannot always be avoided, but sometimes the ideas may be based on myths.

In his guidebook John Sanday writes that "concern for periods and datable styles may, in the case of Nepali architecture, become irrelevant because here the art is expressed in a traditional form as opposed to an individual form." This calls to mind the way in which Gothic architecture was interpreted by people like Eugène Viollet-le-Duc and William Lethaby, namely as the expression of a collective spirit. This interpretation turned out to be nothing other than a projection of a Romantic longing for a return to the feudal society of the Middle Ages, a society in which everyone would have his well-defined place. "It would be hard to devise a more misleading interpretation of Gothic," wrote David Watkin, and he pointed out how this "collectivist and anti-intellectual" view of Gothic architecture contributed to the totalitarian aspects of modernism.[6]

The statement that Nepal's culture is traditional and lacks the stylistic developments we know in the West could be a projection of western ideas on the East. John Sanday's opinion that the "vitality" of Nepal's does not consist "in the development of personal expression" but "in the perpetuation of what is traditionally correct" may perhaps be welcomed by those who earn a living in the traditional crafts. Outside this domain such stereotypes can become dangerous, for instance when the absence of individuality is used as an argument against democracy.[7]

This is certainly not what John Sanday meant. He relates how the traditional crafts were revived by new restoration projects with the help of foreign money. Without this revival the projects would have been impossible, but without the foreign help the revival would not have been possible.[8] The traditional crafts are, so to speak, re-invented by the foreign concern for the continuity of a much-admired culture. From this point of view, it would be strange to call the newly revived crafts the expression of a living culture. The living culture is found outside the World Heritage Sites and also in the many recently painted temples with modern additions.

The gap between the living culture and the culture of scientific restorations is wide: this is reflected in the different ways the historical architecture is dealt with. The clever restorations of the international specialists are transformations from everyday life into a dream of the past as true as one can possibly make it. These restorations represent, so to speak, the consciousness of cultural heritage, the expression of an interest in history. As such, these constitute an importation of scientific research into an otherwise much threatened historical environment. Here history can be revived, but only with the help of artificialities such as dollars, knowledge, and imagination.[9]

The restoration of the Buddhist monastery Ibaha Bahi in Patan (1990 to 1995), a project of Japan's Nippon Institute of Technology, is a splendid example of the scientific approach. The distance between this restored building and the living culture can be demonstrated by the fact that the modern stucco on the front has not been reconstructed, probably because not much of it was left and because of the fact that the stucco could not have been original. By leaving out the stucco, the Japanese have cut one of the threads by which the past was connected to the present. Inside the courtyard some sculptured wooden members had to be replaced because they were lost. The new elements were left unadorned, for example, certain timber members and portions of the balcony cornices, as there was not enough evidence for a reliable reconstruction of the carvings.[10]

## The crafts and historical values

Most will agree that this kind of restraint is laudable in the context of a historically correct restoration, but was it necessary? In the Ibaha Bahi new carvings could, after all, have been added in such a way that the difference between old and new was recognizable, but not disturbing. This issue is much discussed in the Kathmandu Valley, where organizations from various countries introduce their respective opinions in their restoration projects. UNESCO is, of course, in favor of restraint, which means leaving some parts unadorned—blank—as a restoration, according the Charter of Venice "must stop at the point where conjecture begins."

Other organizations, like the Kathmandu Valley Preservation Trust, are less convinced of the universal applicability of the charter. They point out that such restraint diminishes the visual unity and is often unsuitable, as it expresses considerations that may be too far removed from the impression the architecture is trying to make. Abstaining from the introduction of new carvings, which should—it is hardly necessary to add—always harmonize with the existing architectural environment, seems a crude and impolite gesture, a forced course of action, an act of doctrinarian and patronizing legalists. Leaving out decorations in religious buildings in order to comply with international guidelines can only be understood by someone who shows more respect for historical correctness than for the temple as a gift to the gods.

At this point it is necessary to remark that this kind of restraint is exceptional in Europe and it is therefore high time for UNESCO to exert the necessary pressure on national governments there in order to be consistent with their own guidelines. The discussion on this issue started in Europe, remained unresolved, and has now been exported to the East, especially to the Kathmandu Valley.

The Charter of Venice was, I think, mainly directed against the European mania for reducing every monument to its original state and for wiping out the architectural contributions of the nineteenth century. And the prescription that "any extra work which is indispensable must be distinct from the architectural composition and must bear a contemporary stamp" was a deplorable mistake of architects who still gave credence to the artistic principles of the Modern Movement. It is not necessary to damage a monument by introducing modern design.

The experts in Venice overlooked the fact that there are also subtle ways to restore. We should forgive them and forget it. It is enough to show in an unobtrusive way what has been added in order to recapture the beauty of a building. The deliberate display of zealous honesty by showing the scars history has inflicted on a building, or by confronting the defenseless monument with provocative modern design, is a relatively new phenomenon in the world of conservation, probably developed in connection with the rise of modern art theories.

Discussion of this issue became relevant again on the occasion of the restoration of the Sulima Ratneshvara Temple in Patan.[11] The restoration of this temple includes new timber roof struts with new carvings, which are reconstructions on the basis of old photographs, old fragments, and examples from other

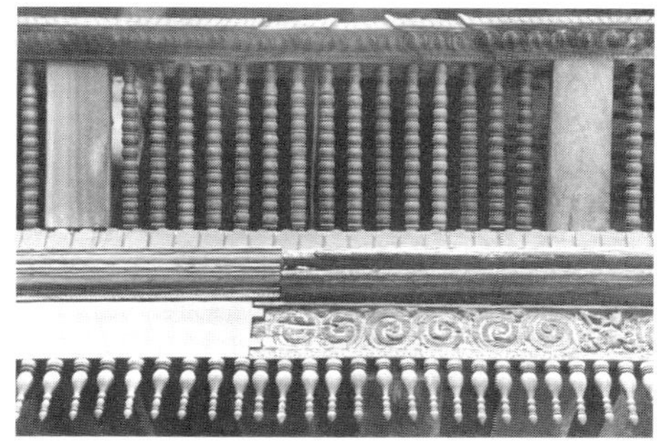

Ibaha Bahi, Patan
Detail of the courtyard balcony

"Where wooden cornices had been lost, they were replaced and the replacements were left unadorned. The new cornices were not decorated with carvings for two reasons: the motifs on existing cornices were difficult to define and therefore not clear enough to serve as models for new carvings, and it was decided leaving the new members plain and unadorned would make it easy to distinguish them from existing older members reused in the restoration. Where new balusters were required, they were patterned on those still found to exist on the balcony of the first floor of the main façade of the east wing. Where possible, existing coping was refurbished and reused or replaced by new coping where this had been lost."
—Takayuki Kurotsu, 1998

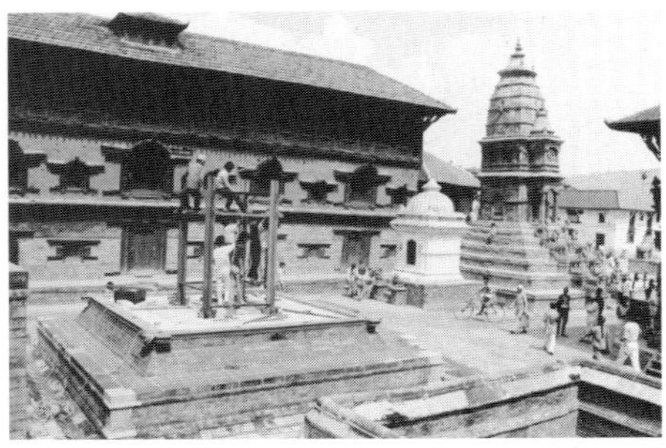
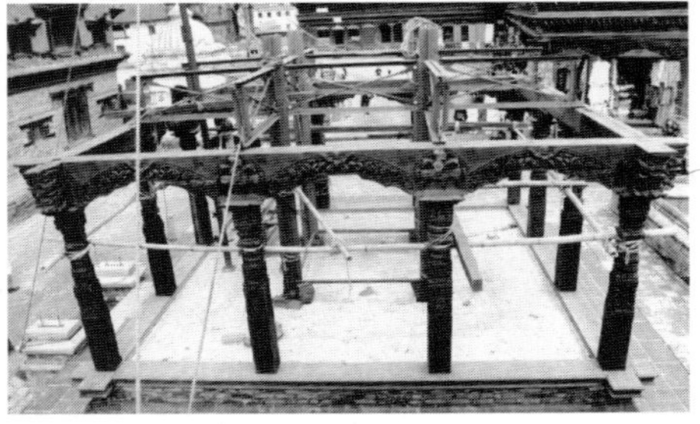

**Reconstruction of the Cyasilin Mandap Bhaktapur Darbar Square**
Four stages of construction between 1989 and 1990: the introduction of the internal steel frame for seismic strengthening and the reconstitution of the historical timber arcade.

comparable temples. According to one viewpoint, the new old carvings are nothing but fake, whereas the other viewpoint defends this approach by pointing out that plain struts represent a typically western attitude that is wholly alien to the local people.

It seems that two different cultures collide in this respect, but perhaps the controversy only exists as long as one follows the rule of the "contemporary stamp" of the Charter of Venice. The historical value of the monument is probably not diminished by reconstructions of lost fragments, as long as these can be distinguished from the original work and as long as the reconstructions are subservient to the existing architecture. The question of how to make such distinctions is a matter of taste. The less obvious the distinction the better, but some distinction would seem to be a gesture of respect towards the old work. While this approach indeed deviates from the Charter of Venice, it is nonetheless no crude violation of it either.

All professional considerations of this kind must be seen in their proper perspective, for when an earthquake has finished its terrible work, the world of preservation must respect the wish to rebuild the devastated architecture in order to recapture the lost habitat. A charter which forbids that is cruel.

Happily there never was much opposition to the rebuilding, between 1987 and 1990, of the seventeenth-century Cyasilin Mandap on the Darbar Square in Bhaktapur. The structure had been devasted during the 1934 earthquake. As in the case of the Sulima Ratneshvara Temple, there has only been some discussion about the completion of carved decorations in the style of the old work. In both cases it was decided to conceal any distinction between old and new. The architects did not dissimulate the steel of the construction inside the Cyasilin Mandap for they wished to express the modernity of the building. The steel stands for honesty and the carvings for the continuity of the living crafts. The steel represents the western attitude as it is in harmony with the "contemporary stamp" of the Charter of Venice. The carvings represent the local traditions.

This is a violation of the charter because the distinction between old and new carvings has been dissimulated. Here *les extrèmes se touchent* and this paradox might disturb our tourist who has, of course, no detailed knowledge of professional debates. Perhaps the paradox could have been avoided by concealing the steel and not concealing the difference between old and new carvings. Concealing the steel might be dishonest in western eyes, but it pays respect to the spirit of the monument.

Showing some difference between old and new carvings (impossible to discern from some distance) might also be a form of paying respect. If the craftsmen do not want to change their art, if they want to continue their own culture, nobody can blame them, but paying respect to the arts of their own past does not force them to blot out the distinction between their work and that of their ancestors. Is it necessary for the "living crafts" to deny the difference between the past and the present?[12]

Some people believe that there are fundamental differences between the West and the East on this point. In eastern cultures, they say, the historical substance as such is of much less importance than the *genius loci*. Preservationists in the West are believed to be more concerned with the material aspect of the monuments than their colleagues in the East. This difference would be based on "underlying philosophical approaches to the cosmology of the world," as Chen Wei and Andreas Aas wrote.[13]

Defining cultures and nations in such general terms may be an obstacle to better understanding between different cultures because such definitions are nearly always used to enshrine identities and mostly based on myths. In these kinds of comparisons the East is always represented as the world of mystery and the West as the world of reason. Take, for instance, what Sir Alfred Lyall once said to Lord Cromer: "Accuracy is abhorrent to the Oriental mind." Cromer added that the European "is a natural logician," whereas the reasoning of the Oriental is "of the most slipshod description."

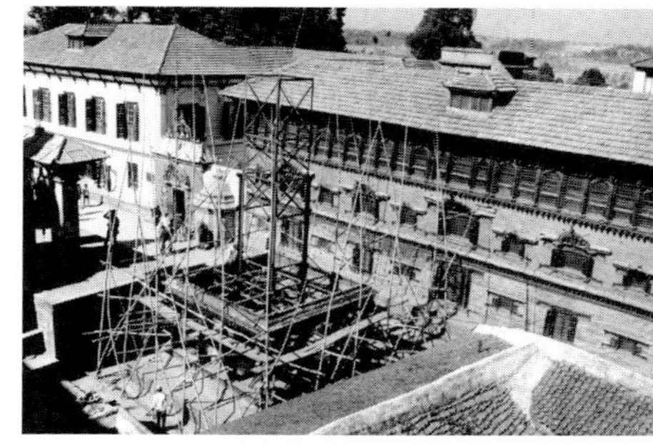

This was written in the beginning of the twentieth century. We know now that it reveals more about the state of mind of the European rulers than of those who were ruled by them.[14] In the beginning of the nineteenth century the German philosopher G.W.F. Hegel prepared the way for these kinds of orientalist stereotypes by explaining that the Indian mind lacks a sense of history and objectivity. "The Hindoo race," he wrote, "has consequently proved itself unable to comprehend either persons or events as part of continuous history, because to any historical treatment a certain objectivity is essential..."[15]

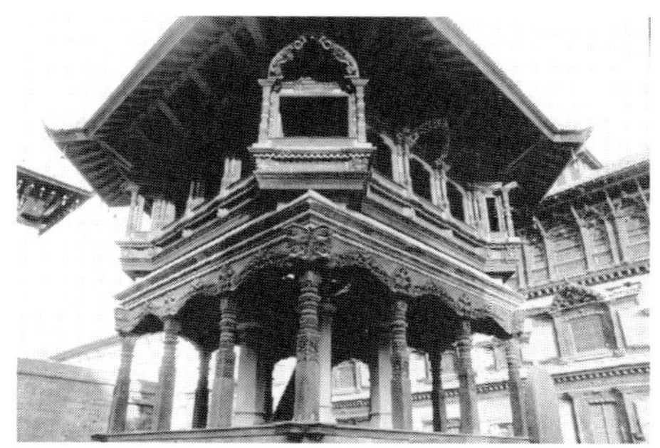

Our tourist, who certainly did not expect to end up with this kind of pedantic judgement, begins to understand that people in the East sometimes define their own culture according to concepts that were developed in the West.[16]

The orientalist view of the East as a static and unchangeable culture, in which traditions remain always the same and are not subject to the influence of temporary circumstances, may have been a creation of the West, but it can indeed also be found in the East. "We Indians," said the Indian psychotherapist Sudhir Kakar, "use the outside reality to preserve the continuity of the self amidst an ever-changing flux of outer events and things."[17] But who is entitled to speak for all the people of a culture?[18]

In 1999, the municipality of Kathmandu announced the reconstruction of the Akash Bhairav Temple at Indra Chok. This temple had been modernized in the first quarter of the twentieth century to include many non-traditional elements. The project to remove these elements and to reconstruct the original appearance of the temple is probably based on concepts from the West. In this case the East seems to adapt a European tradition of reconstructing the original appearance of the monuments. This tradition goes back to nineteenth century architects like Eugène Viollet-le-Duc.

The irony here, however, is that nowadays many experts from the West reject this tradition and are recommending against the removal of alterations made more than a generation ago that should, for this reason, be valued as an integral part of the historical fabric. It seems that the municipality of Kathmandu is as old-fashioned as the Minister of Culture of France, Jack Lang, who in 1990 gave permission to destroy the nineteenth-century restoration of the Saint-Sernin in Toulouse. This romanesque church had been restored by the famous French restorer Eugène Viollet-le-Duc in 1860 and has now been *dérestaurée* by his contemporary successor, Yves Boiret.[19]

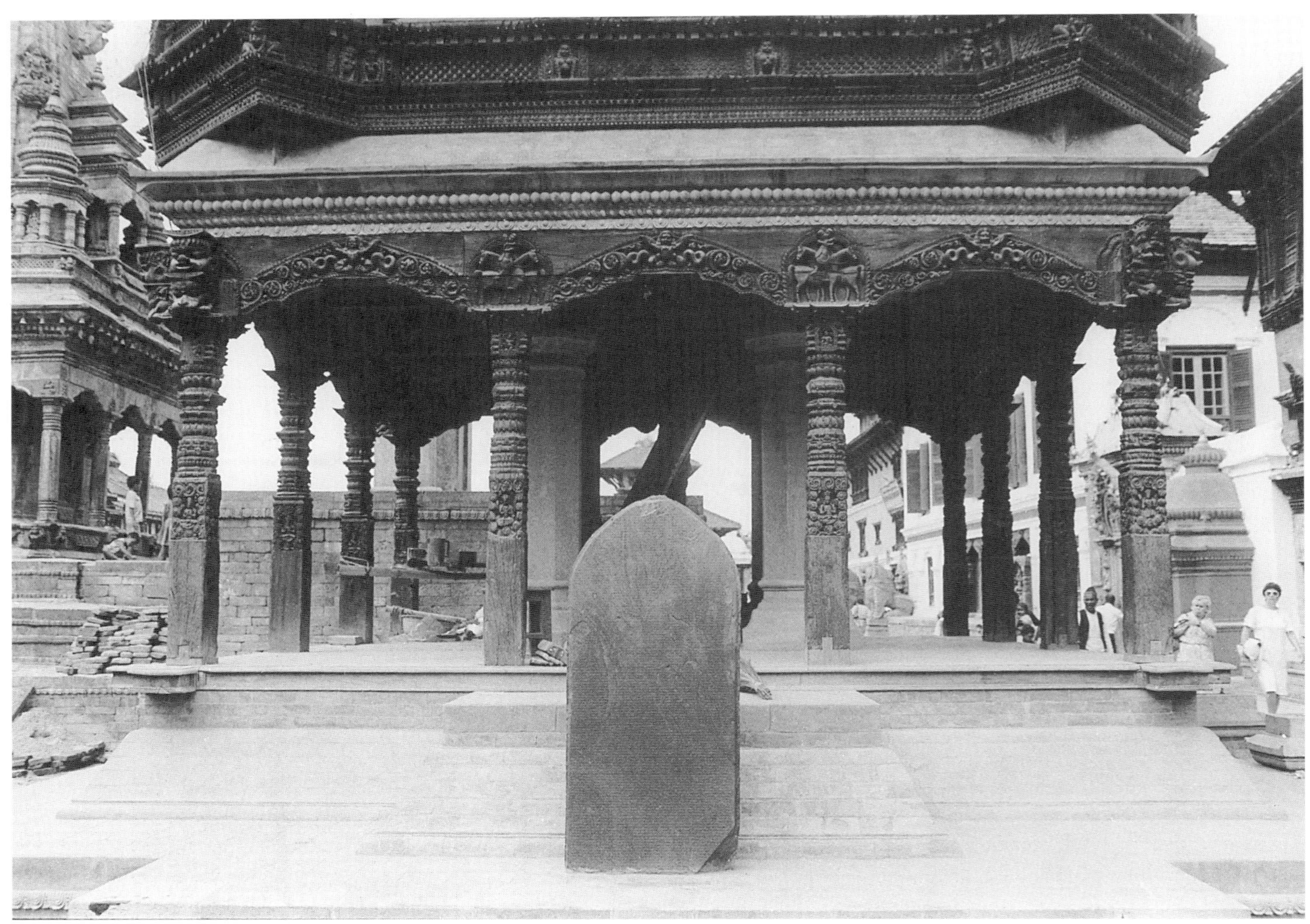

**Cyasilin Mandap, Bhaktapur**
Eight of the twelve pillars survived the earthquake of 1934 and were reinstalled during the 1987-1990 reconstruction. Five of these had rotten bases and were fitted with new feet joined in cruciform fashion, a traditional Newar carpentry technique. Other historical fabric that was reused included thirty percent of the lintels, four capitals, and three half-capitals.

# Techniques in the Architectural Preservation of Nepal
## Thoughts about Diversity of Practice in the Repair of Timber Pillars

Niels Gutschow

Much discussion has taken place about appropriate goals for architectural preservation in Nepal. The globalization of standards and different interpretations emerge as key topics. My particular interest as a documentation specialist is to collect materials that can serve as concrete contributions to these discussions. To this end I present three different solutions to a specific conservation problem, the repair of damaged pillar bases. These were part of three different restoration projects, all of which were implemented in Nepal with international technical and financial support between 1987 and 1997.

Cyasilin Mandap

The reconstruction of the lost Eight-Cornered Pavilion, Cyasilin Mandap[1], on Bhaktapur's royal square (1987 to 1990) was a gift of the German Government to Nepal. The project design was based on the historical photographs of Gustave Le Bon (1886) and Percy Brown and Giuseppe Tucci (ca. 1920). The detailing of this, one of Nepal's most intricate historical structures, relied heavily on the expertise of Surendra Joshi, builder and site manager, and Radhe Shyam Silpakar, head carpenter and master carver.

Ibaha Bahi

The dismantling and rebuilding of the Ibaba Bahi[2] in Patan, a seventeenth-century monastic building, took place between 1990 and 1995, after designs by Katsuhiko Watanabe in collaboration with Jun Hatano and Takayuki Kurotsu from the Nippon Institute of Technology. Site supervision was carried out by the Department of Archaeology, complemented by the Japanese architects on short-term supervisory missions.

Patan Palace

The restoration of Keshav Narayan Chok[3], part of Patan's palace complex, and its adaptation as a museum were executed with technical and financial support from Austria. The project began in 1983 under the guidance of architect John Sanday, who restored the north wing and northwestern tower. Architect Götz Hagmüller completed the restoration of the building and an extended program for the new museum (1986 to 1997). Several wings of the palace were dismantled based on the architect's decision that these structures, poorly reconstructed after the 1934 earthquake, disrupted the architectural continuity of the palace complex. Moreover, they were not structurally sound enough to accommodate future museum requirements. The northeastern wing was rebuilt in stages between 1993 and 1997, incorporating as much historic fabric as possible. This work eliminated four modern windows added in the 1950s and reshaped the top floor to accommodate new guest studios. The new roof configuration was loosely based on seventeenth-century examples.

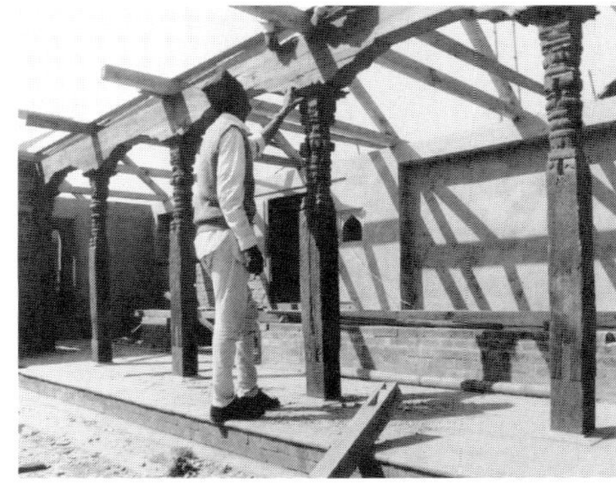

New roof terrace, northeast wing, Keshav Narayan Chok, Patan Darbar, 1997
While the configuration of pillar, capital and lintel follows traditional models, the pillars were elongated by 20 cm, thus changing their proportions considerably.

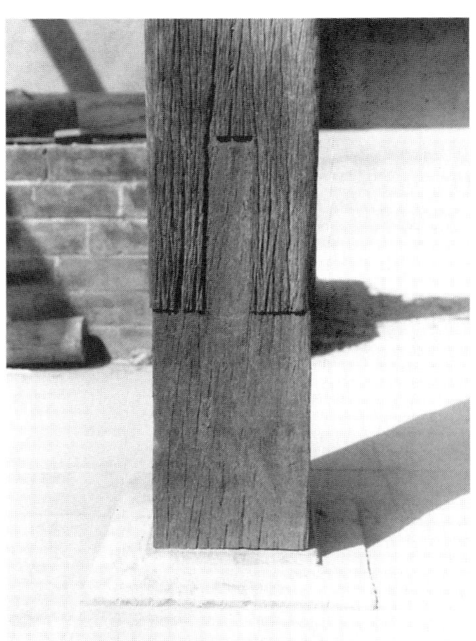

Pillar detail, roof terrace, northeast wing, Keshav Narayan Chok; this cruciform joint is a traditional Newar carpentry detail.

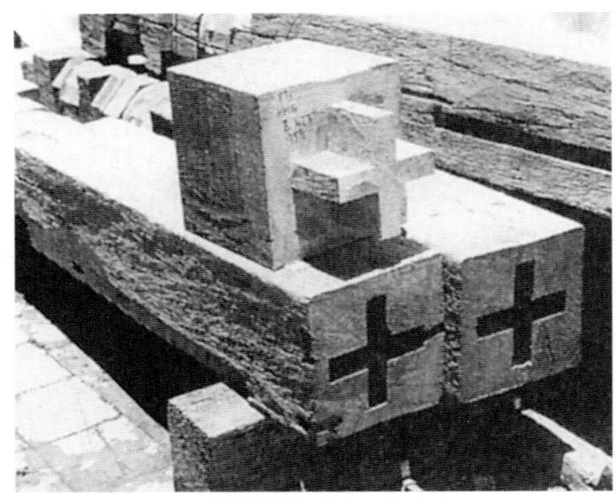

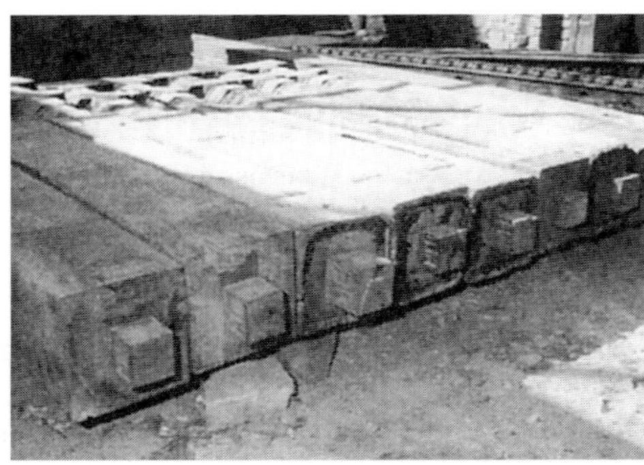

**Details of column repairs at Ibaha Bahi**

"As far as possible, pillars were hollowed out to remove parts that had rotted or were decayed but the surface was retained. Repairs were effected by inserting wood plugs by means of epoxy resins. Some pillars needed to be joined at the point where they had rotted. A cruciform plane splice, a traditional form of splice used in Nepal, was used for these joints. In addition, a Japanese technique of a cruciform splice was also employed inside the pillar as a means of retaining the original surface. A lead plate was inserted between each base stone and the pillar above it in such a way that it was not visible. The lead plate adheres to the base stone and serves as a form of damp-proofing."
—Takayuki Kurotsu on the repair of the pillars at Ibaha Bahi

The problem: deterioration of pillar bases

Ground floor *loggias* (*dalan* in Newari) with timber pillars are a common feature in traditional Nepali buildings of all eras. Despite the generous overhangs of the traditional roofs, the timber pillars receive little protection from rain. The overhang is normally designed so that water falling off the eaves falls outside the plinth of the building onto pavement that is 30 to 50 centimeters below the stone bases, *tepulvahan*, of the pillars.

Nevertheless, wind-driven rain causes the timber tenon of the pillar (which keys to the stone base) to deteriorate. Rot from weathering often extends 20 to 30 centimeters up the pillar shaft, threatening the structural cross section. This problem is not new: at innumerable historic buildings replaced pillar bases attest to the deficiency of the traditional configuration. One can even identify the range of typical solutions executed over the last two centuries by the Newar craftsmen. In their solution, the rotten ends of the weathered shaft are cut off and new timber pieces added with a cruciform joint. This cross joinery is never concealed.

## Three solutions

### Cyasilin Mandap

The traditional solution described above was used in the Cyasilin Mandap project, most specifically for the repair of five elaborately carved timber pillars original to the seventeenth-century construction. It should be added that the architects felt it necessary to supervise these repairs. The local carpenters, direct descendants of those who 300 years earlier had constructed the original building, would certainly have cut off more of the damaged historical pillars. Also, in an effort to maximize joint strength, they would have made the cruciform joint longer and thus more visually prominent. Our foreign approach sought to retain the maximum amount of historic fabric and minimize the visibility of the intervention, ideas alien to local craftsmen.

### Ibaha Bahi

While dismantling and rebuilding Ibaha Bahi, the Japanese architects found that almost all of the pillar bases on the ground floor needed consolidation. In cases where only the column tenon had rotted, the tenon was replaced and joined with epoxy resin. When there was more damage and the pillars had to be cut, the architects retained as much of the outer surfaces of the shaft as possible and inserted new structural cores. This was based on analysis that structural deterioration was sometimes confined to the pillar core. Damaged portions were thus removed and cruciform jointing achieved, additionally reinforced with epoxy resin. The ultimate goal of this intervention was to retain as much of the original surface as possible while minimizing the visual impact of the joint. Thus, while the traditional joint comes all the way to the outside and is visible, the modified solution concealed some joinery and was more difficult to execute. The traditional repair method was thus modified to create a hybrid solution.

### Patan Palace

During the dismantling and rebuilding of the northeast wing, four of the twelve ground-floor pillars needed repair. This stand of exceptionally beautiful early seventeenth-century pillars was not original to the building, but rather a secondary installation from another lost structure. The architect's solution to the problem, like the preceding examples, attempted to retain maximum historical fabric and make the intervention unobtrusive.

The lower pillar ends were cut at the point where the interior fabric was strong enough to accept a cruciform joint. This level, however, was not at the height where the pillar's cross section retained its original volume, but rather some 30 centimeters below where the weathering had already led to a reduction of the original cross section. In this specific case, where the pillars were more than 20 centimeters square, the remaining cross section was still considerable. The craftsmen cosmetically rendered the new "feet" to match the weathered surface of the old section with which they butted, creating a continuity of scars that only a professional observer can distinguish as a joint between old and new wood.

While designing the top floor reconstruction, the architect decided to elongate salvaged historical pillars from another site in order to achieve door heights appropriate for western visitors. These pillars were not damaged, but the problem of adding to them was similar to the previous examples. New ends were joined to the historic pillars using the local solution with visible cruciform joints. The tall proportions of these lengthened members do not conform to the local canon, but the opportunity to reuse historical elements was more important than this formal consideration.

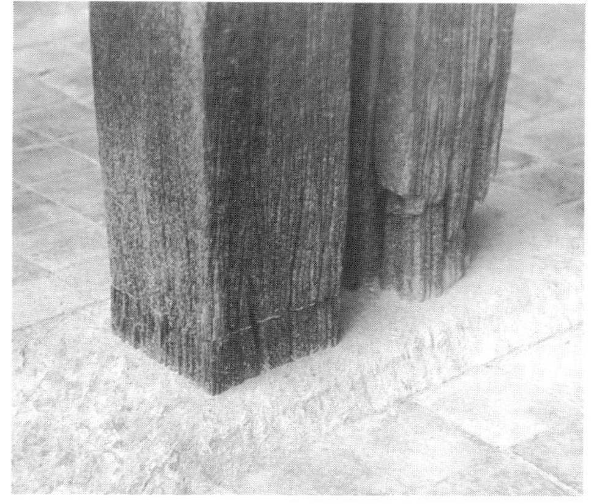

Ground floor pillars, northeast wing, Keshav Narayan Chok
The new extensions are joined to the old pillars with a concealed cross-joint. The surfaces of the new pillar feet match the weathering of the old pillars.

## Dilemma between traditional craftsmanship and the impulse to conserve

Local craftsmen have a solution for repairs. It would be appropriate to maintain as historical and structurally sound, but in the context of international preservation standards is not acceptable because it does not retain as much of the historical fabric as possible. The western preoccupation with the value of tangible authentic material is well illustrated by the ancient and well known story of Theseus' boat.

This was the old boat that, as more and more of its pieces were replaced over time, begged the question whether the boat could still be considered Theseus' boat. Was it the material that constituted the vessel or was it the form? Nepali craftsmen would answer without hesitation: replaced materials do not change the fundamental quality of an object. We western conservation architects are less clear. My experience documenting Japanese conservation practice in recent years suggests that their traditions might have disassembled the damaged boat at an early stage in its deterioration to reproduce it with all new wood, a more faithful record for the future than the piecemeal-repaired later boat of Theseus or the rotten original.

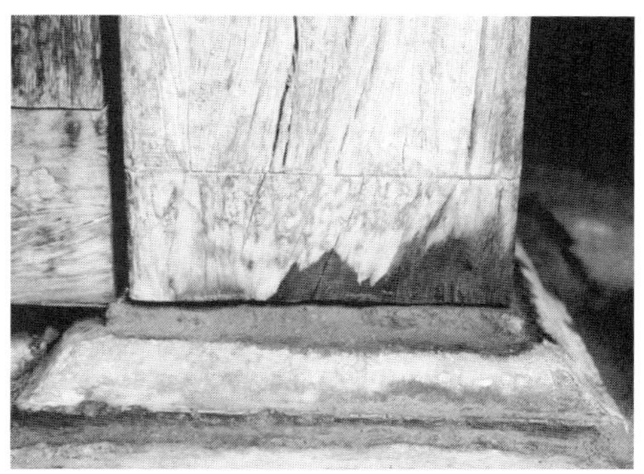

Ibaha Bahi
A historical pillar, repaired and re-installed. A thin line at the base of the pillar marks the joining of old and new.

The exceptional value that is attached to historical fabric gives rise to many acrobatics in our field, all undertaken to allow the survival of time-worn surfaces that traditional repair methods in Asia would eliminate. It can also be mentioned that our aesthetic sense—thanks to the Romantic Movement—even finds damaged surfaces beautiful, an idea foreign to Asia's traditional craftsmen. Does this somehow limit the role of traditional craftsmanship in international conservation projects? At this point in time, new aesthetic values are imported to Nepal quickly and filter into the trades. An African sculpture, for example, once commissioned in Kathmandu, becomes part of the repertoire of local carvers. The responsible conservation architect must also address the preservation of the role, skills, and methods of traditional craftsmen, even if sometimes at the expense of historical fabric.

I have chosen these examples for their thoughtfulness and out of respect for the professionalism that went into such hybrid solutions. At the same time, I respect the traditions of Newar carpenters to the extent that I would rather not interfere in their repair techniques. Their decisions are not based on intellectual considerations or courses taken in school. In the houses of their ancestors they practice skills handed down from father to son through the generations. Their processes, thinking, and artistic abilities are authentic. I would thus propose special consideration be given to support their practice, a true expression of a living heritage.

# Conservation as a Critical Activity
## The Sulima Strut Story

A.G. Krishna Menon

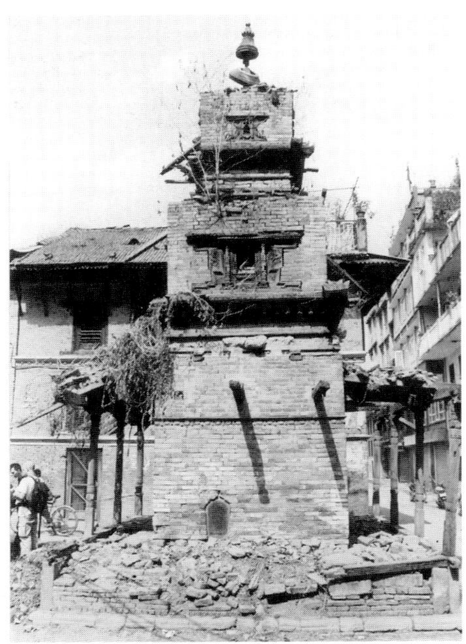

**The Narayan Temple at Tumbaha, Patan is typical of hundreds of historical ruins in the Kathmandu Valley. Its restoration was recently completed by the Kathmandu Valley Preservation Trust.**

It is one of the paradoxes of globalization that even as it imposes transnational values and processes on local cultures, it simultaneously gives these local cultures a "presence" they never had before. The more globalization disrupts, displaces, and overlays local traditions, the more one realizes the significance of what is lost in the process. The interdisciplinary and intercultural scholarship encouraged by globalization brings to light the existence and logic of previously obscure indigenous knowledge systems and practices. This scholarship creates provocative voices of dissent that question the very premises underlying globalization, and provides the raison d'etre to resist—or at least direct—its further progress. This is the message of the Sulima strut story.

The Sulima strut refers to the restoration of the fourteenth-century Ratneshvara Temple in Sulima, Patan from 1996 to 1999. Specifically, the story highlights the issue of the replacement of lost carved timber elements as part of the restoration work. These replacements were carved by contemporary craftsmen and purport to be "authentic" equivalents to the original. Such claims challenge the hallowed principles of conservation that prohibit imitative replication of lost architectural elements. The conventional orthodoxy of conservation practice requires that ancient buildings be kept in roughly the same state that they were found, as stabilized ruins. "Good" conservation procedure thus only attempts minimal intervention to maintain the original integrity and authenticity of the remaining fabric of the building or ruin.

In the Ratneshvara Temple project, however, a ruin was largely restored to an "original" state. There is little evidence of the "golden stain of time" or the possibility of distinguishing between the old and the new parts of the building in the restored monument. Indeed, much of what one sees is not "original," and John Ruskin would certainly have fulminated that the building is a lie. Nevertheless, the heresy perpetrated here merits serious consideration—not only because it questions the authority of "universal" conventions in the context of Nepal, but also because it provides a compelling rationale to conserve a living tradition facing extinction.

Many would agree that the attitudes governing the conservation of cultural heritage ought to be specific to each culture. But in practice this is not so; throughout the world the "official" values governing conservation practice are imbued with the ideals established by John Ruskin and his colleagues in England during the nineteenth century, and consequently reflect a thoroughly Eurocentric point of view.

These ideals are disseminated through the various charters of UNESCO, most notably the 1964 Venice Charter. The principles of conservation have, of course, broadened to acknowledge other imperatives including those of "living cultures," but the orthodoxy defined by the Venice Charter nevertheless prevails and dominates official policy. In many developing countries, where traditional skills and practices survive, the implications are profound: the universalization of conservation policy breaks the continuity of indigenous traditions. Eurocentric norms are inimical to indigenous practices of conserving (or not conserving) ancient buildings because they make the traditional craftsmen and their skills redundant. This impoverishes local cultures and destroys the organic bond that existed between traditional knowledge, traditional practices, and the monument. The stabilized ruin idealized in European cultures holds little meaning in traditional societies.

And yet, when these societies set about to conserve their monuments, they adopt Eurocentric norms. The need for international financial assistance to undertake conservation works and the aura surrounding the UNESCO stamp of approval ensures the adoption of such norms even when viable, traditional alternatives exist. What "foreign experts" represent are the "modern" and "progressive" principles of conservation. The desire to align with them is a potent force in developing countries.

It is not surprising, therefore, to find that the Archaeological Survey of India or the Department of Archaeology of Nepal, or their counterparts in other developing countries, are turning their backs on centuries-old traditions, diligently emulating the precepts enshrined in the Venice Charter. Its allure is the power of globalization.

As I mentioned, however, within this homogenizing influence of globalization, and often as a result of it, is the possibility to reveal the specificity and efficacy of traditional local practices. And the critique of Eurocentric conservation can come from the very agents of these practices: foreign experts working in the field. The understanding of local practices makes the limitations of Eurocentric principles more clear to the foreign experts whose unique position allows them to appreciate and articulate differences. Thus, in places like Nepal, the outsider is potentially both the agent of change and the one to question it.

Furthering the new visibility of traditional practices also ensures that they are reappropriated by the local society. This process of going "back to the future" can be seen at work in Patan and Bhaktapur where conservation work was initiated two decades ago. Projects undertaken there by foreign experts were within the bounds of Eurocentric orthodoxy even if they tested its limits, as did the reconstruction in 1987 of the lost Cyasilin Mandap in Bhaktapur. In the restoration of the Ratneshvara Temple, however, the boundaries have been breached: here it is outright apostasy. Considering the heritage value of the monument, this order and extent of restoration work would not have been "officially" permitted elsewhere. It is for this reason that the work is significant at one level and remains problematic at another.

There is, of course, the dominant role of the foreign expert and the source of funding to consider while evaluating the polemic context of this and other conservation projects in Nepal. Why is it necessary to rely upon foreign expertise and funds in order to restore valuable traditional heritage? Has this heritage lost meaning in local society, but gained meaning outside? Is "sovereignty" an issue in the global marketplace of conservation?

In earlier times a feudal elite constructed and maintained temples such as the Ratneshvara. There was a concordance between the aspiration and activities of different classes in that society because the culture within which they operated was homogenous. The process of modernization has eroded the organic relationship that existed earlier between patrons, craftsmen and the pervasive socio-cultural ideals. The government bureaucrat has replaced the feudal patron in matters of heritage

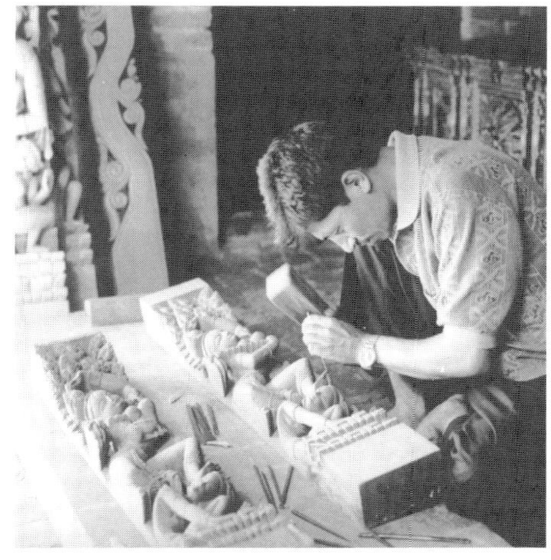

**Master carver Indrakaji Silpakar at work on Sulima struts**
Indrakaji, who learned his skills from his father, comes from a long line of carpenters and carvers.

management. As a consequence, there is today a widespread indifference to conserving architectural heritage. Traditional knowledge and skills are still available, but are not put to use.

The state is unable to remedy the situation because it has neither the will nor the imagination to tackle such problems. Its urgent agenda does not include heritage, thus setting in motion a familiar pattern of the attrition of ancient monuments. This sets the stage for the entry of foreign expertise and funding. Although Nepal has undoubtedly benefited from such interventions, the role of an external agency with altruistic intent raises uncomfortable questions, especially from a post-colonial perspective. The focus of these questions sharpens when the ideology of conservation is "subversive," as with the decision to replace Sulima's wood struts.

One must evaluate the role of the foreigner, both official and otherwise, in mediating local cultures. In the Ratneshvara project, the foreign and the local have coalesced with a common purpose not unlike the manner in which the foreign and the official invariably align in the process of modernization and globalization. However, an ethical distinction between the two situations should be made. By relying on local traditions and skills, one enriches local cultures, while relying on Eurocentric norms of conservation does not. Both have the propensity to distort future developments because the local lacks a voice. This is the problem with the conservation work undertaken by foreigners in Nepal.

The only safeguard to this propensity is a critical sensitivity of analysis and action on the part of the external agent who must evaluate simultaneously the relevance of Eurocentric as well as local traditions in conservation. The Nepali experience should not be used to unearth local allegories of western theoretical preoccupations: this is the classical trap of Orientalism. On the other hand, it would be wrong to debunk all western claims by referencing the uniqueness of Nepali culture; this is the classic trap of cultural essentialism. One is thus confronted by the Scylla of universalism and the Charybdis of particularism. What is compelling in the Sulima strut story is the exemplary manner in which these issues have been mediated.

In order to understand this reading of the story, the issues must be considered in the context of contemporary Nepal. This situation can be diagrammed (see illustration on opposite page) as follows: in this composite diagram, both society and the monument in question are in the beginning located at point A, sometime in the distant past. The X-axis represents Time. The Y-axis calibrates two developments: upward, to indicate the modernization of society, and downward, to indicate the deterioration of the monument. The X-axis also represents the idealized "steady-state" condition of the monument, had it not deteriorated over time or been pillaged by art thiefs as it was in the 1970s, or if it had been continuously maintained and upgraded over the years. Obviously, this did not happen and in the diagram the ruined monument is located at point B, well below the "steady-state" condition.

Furthermore, at the time when conservation is mooted, the condition of the monument is at Point B, while the level of modernization of society is at point D. In parallel trajectory, the condition of the skilled wood carver, or silpakar, is at point C, still living, but declining.

Given these conditions, the future of the monument at point B has three possibilities. If nothing is done, then it will move towards B1, that is, continue its trajectory of deterioration. If one applies Eurocentric principles of conservation,

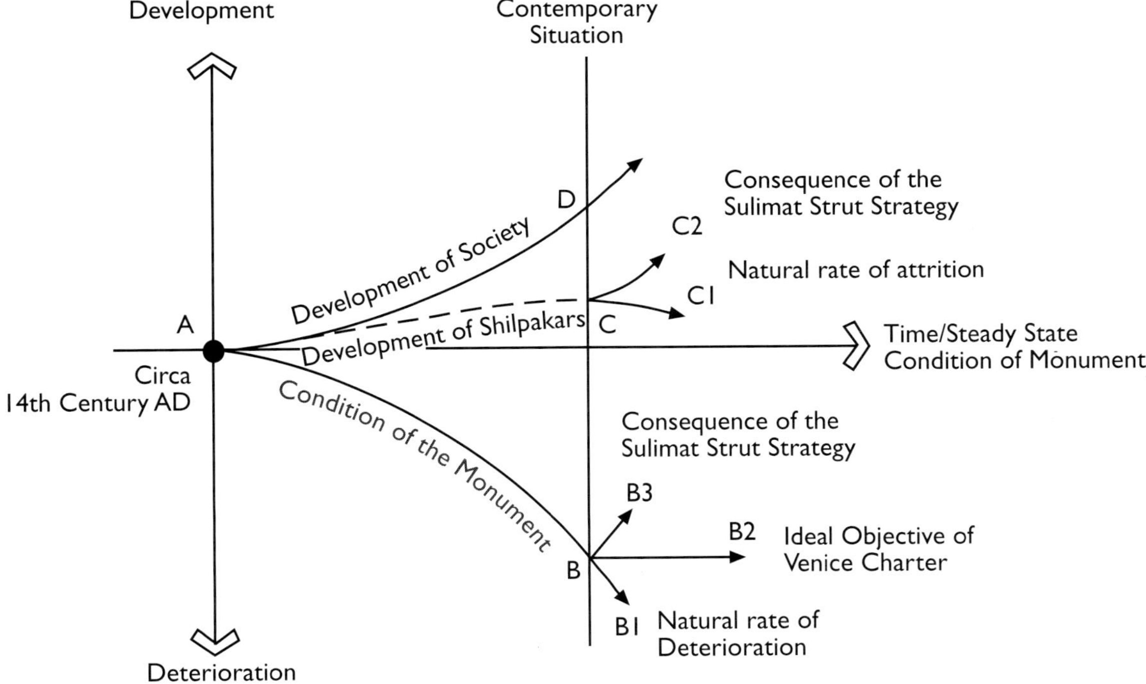


then (as an ideal possibility) one would move towards B2, roughly parallel to the X-axis but below it. The building would then be a stabilized, in this case pillaged, ruin. It would also have little meaning in the local society. But the strategy employed in the restoration of the Ratneshvara temple moves the monument to point B3, closer to the X-axis, that is, closer to its original form.

The issue to consider should be the appropriateness of the strategy within the Nepali context, rather than its conformity to international norms. This would depend on whether the local constituency would prefer to have a resurrected temple, a stabilized ruin, or a deteriorating heap of rubble. The Sulima strut story hinges on the assumption that the local people prefer a resurrected, if not an entirely new, temple.

In deciding, the role of woodcarvers, or silpakar, must also be brought into focus. If no initiative to improve their prospects and social status is taken, the gap between C and D will widen, and the silpakar would be driven to point C1. However, the strategy to take the monument to B3 introduces a contingent possibility of taking the silpakar to point C2, thereby reducing the gap between C and D. Many development professionals would agree that this is a worthwhile objective to pursue.

Eurocentric practices, focussing as they do on the monument rather than the silpakar, preclude this possibility. The distinction between conserving monuments and conserving the skills that built them must therefore be polemecized into a critical culture of conservation wherever traditional practices still survive. The almost complete restoration of the Sulima Temple exemplifies these issues in a compelling manner. This is the significance of the Sulima strut story, but there is also great irony in its message: such critical thinking wouldn't have been possible without the outsider or foreign funds. When the implication of this message sinks in, we will find it both salutary and tragic.

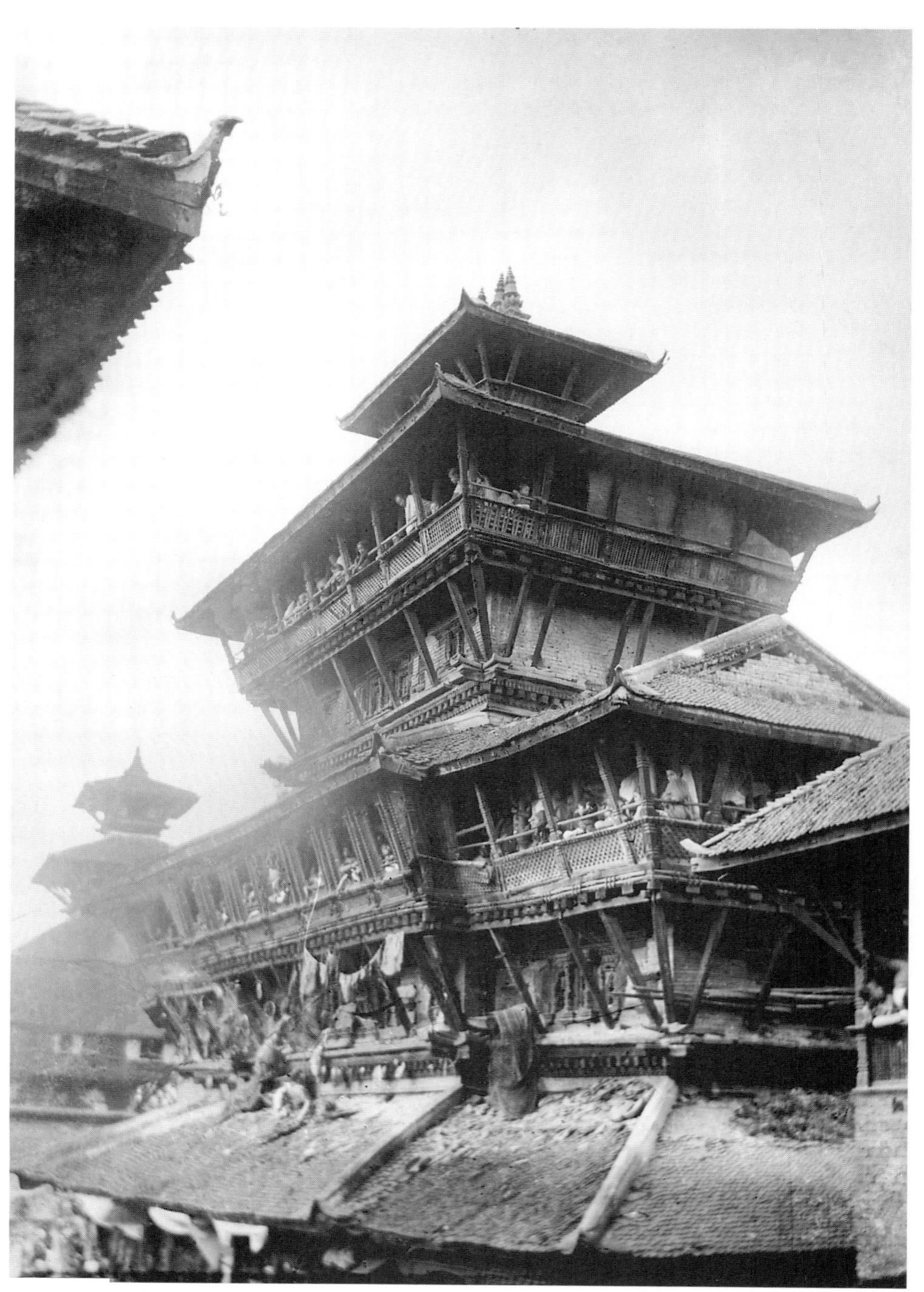

Kabindrapur Sattal
Kathmandu Darbar Square (ca. 1920)



The Sulima Pagoda

# Love and Architecture
## Modernity Comes to Nepal

Rohit Ranjitkar

In Nepal most temples and a variety of other religious structures are still centers of active worship. Nearly all people have direct and personal connections to these houses of the gods. This ongoing devotion is, nevertheless, something of a contradiction: if they love these places, why are the built structures under threat?

A first important reason is that the local devotees actually love the deities within, not the building fabrics and especially not when the building fabrics are old. It will come as no surprise to most professionals that in Asia the patina and visible age of old structures are not considered beautiful. The temple fabric—layered, rebuilt, repaired and renewed—is an expression of their love for the gods. This is votive architecture. This is architecture for the gods, not for people. It is a process that, unlike western preservation practice, adds not subtracts.

Until 1970, the isolation of Nepal and survival of the building crafts guaranteed a great deal of artistic continuity in the evolution of monuments. No guidelines were necessary in this conservative and traditional world. Today there is a new aesthetic contradiction: clear love for the gods fuels ongoing votive architecture, but interventions conceived in the modern spirit often scar or destroy earlier structures. People believe in the superiority of modern materials and new fashions. Guidelines cannot convince them that these are not the best things to offer to their gods. This is still love.

This belief in the goodness of materials is not without practical concerns. The donors believe that modern finishes in cement, concrete, and enamel paints are more durable and that maintenance will be reduced. In the past, reducing maintenance was not a goal as life centered around the temple. In a modern Nepali's life, however, there is less time for these activities. Decisions to replace high-maintenance traditional tiles, mud, and timber features with modern substitutes thus reflect a willingness to pay with money, not time.

Parallel to the change in the palette of materials has been a change in the actors. The modern cast of characters includes national, municipal, local, and even international players, many of whom do not have a personal relationship with the god or building. Bureaucratic structures and government procedures introduce further layers between temple and donors. The tendering process by contractors, for example, brings outsiders to work on a building when traditionally neighborhood craftsmen would have been engaged. Government procedures and "standards" generally do not encourage creative or high-quality work, although there are important examples when the personal commitment of an individual within the government system is able to conquer hurdles to achieve higher standards in the conservation of a historical structure.

### Am I an outsider?

I am a student of architecture and Nepali history. Like many of my foreign colleagues I love these temples. At the same time, I must admit that I worship a different god: I worship the historical and artistic inventiveness of my ancestors more than the deities housed within the temple walls. I wouldn't mind if a significant monument were restored even without its god. There are still, however, very few devotees of Nepal's architectural history in the local community. International art collectors and thieves seem to be the only other significant population sharing this particular love.

The challenge to save the historic structures of Nepal for my grandchildren requires concrete action. With the Kathmandu Valley Preservation Trust, I am able to restore a small number of monuments to the highest-quality standards. These concrete achievements have the potential to influence other projects in the same positive ways that the artistic achievements of my ancestors triggered subsequent architectural invention. These accomplishments may also, in the long run, prove more effective than the reports and guidelines of government agencies and visiting experts, which though numerous have thus far proven fruitless.

The conservation projects also provide critical and much-needed opportunities for Nepali professionals, craftsmen, and draftsmen to work close to the monuments. A draftsman's four-month assignment to prepare detailed carving documentation, for example, creates and affirms love between object and person. This is itself a votive act consistent with Nepal's history. In the end I believe that such love is the best hope for preserving more of Nepal's extraordinary architectural heritage.

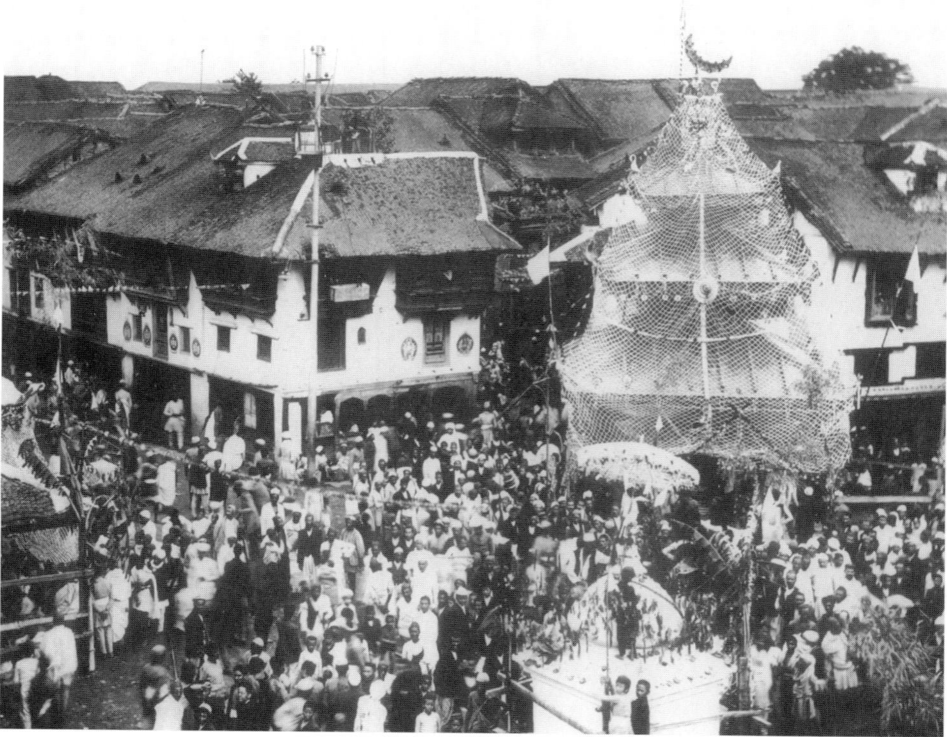

**Annapurna Temple, Kathmandu**
The Lachhavati hom ritual, celebrated circa 1920, included the dressing of the temple with a sacred net of puffed rice. Out of devotion to the deity, this celebration was recreated as recently as 1999.



**The Sulima Pagoda**

# The Original, Replicas, and Reality at Sulima Temple

John H. Stubbs

"Why not just call all restored buildings reconstruction, and be done with the question?" asked architect Krishna Menon from Delhi on viewing the recent Sulima Temple restoration in Patan. To re-conceptualize and redefine all architectural conservation interventions as such would greatly simplify debate on the matter of how far one can go in preservation projects before historic architectural character and fabric become essentially something new. To add to the dilemma, physical evidence at other Newar buildings that survive today in the Kathmandu Valley suggests that local builders throughout history regarded such concerns as irrelevant.

The recent restoration of the Sulima Temple, possibly Nepal's oldest pagoda-style temple, by the Kathmandu Valley Preservation Trust (KVPT) continues a legacy of repairs to the 700-year-old structure that may have included as many as eight major preservation-minded interventions. Despite these periodic changes, each of which included the integration of some new elements to the exterior of the building, the original shaivite sanctuary with its linga icon is thought to have remained unchanged since its original construction.

When research and planning for the restoration began in 1996, Sulima's masonry structural core was 80 percent intact. Only 75 percent of its exterior wood ornamentation and its two-tiered roof slopes were in place. Both roof tiers, which had been replaced in the past 30 years, were extensively deteriorated. The most critical losses to the building were most of its finely carved ornamental struts that were stolen in 1975; the eight surviving corner struts saved the roofs from collapsing altogether after this act of vandalism.

The recent restoration to protect surviving carvings was mandated by the poor condition of the building, especially its roofs, and a need for improving the temple's earthquake resistance. This first scientific restoration intervention at the site involved the careful disassembly of the remains of the roof structures, and their reconstruction using as much original or early architectural fabric as possible. The various missing elements were painstakingly replicated based on historical and physical evidence and research.

Several factors justified the Trust's decision to intervene and restore Sulima Temple: (1) the building's outstanding architectural significance; (2) its relative completeness and the fact that at least one of every missing or badly damaged element had survived; (3) photographs of the building taken in 1968 when the building was almost completely intact; (4) the rigorous documentation and analysis of the site prior to intervention; and (5) the availability of highly skilled architects, historians, and local craftsmen who were in agreement on a plan to restore the building to its most developed and artistically coherent previous appearance.

After scrupulous documentation, analysis, and project planning, funding and approvals were obtained and the restoration project began in June 1996. Funding for the project was secured by the KVPT from Himalayan Bank (Nepal) and the Robert W. Wilson Challenge Grant of the World Monuments Fund. Both the archival photographs and archaeological evidence allowed for the accurate reconstruction of Ratneshvara's most prominent exterior features, its raised brick masonry platform, and both roof tiers including its impressive bell shaped copper finial. Surviving finely carved woodwork at the openings and blind niches were cleaned and preserved in situ.

The main challenge of the project was the question of what to do with the various missing carved ornaments, including fourteenth-century roof struts, the *tympanum* (*torana*) over the east portal, and various missing or badly deteriorated details at existing door and window surrounds. The time came to decide if these finely carved *lacunae* or lost details could be accurately replicated.

Some asked if such an approach would comply with the principles of modern architectural conservation defined in the Venice Charter. Of particular interest was whether such interventions would be consistent with Article 12, which states, "Replacements of missing parts must integrate harmoniously with the whole, but at the same time must be distinguishable from the original so that restoration does not falsify the artistic or historic evidence." An even larger question is whether the 1964 Venice Charter even applies in Nepal, a country with unbroken crafts traditions located thousands of miles from Western Europe.

After preparation of full-scale drawings and a review of samples, the decision to replicate the vanished sculpted architectural details was made. Because the struts, the torana, and other details serve essentially as artistic embellishments, their modern replacements were both physically and visually integrated into the

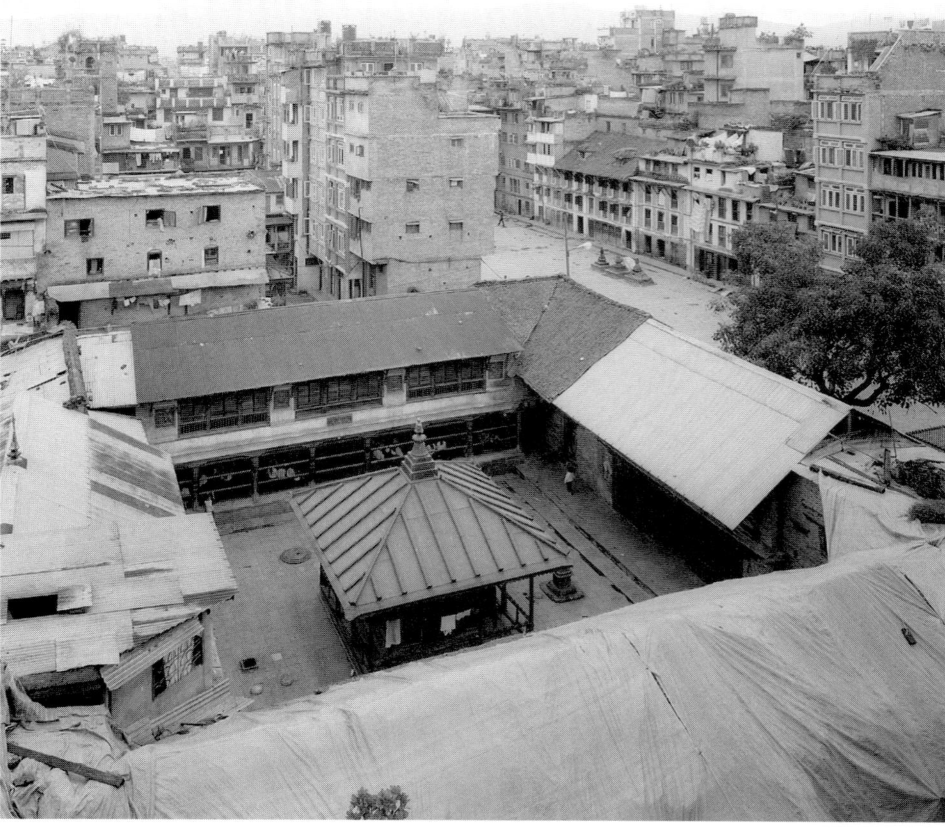

**Itum Baha, Kathmandu**
A Buddhist monastic quadrangle (left) in the old city and religious center since at least the thirteenth century, Itum Baha is the next collaborative effort of KVPT and the World Monuments Fund. It has been included in the World Monuments Watch 2000.



**The Sulima Pagoda**

whole. This principle, which is used more widely in the conservation of art objects than in architectural conservation, is relevant here since these particular components can easily be termed art objects. The results seen today at Sulima Temple are impressive, mostly due to the extremely fine new carvings of local sculptors Indrakaji and Hari Silpakar, who descend from generations of Newar wood carvers in nearby Bhaktapur.

As to whether the overall intervention at Sulima could be termed reconstruction or restoration, it would have to be termed the latter as the core structure, the shrine within, and nearly all significant remaining historic fabric were retained. The only structural components that were replaced were roofs that had been periodically replaced over time.

As for replacement of the missing wooden elements in the traditional manner, anything other than the replication of these details, such as using uncarved anonymous substitutes, would have lessened the character of the historic building and created an ambiguity in the temple's religious program. The distinction between old and new has discretely been accomplished by two means: each newly replicated element is date stamped on the *verso*, and a detailed record of the entire project has been placed in the KVPT's newly established archive at Harvard University.

Significantly, the justification for replicating the lacunae of Sulima lies in the fact that these kinds of replacements have been practiced in Kathmandu for nearly a millennium and continue to be a part of the living tradition. This undoubtedly has a bearing on why modern locals give the Sulima restoration a high approval rating.

Continuous use, regular maintenance, and sympathetic repairs of the temple by local worshippers over its long history are what preserved this remarkable structure to this point in time. Therein lies another valuable lesson of the restoration project: the importance of regular maintenance and continuous use.

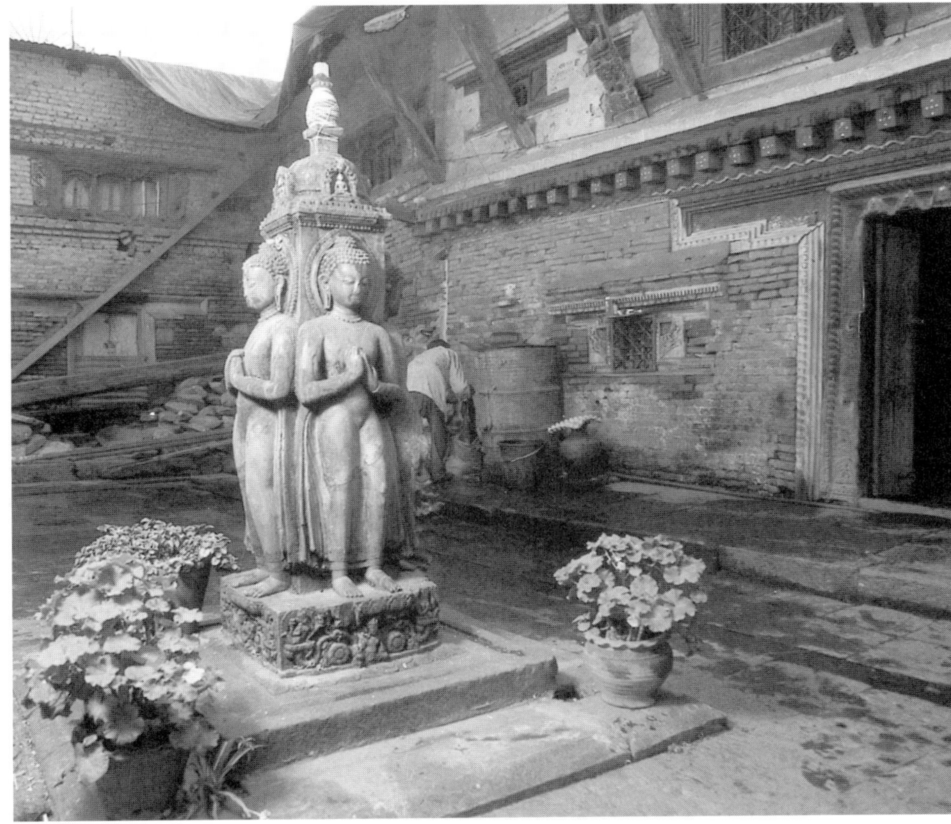

While the Trust's early projects represented critical interventions to save buildings that would have been otherwise lost, the Sulima and Itum Baha projects respond to a new need: the development and popularization of more sophisticated and rigorous approaches to Nepal's conservation challenges. Numerous preservation projects have sprung up in the public and private sectors recently; their success will depend on the application of sensitive approaches to questions about retention of historical fabric, seismic retrofitting, and adaptive reuse strategies.

# Venice, Burra and Kathmandu

Sharon Sullivan

The Venice Charter lays down the basic philosophy and conventions for the conservation of historic monuments, often referred to in the Charter as "ancient buildings." This is my reading of some key articles of the Charter, which relate to restoration:

The definition of a historic monument may include an urban or rural setting, when that setting provides evidence of "a particular civilization, a significant development, or an historic event" (Article 1). Historic monuments should be conserved as both works of art and as historical evidence (Article 3). Traditional settings should also be conserved (Article 6). Using the monuments for a socially useful purpose may help with their conservation, but such use may not alter the "lay out or decoration of the building"(Articles 4 and 5) and additions can only be allowed if they do not detract from the monument as a whole in its setting (Article 13).

The aim of restoration is to preserve and reveal the aesthetic and historic value of the monument, by respecting the original materials and authentic documents. Restoration must not be conjectural, and any new work—the restoration of missing parts—must be both harmonious and distinguishable (Articles 9 and 12). Proven modern techniques can be used where traditional technology is inadequate (Article 10).

Evidence of all periods of the development of the monument must be respected, and removing this accretion to reveal earlier periods can only be justified in exceptional circumstances and conditions (Article 11). Scientific techniques must be used when excavating archaeological sites and ruins, and conservation of the exposed remains should be ensured. All reconstruction work should be ruled out a priori at such sites where only anastylosis will be acceptable (Article 15).

Why did the practitioners of the 1960s find it necessary to write and endorse such an international charter?

One answer is that physical intervention at a site with the aim of conserving it can, in fact, destroy much of its cultural value. There were by the 1960s, in the view of the Charter writers, at least two centuries of well-meaning damage or destruction perpetrated in the name of conservation. The main danger, which needed guarding against, was the attempt to renew or replace missing elements that could have the effect of destroying historically significant fabric, of damaging the integrity of original works of art, or confusing old fabric with new, thus inadvertently misleading the modern viewer with an experience that was not wholly authentic.

The Charter has been widely accepted, and it has prevented much well-meaning but ignorant damage or destruction to important monuments. Underlying the Charter is the strong tradition of the aesthetic and historic value of places where the ravages of time can clearly be seen, and in experiential terms, the undeniable fact that many such places raise strong emotional reactions in the educated western visitor. They connect us with the past history of humanity, and at the same time give us a strong nostalgic feeling of its distantness and the impossibility of fully recovering it in the present.

Another underlying assumption of the Charter is that it is for the protection of monuments of architectural or aesthetic value. Article one states that "the concept of an historic monument embraces not only the single architectural work, but also the urban or rural setting in which is found the evidence of a particular civilization, a significant development or an historic event." However, the emphasis in the Charter is clearly on the word monument—in the sense of a building, structure or substantial locus of material evidence—and the articles of the Charter are devoted to ensuring the conservation of the fabric of such monuments. It seems clear to me therefore that the main concern of the Charter is to protect the historic and aesthetic value of important material remains *in situ*.

Another underlying assumption of the Charter is that the significant fabric of the monument was created in the past. The Charter does not prevent ongoing use; but the assumption is that while past additions, changes and diminutions through loss or damage over time will be a significant part of the historic value of the monument, and should be conserved, contemporary changes, which might arise from continued use, are not significant, and do not merit conservation. In this sense, the Charter is intended for the conservation of monuments whose only contemporary cultural value relates to their original creation and past development. So, while the Venice Charter is often taken to be applicable to all historic monuments of cultural value, it is clear that in fact it only applies to a limited range of cultural values.

I do not think the Charter's drafters had these limitations in mind, in a conscious way; but the monuments, which they were intent on protecting at that time, certainly had these characteristics.

A contemporary problem in our conservation practice is that the conservation definitions and precepts of the Venice Charter have been widely interpreted as being applicable to all historic monuments or heritage places. They are not. In particular, the Venice Charter assumes that the primary value of historic monuments is their aesthetic or historic significance, and it lays down rules specifically for the conservation of these two sorts of value.

Heritage places may have other types of value, which require consideration of a wider range of issues for their conservation. A clear example is the contemporary, but strongly traditional, cyclical rebuilding or refurbishment of some ancient heritage places in Asia, where the process of renewal is clearly part of the contemporary social value of the place.

Another example is an Australian Aboriginal art site that contains a series of paintings, some of which might be 10,000 years old, but which is still a part of traditional life and subject to renewal and change as part of a very long tradition. Here we can readily see that conservation of that tradition of change will, in fact, enhance and carry forward into the future the significance of the place, even though some of the original, important fabric might be lost in the process.

In a third case, the appearance of a temple in a traditional medieval city's contemporary streetscape may be very significant for the present integrity of the streetscape and its use by the inhabitants. Leaving the temple as a ruin with minimum physical intervention may preserve some of its significance, but may be offensive and distasteful in the context of a living traditional community.

The Burra Charter, an adaptation of the Venice Charter by Australia ICOMOS, seeks to resolve this problem in two ways. It broadens the definition of cultural significance to include "historic, aesthetic, scientific and social value for past, present and future generations." More fundamentally, it introduces the notion of assessment of the cultural significance of a place, prior to determining appropriate conservation or restoration values; and it makes decisions about this policy and rules for its implementation dependent on this assessment of significance.

In this way all the values that a site has are discovered and made visible. Any potential conflicts between, say, historic and contemporary social values can be analyzed and resolved. Recent amendments to the Charter have further clarified some elements of significance—for instance by pointing out that a society's association with a site or its continued traditional use over a long period may be valid elements of significance that require a different set of management guidelines.

It seems to me that the process of significance assessment should be at the heart of any conservation plan for a heritage site, and that such an assessment can guide us in selecting the correct conservation treatment for a particular site—that is, a treatment that will conserve all elements of significance. Such a solution will follow the general philosophy of the Venice Charter, but may require variation and modification to ensure conservation of all values, as in the examples given above.

So, a decision about whether to replace lost wooden carving elements in a temple in Kathmandu with new carving done in the traditional way by local craftsmen should depend on a careful assessment of all the cultural values the temple has. These values might include a range of contemporary social values, the conservation of which might need a different approach to that laid down in the Venice Charter.

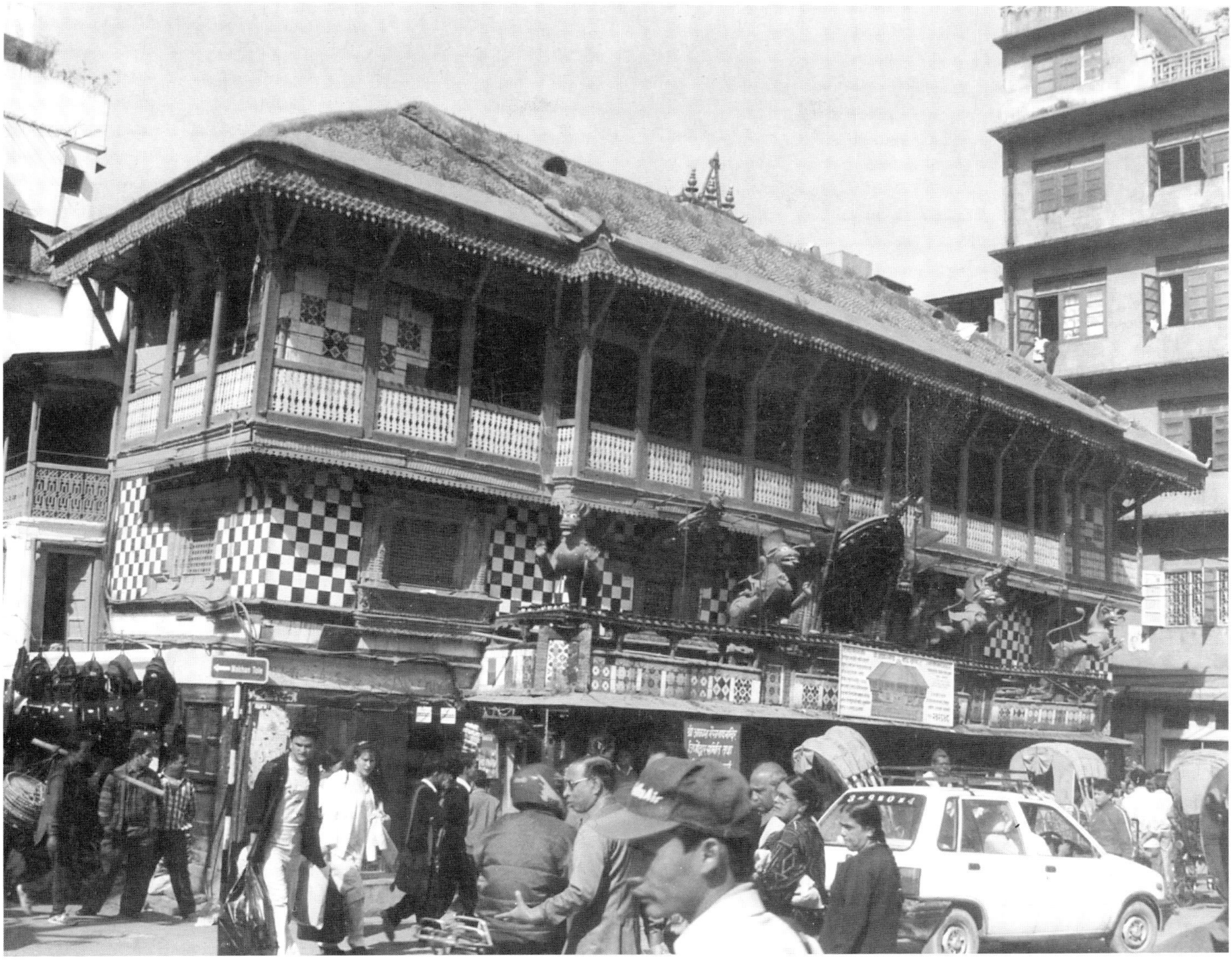

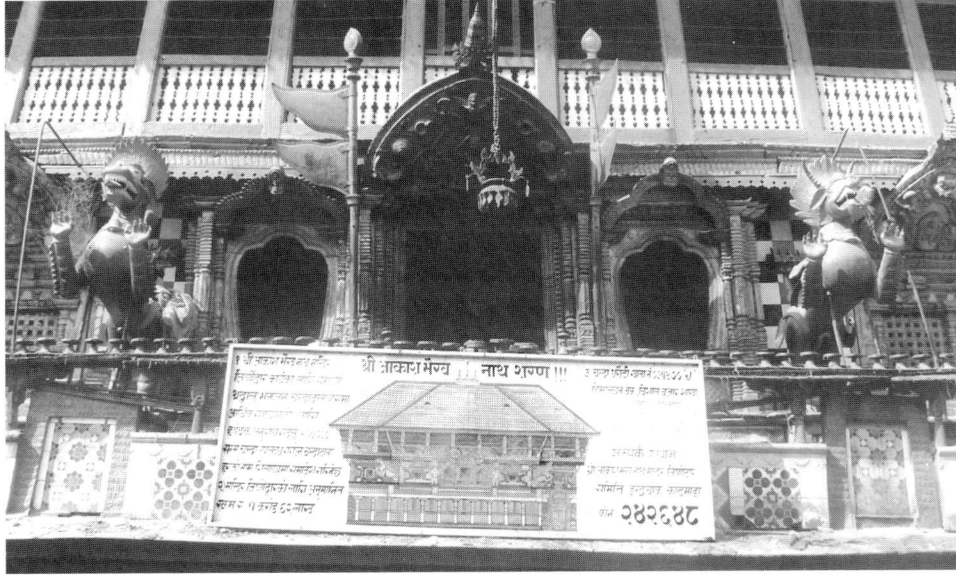

**Akash Bhairav Temple**
**Indra Chok, Kathmandu**

The signboard (left) announces the planned return to a more "original" state, wiping out all twentieth-century layers such as the polychromatic tile and painting (shown above).

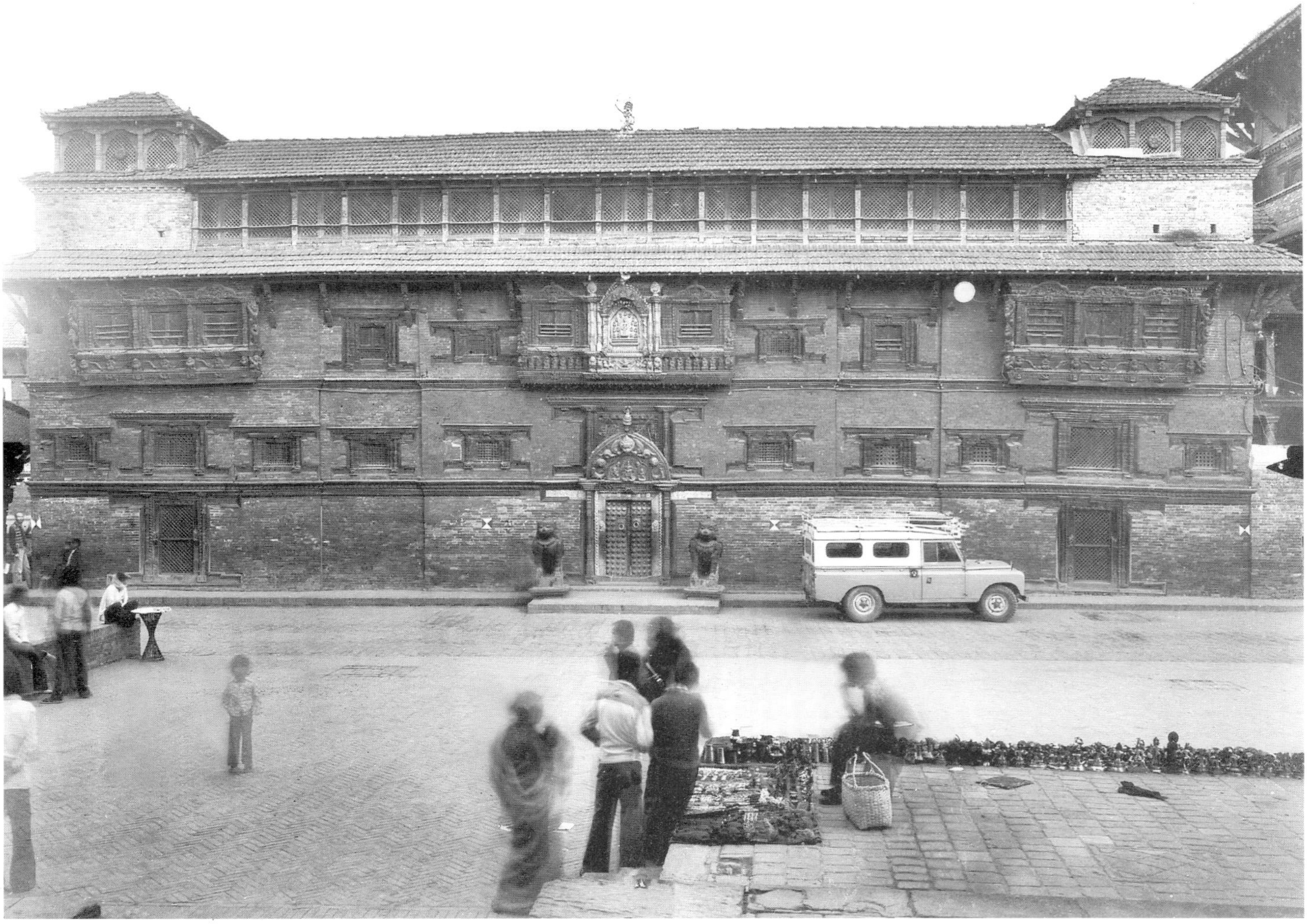

**Patan Museum**
The restoration and adaptive reuse of
this palace as a museum involved
redesigning and rebuilding the upper
levels and the roof. The principal façade
in 1980 (top) and after restoration (right)

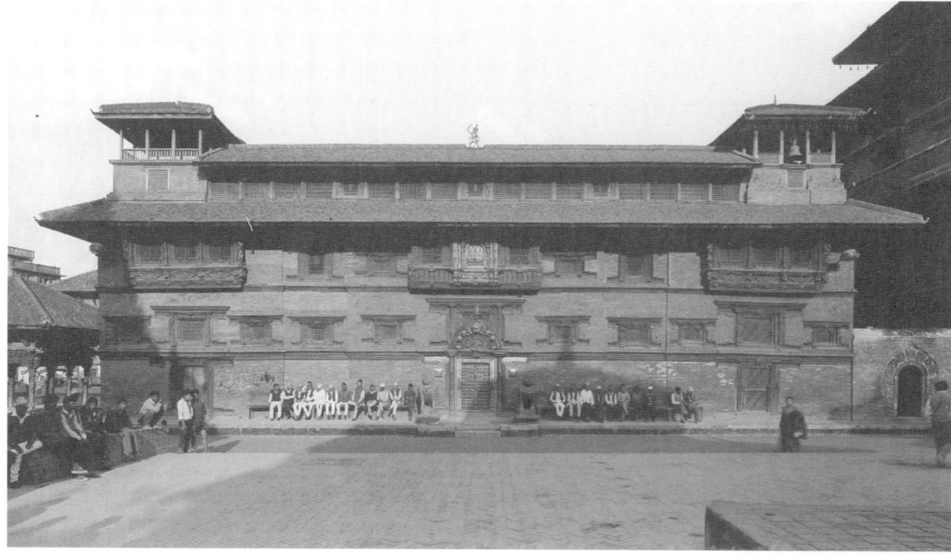



The Sulima Pagoda

# The "Art" of Conservation
## Subjectivity and Contradictions in an Architect's Conservation Practice

Erich Theophile

My first serious introduction to building conservation was in 1988, when I came to Nepal to volunteer with architect Götz Hagmüller on the restoration of the Patan palace and its adaptation as a museum. At that time Götz was planning to rebuild the main roof, which involved complex intersections of balconies, galleries, and towers on the principal façade. There was clearly no "correct" solution based on the contradictory and limited historical evidence, not to mention the multiple goals of the adaptive reuse project. The exercise had to reconcile historical photographs, surviving original structure, various layers of nineteenth and twentieth century additions, as well as project budget constraints and the practical concerns of a new museum.

I witnessed with pleasure a great architect solving a complex design problem, balancing numerous considerations to arrive at an elegant and practical solution. The realization that building conservation could engage so many of one's design abilities greatly influenced my own career choices. I stayed in Nepal, in fact, to pursue such projects because sensitive and creative approaches to historical buildings seemed to be few. I even sat down that week and wrote an article documenting and analyzing "the design process" I had been so fortunate to witness.

I never published that piece, however. In a subsequent meeting with an international conservation expert I was told that although "interesting," the article was better not circulated because "it might raise doubts about the scientific-ness of the project." Playing down the architect's role as designer was an essential aspect of the conservation politics scene in Nepal. A focus on creative contributions might jeopardize foreign funding of the "conservation" project, not to mention invite criticism from other experts in the field. Even Götz himself, in later documentary articles, played down his architectural contribution, preferring a sanitized, "politically correct" construct of the design process. In these articles he described the restoration and museum design as the rather inevitable, scientific outcome based on rational deliberations to preserve historical fabric.

After fourteen years of practice, I'm distressed by this intellectual dishonesty, the characteristic downplaying of subjective design choices in the field of historic preservation. I'm saddened by reports from recent conservation program graduates that practice is taught more like dentistry than design. Gaps between theory and practice rarely are considered. The conservation architect supposedly follows a scientific process to solve a design problem in which "authenticity" and retention of historical fabric constitute the only acceptable criteria. It is not that I don't cherish authentic historical structures, I just think that suppression of the multiple agendas that drive historic building projects is destructive to intellectual development in the field. Following are some personal formulations for expanding the range of dialogue in the field.

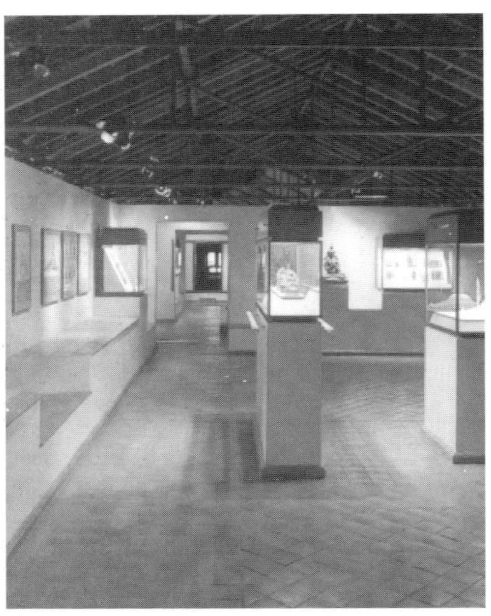

**Patan Museum**
**The rebuilt east wing of the palace**
**juxtaposes a new steel roof structure**
**with traditional floor and wall finishes.**

## "De-vilification" of the architect

According to stereotypes in our field, non-architects emphasize the choice of technically up-to-date chemicals and repair techniques, and architects "destroy" historic buildings. Even such greats as Sir Bernard Feilden resonate a generally negative picture of the architect's role in his textbook, *Historic Building Conservation*. Are conservation technicians similarly disparaged when fabric is maintained at the expense of a better solution?

New formulations for the field of conservation must include at least the possibility of a valuable, perhaps irreduceable contribution by the architect. Somehow only the field of adaptive reuse specifically invites this role, although the artistic or interpretative "presentation" of an historical building can also be such a design-intensive question. To vilify the architect's contemporary contribution suggests a serious contradiction with the generally accepted notion to preserve multiple layers of historic structures. Are we different from all the previous generations of actors who worked on these buildings? Are we truly able to separate ourselves from history or are we just pretending?

## Terminology

Beware of technological and quantifying arguments in conservation projects: they are inevitably invoked to justify more important, but disallowed choices. We often chuckle at the overuse by our Asian partners of the word "scientific," but as conservation architects we consistently use such constructs to organize presentations of our work—like the ubiquitous "historic structure report" universally used to package repair and design proposals. A good historic structure report should be seamless and include little mention of contradictions, compromises, and subjectivity.

## Diversity and dialectic

While working on the Sulima Temple, I never considered doing anything to the exquisite and time-worn wall niches. They were exquisite (I used photographs of the niches for the fundraising literature) and didn't seem to need any intervention. I was hesitant when my partner, Niels Gutschow, proposed replacing the lost colonnettes. I imagined that these new elements would disturb the presentation of the timber elements' patina.

We discussed our approaches measuring Niels' belief to repair the building as a local carpenter or carver would go against my instinct that the new additions would be distracting. We decided to try an experiment on one façade. During the installation of these new pieces, I was moved by the transformation of the niche and the reading of the façade. The façade's original depth was suddenly made palpable by this new layer. The depth of carvings and brickwork is, in fact, an extraordinary feature of this architecture, especially in these earliest structures in which carvings are generally deeper. The lesson of the story is that collisions of viewpoints are educational. But how to incorporate a dialectic method if aesthetic impulses, alternative ideas, and maybe even obsessions are not invited by professional discussion?

## The power of beauty

Much of the restored Patan Museum could have been designed differently in order to preserve more historical fabric than the present configuration. The project was even condemned and almost shut down by a visiting ICOMOS conservation conference. But the brilliance of the whole with its mix of modern. historical. fake. and authentic fabric is an undeniable success.

Its impact is significant in this region where historical buildings have only rarely been considered for new or contemporary uses. It's also the first time the Nepali public has seen a historical building artistically presented and has already spawned a number of adaptive reuse and repair programs where historic buildings would have been otherwise lost. Do we think we know enough to discourage diversity in conservation practice that would allow such breaking of the rules?

## Living design

It's no accident that we have this discussion in Nepal. where norms of international and local practice collide. Given the infrequent. short visits of foreign critics and the vagueness of local norms. we have to solve problems ourselves. In the context of the success of the newly made Sulima struts. I was very curious to hear from John Stubbs about a comparable question back home in the United States. the replacement of the *porte cochère* of New York's Ellis Island Visitors' Center. The reconstruction of the lost feature was proposed based on surviving working drawings.

The parallels to our Sulima project were remarkable: Indrakaji. the master carver. seemed a living comparable to the surviving shop drawing of the *porte cochère*. The reconstruction was judged "misleading" by the Landmarks Commission and disallowed. This story suggests the valuable opportunity Nepal offers to engage designers and artisans in the design and realization of historical architecture. as this book attempts to document. In New York. only the memory survives.

*   *   *

If accepted as an art. the field of architectural conservation might live more easily with the undeniable diversity of practice. Until today. this diversity has not been reconciled. except when identified as an historical. autochthonous approach like the over-cited Japanese cyclical rebuilding of Ise. But. we need new approaches. That UNESCO reprimands of Nepali practice today read the same as antiquarians' condemnations of "over-restorations" in the nineteenth century suggests that we still don't know how to assess our own work. If the goal of "aesthetic unity" or the practice of "design beyond the point where conjecture begins" are disallowed by norms and international charters. is our professional involvement not a lie?

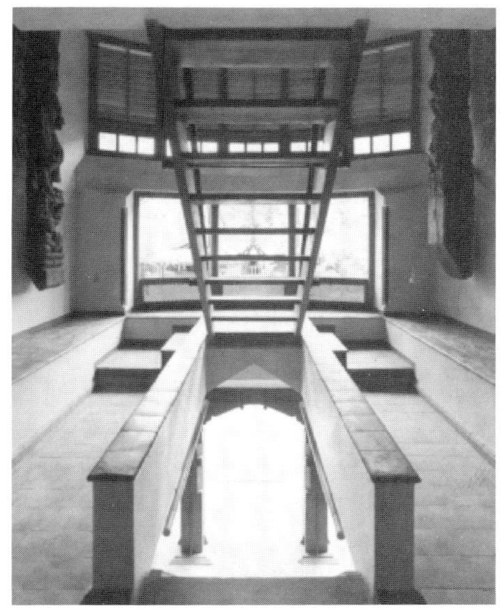

**Patan Museum**
**The traditional ladder stair of Nepal is integrated in a new design for the museum's principal stairhall.**

# POSTSCRIPT

## In Search of Architectural Authenticity at the Foot of the Himalayas

Eduard F. Sekler

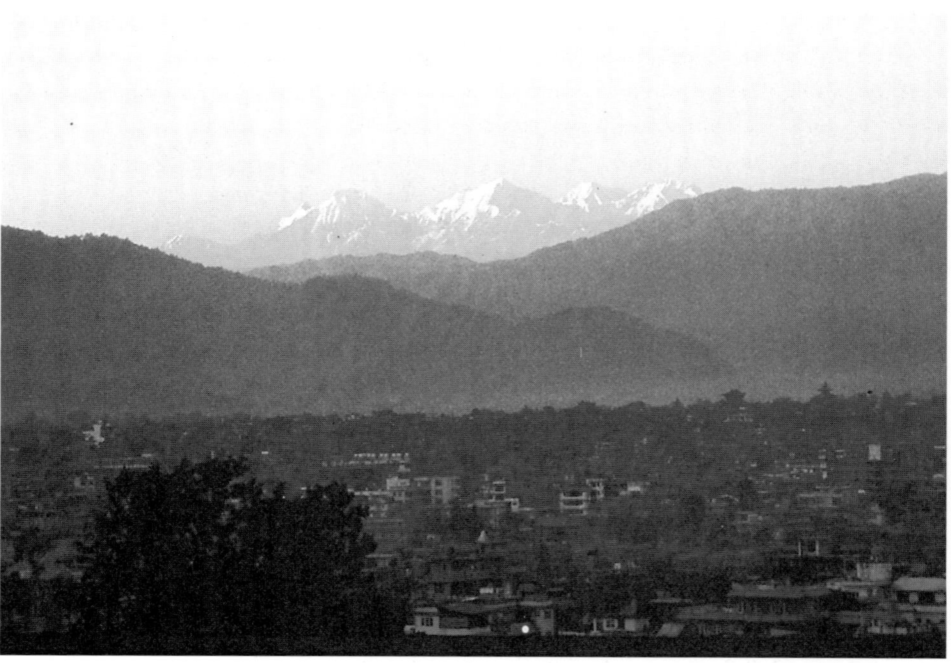

**Kathmandu with the Himalayas in the background**

Today the term "authenticity" is used frequently in architectural discourse, but not always with a precise definition of its meaning in the context in which it occurs. Consequently, there are many opportunities for misunderstanding in an age when digital manipulation and mixing up the virtual with the real are widespread. Not surprisingly, a recent article in *Historic Preservation* could suggest, "Something authentic is simply something that looks as you imagine it might, based on a lifetime of movies and television."[1]

In confronting such a situation, it is useful to discuss the issue of authenticity in some detail. There are few places where this can be done better than in the Kathmandu Valley, not only because of its wealth of precious historic buildings, but also because it is so inseparably linked to the Himalaya. A background of high mountains like these is a permanent remainder of what is meant when one speaks of authenticity in the sense of something truthful, genuine.

These mountains, being natural facts, brook no doubt about their authenticity because here this quality is based on a facticity one cannot ignore except at a risk. Facticity is also a characteristic of architecture as a quality that distinguishes the built works from works that are textual or virtual, as Georg Böckler recognized already in the seventeenth century, when he wrote: "The art of building does not consist of words, but of a visible and tangible demonstration."[2]

Prior to discussing some examples that illustrate issues of architectural authenticity in the Kathmandu Valley, the origin and application of the concept of authenticity deserve a brief mention. In ancient Greece an authentes was an absolute master, but also anybody who himself carried out something, or completed something by his own hand. The adjective *authentikos* (authentic)[3] consequently denoted something that had a certain, recognized author and therefore could be trusted and vouched for. In this sense the word was also taken over into Latin.

Writing about modern art and referring to the original sense of authentes as somebody "having complete power over something," the literary critic Lionel Trilling could state, "the work of art is itself authentic by reason of its entire self-definition: it is understood to exist wholly by the laws of its own being..."[4] But there is one art—the art of building, architecture—where the "laws of its own being" include laws that tie it unavoidably to the realities of "objective facts invariant under specified transformations" (Robert Nozick) and to the needs of society and of daily life. When these constraints are ignored in badly designed or badly constructed architecture, a building can kill—just as a mountain can kill if the constraints it imposes are ignored.

In the realm of historic conservation, the UNESCO International Convention for the Protection of Cultural and Natural World Heritage of 1972 caused a renewed and very thorough discussion about the concept of authenticity. This was due to the well-known passage in the UNESCO Operational Guidelines stipulating that, among the criteria affecting decisions about inclusion in the World Heritage List, the work or site under review must "meet the test of authenticity in design, material, workmanship or setting and in the case of cultural landscapes their distinctive character and components (the Committee stressed that reconstruction is only acceptable if it is carried out on the basis of complete and detailed documentation of the original and to no extent on conjecture)."[5] Not many monuments fully possess all the stipulated authenticities, because with the passing of time, unavoidable—and avoidable—changes tend to occur. There is a moment, however, when the degree of change has become so great that one must admit that authenticity has been lost in the process.

International conferences in Bergen, Nara, and San Antonio, Texas, were dedicated to the difficult task of clarifying all that is really involved in the "test of authenticity." At Nara it became clear that in different parts of the world fairly different opinions prevailed about what the word authenticity denotes—provided that one could even find an exactly corresponding translation of the word. Regarding Japan, for example, Nabuo Ito explained, "Unfortunately, the Japanese language, and probably many other Asiatic languages, has no proper word for authenticity, but has only new equivalent words for it...namely genuineness and reliability."[6]

In the United States, the language includes the word authenticity, but, according to a report by US/ICOMOS, "the term integrity is generally used in place of authenticity and is defined as 'the ability of a property to convey its significance' (U.S. Department of the Interior 1991)."[7] This substitution is not an entirely happy one, because according to the dictionaries the inherent emphasis of authenticity is on "an origin that cannot be questioned," while integrity emphasizes the "unimpaired condition" and "the state of being complete." Moreover, among the seven qualities that are enumerated as the elements of integrity, one is hard to define by criteria that can be validated unequivocally: "feeling," is mentioned together with design, materials, workmanship, setting, location and association.

"Feeling" clearly does not belong to the same realm of discourse as the other criteria. It is highly probable that qualified judges will be able to arrive at an agreement on questions of design, materials, workmanship and so forth, but not on questions of feeling because this quality is "subjective" in a manner the other criteria are not. "Feeling" is also mentioned in the Nara Document on Authenticity (see below), where, moreover, "spirit" is added to the list of critical factors. Without wishing to deny the importance of "feeling" and "spirit" (in the sense of *spiritus loci*) when considering historic monuments and sites, they are in a different category from the other criteria and consequently also ought to be treated differently in the evaluation process.

The last portion of the Nara Document on Authenticity (1994) concerns issues of value and authenticity and states (in excerpt):

> Conservation of cultural heritage in all its forms and historical periods is rooted in the values attributed to the heritage. Our ability to understand these values depends, in part, on the degree to which information sources about these values may be understood as credible or truthful. Knowledge and understanding of these sources of information, in relation to original and subsequent characteristics of the cultural heritage, and their meaning, is a requisite basis for assessing all aspects of authenticity....

> Depending on the nature of the cultural heritage, its cultural context, and its evolution through time, authenticity judgements may be linked to the worth of a great variety of sources of information. Aspects of these sources may include form and design, materials and substance, use and function, traditions and techniques, location and setting, and spirit and feeling, and other internal and external factors. The use of these sources permits elaboration of the specific artistic, historic, social and scientific dimensions of the cultural heritage being examined.

## Definitions

> Conservation: all operations designed to understand a cultural heritage, know its history and meaning, ensure its material safeguard and, as required, its presentation, restoration and enhancement. (Cultural heritage is understood to include monuments, groups of buildings and sites of cultural value as defined in Article One of the World Heritage Convention).

> Information sources: all material, written, oral and figurative sources that make it possible to know the nature, specifications, meaning and history of the cultural heritage.[8]

This is a brilliant and at the same time potentially dangerous formulation. It is brilliant because it does cover all aspects of evaluative decision-making about the conservation of cultural heritage under one umbrella, namely that of the semantic quality of information. Because this involves a great deal of discourse, there is, however, the danger inherent that in some, albeit rare, cases the profound concern with facticity essential for succcessful work in historic conservation may be overwhelmed by splendidly presented but highly debatable or even fallacious theoretical arguments. From the point of view of the historian and theorist who constructs a narrative, authenticity may indeed not appear as a "rock of faith"[9] on which to base evaluations, but for the architect/conservator who needs to be pragmatic, there is no better guidance than to search out and respect what is authentic.

The need to clarify what values are involved when dealing with historic conservation was met by the Austrian art historian Alois Riegl in his seminal essay of 1903, *The Modern Cult of Monuments*,[10] in which he distinguished between values referring to the past of monuments and values that are conditioned by the present. He wrote this essay as part one of a tripartite work that consisted of this piece as the preparatory memorandum for the first law about the safeguarding of historic monuments in the Austro-Hungarian Monarchy plus the commented draft of this law, and its operational guidelines.[11] Only the first part has been translated into English, which made it impossible for English-speaking readers to fully comprehend its meaning.

Riegl was conservator general in the organization that in the Monarchy took care of the "artistic and historic monuments" and his goal was to stress that anything that had age value deserved protection, regardless of its art value or lack thereof. Whose values Riegl had in mind when he formulated his definitions becomes clear from his following statement that anticipates what later the law defined as the purpose of historic conservation: to deal with monuments the protection of which "is in the public interest":

> Nobody will not recognize that the coming into existence of the age value is nothing else than a special manifestation of the general social movement. One finds something in a monument that concerns everybody without exception, and from this one derives the justification for removing the disposition about it from the individual...and to transfer it to the state as the sum of all its individuals...[12]

It is remarkable that at this early stage in the development of a theoretical framework for historic conservation, Riegl already stressed conservation's relation to "the general social movement" (*allgemeinen sozialen Bewegung*). This social aspect has been greatly stressed in recent years, for example in the extensive research report Values and Heritage Conservation published by the Getty Conservation Institute.[13]

Each of Riegl's five values can be related to a corresponding kind of authenticity: the "age value," which accrues to a property simply by the passage of time, the "historic value," which means the value as a piece of unaltered historic evidence, and the "commemorative value" that refers to monuments that were created to memorialize somebody or something. These first three values are what people generally have in mind when they speak of historic authenticity.

Independently of age, the next value, "use value" has its correlate in the functional authenticity of an historic property, with religious use and religious authenticity as examples of special importance. Religious authenticity may be completely independent of historical authenticity and arguments are pointless that fail to heed this difference.

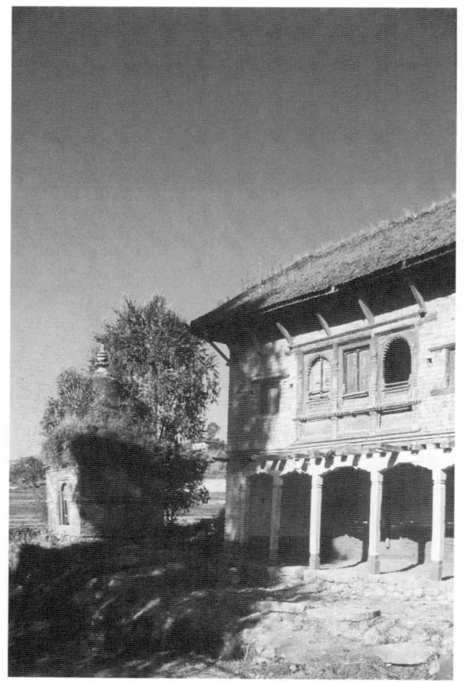

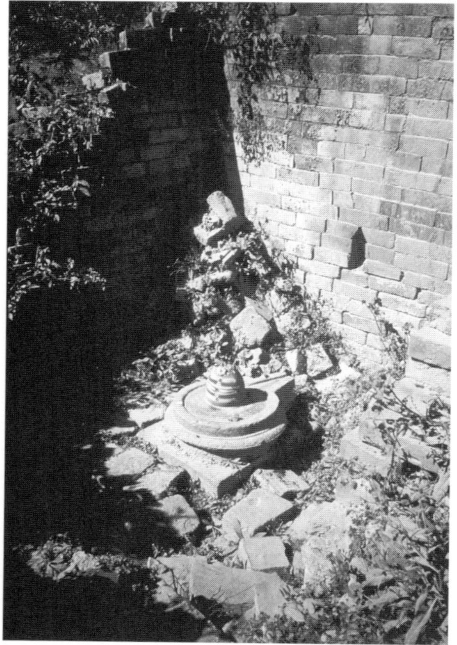



The "art value," finally, which refers to the way in which the artistic worth of an historic monument is estimated, depends on a number of factors. In addition to the creative capacity and skill of the monument's maker, they include the "artistic volition" of the period when the estimation is made: postmodern architects of the 1980s admired Victorian buildings that thirty years earlier their architectural predecessors had intensely disliked.

Japan, as is well known, provides one of the most important examples of the fact that for a monument of outstanding cultural and historical significance, the Ise Shrine, the historic age of the building material can be unimportant; the complex is regularly rebuilt after 20 years—albeit in exactly the ancient form. If one speaks of authenticity here, only the religious and formal, not the material authenticity can be referenced. Nobuko Inaba has explained that this regular rebuilding has nothing to do with conservation technique and is not a common practice in Japan. "It is part of the ritual practice of the Shinto religion;...the only shrine which has continued the tradition...in its pure form is the Ise Shrine...."[14]

Examples like Ise or the Athenian Acropolis must have been what the authors of the Statement by Greece on Authenticity had in mind when they deposited this document at the session of the World Heritage Committee in Kyoto in 1998. It begins by stressing that "authenticity is a complex concept and the employment of the word authenticity, without the provision of an appropriate specification, is without any valid signficance."[15] The correctness of this statement can be corroborated by many convincing examples taken from the practice of historic conservation in the Kathmandu Valley.

In 1985, on the road from Banepa to Panauti, a *sattal* (rest and meeting house) stood next to a small ruinous Shiva sanctuary where, as in so many other instances, unhampered plant growth had ruined the building. In 1991, the little shrine was in better condition, though plant growth had set in again. By 1994, the plant growth had become a real menace once more and three years later, all that remained of the building were wall fragments and the sacral Shiva *linga*, freshly painted as evidence of ongoing worship despite the lack of the built sanctuary. The functional, religious authenticity of the sanctuary was untouched by the loss of its shelter, the formal and material authenticity of which was gone. "But we can rebuild it" the then head of the Archeology Department said to me, as we gazed at the scene.

This brief assertion taught me a lot about the way cultural tradition influences concepts of authenticity in different parts of the world. He was, of course, right because he was correct in assuming that the formal language and the building technique of the lost shrine were known to local craftsmen who could more or less replicate it, though they might use new machine-made bricks and a stronger mortar instead of more traditional materials. After its consecration the new building certainly would have complete religious authenticity, but it would lack authenticity as evidence for a scholarly or scientific study about certain details of historic Shiva shrines.

When one considers some of the historic monuments of the Kathmandu World Heritage Site, one is confronted with striking examples of varying authenticities found at a single monument. The religious authenticity of the great *stupa* at Boudhnath, for example, remains intact, but the spatial authenticity of its setting has been irrevocably compromised by the numerous tall new buildings in its immediate vicinity and by a very large new hotel recently built nearby. Here, as on many other occasions in the Kathmandu Valley, the greatest danger for the historic authenticity of an important monument was not anything happening to the building itself, but the persistent encroachment by disturbingly inappropriate and often high new buildings in the neighborhood.

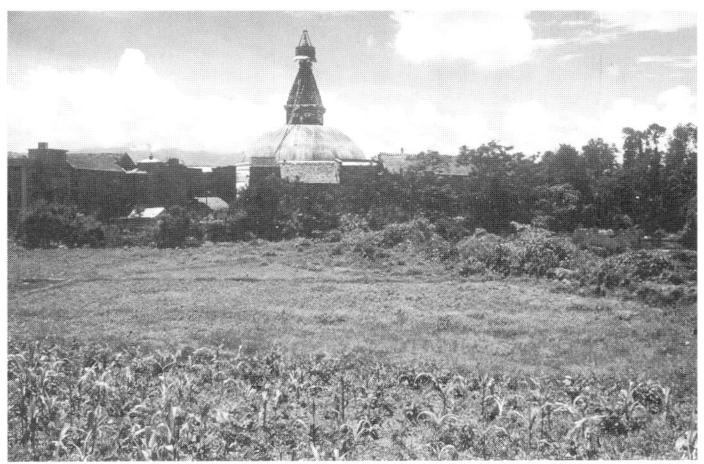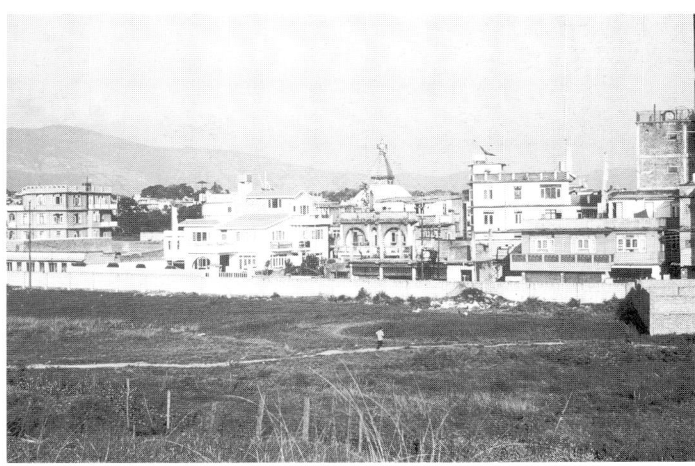



The religious authenticity of the Pashupatinath zone remains untouched by the fact that many of its small shrines threaten to lose their historic authenticity of form and material because they are severely dilapidated and there is a lack of timely safeguarding. By contrast, the historical and formal authenticity of the Swayambhu site has been affected by numerous well-intentioned recent "improvements and beautifications" that were generally considered a welcome strengthening of the site's functional, religious authenticity, but certainly were not welcome from the point of view of historic authenticity and authenticity of setting.

I do not believe, however, that in cases where the survival of an authentic religious function guarantees the continuation of religious authenticity, the wish to safeguard the historic authenticiy of form and material in a World Heritage Site becomes irrelevant. To ignore the quest for historic authenticity would deny the complexity of legitimate interests that interact in a society.

Scholars who are concerned about the value of surviving monuments as veridical sources of historic information to be preserved for future generations have a right not to be ignored. Such is true even if the artistic and historic authenticity of an element from the past may be of little or no interest to many present inhabitants of the Kathmandu Valley. Those residents, incidentally, share such an attitude with many contemporaries not only in Asia, but in the rest of the world, as anyone can testify who works in the field of architectural historic conservation.

The argument that the culture of the Himalayan countries and Southeast Asia has no tradition of caring about the preservation of authentic cultural heritage can

*above:* **The great Stupa of Bodnath in its rural setting, 1978**

*above, right:* **The great Stupa of Bodnath dwarfed by encroaching new buildings, 1991**

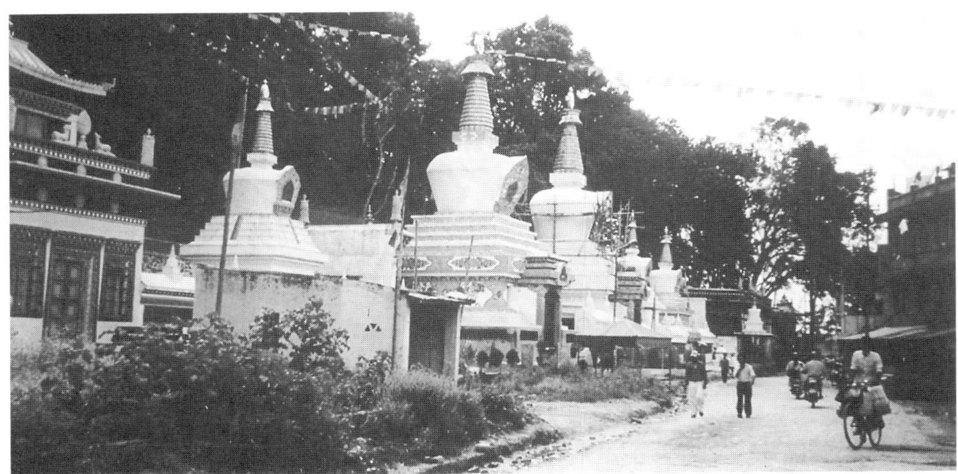

**Stupas of the Tibetan type (*chorten*) recently erected as an improvement and beautification at the Swayambhu monument zone**

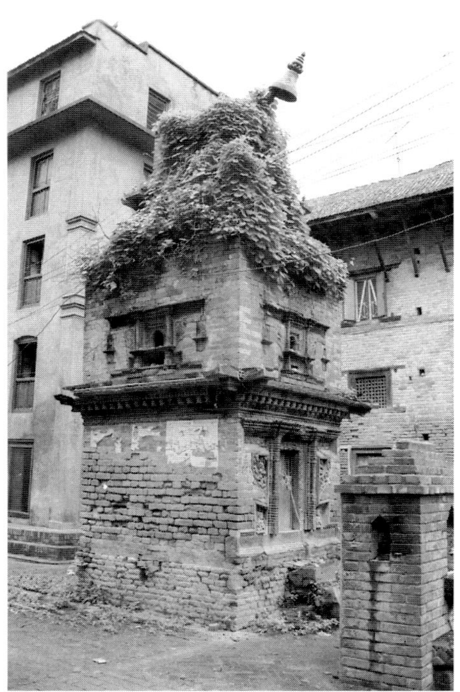

The ruinous Kulima Narayan temple, Patan, in 1996

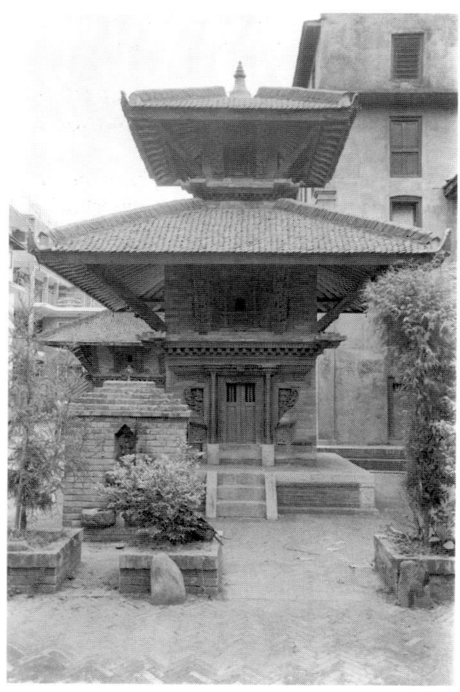

The Kulima Narayan Temple, Patan, after restoration by the KVPT
Some replacements for lost carved struts were left uncarved because it was impossible to establish conclusively what they had looked like.

be refuted on several grounds. One is the influence of Buddhism with its appreciation of the commemorative value of a monument; as Nabuo Ito put it: "With the introduction of Buddhism, the preservation of art and architecture was recognized... The historical background of modern philosophy of preservation of cultural heritage lies in this tradition of Buddhism."[16] In the Kathmandu Valley, a telling example of historical Buddhist restoration activity at the Swayambhu *stupa* has been fully documented by Bernhard Kölver.[17]

Hindus also appreciated the commemorative value, as is proven by inscriptions such as the one dated CE 1575 relating to the recently restored Tum Baha Narayan Temple in Patan.18 The temple is dedicated to the memory and blissful afterlife of a son who died in a landslide. It is also relevant that there is a Sanskrit term, *jirnodhara*, that occurs in early texts and that has been translated as "repairs or renovation and conservation" in D.C. Sircar, *Indian Epigraphical Glossary*, Delhi, (Motilal), 1966.[19] In the past, moreover, renowned pandits are known to have worked assiduously to preserve the authentic version of the ancient Sanskrit texts of the Vedas.

In Europe too, the search for authenticity began among the scholars concerned with the text of ancient documents long before it also occurred in relation to historic architecture. Would it not be impermissible arrogance to negate the possibility that eventually a similar broadening of critical interest from texts to architecture is likely to occur elsewhere? And does acknowledging this possibility not imply the demand to preserve valuable cultural heritage with its historic authenticity intact? It is also significant that in all Himalayan and Southeast Asian countries, the public interest in the preservation of authentic cultural heritage found expression in the legal prohibition of the export of historic works of art and archaeological finds.

To preserve authenticity as much as possible is a basic assumption and prime motivation in all serious historic conservation work. But local conditions in the area where the work takes place, and changes in the understanding of what authenticity means, may be responsible for far-from-uniform results in different cultures and over a span of years during which "artistic volition" changes.

The Kathmandu Valley Preservation Trust (KVPT)[20] since its inception has had to deal with this issue. Its various attempts to do so (see photographs on the left) provide intriguing material for analysis, interpretation, and evaluation. The discussion has not been conclusive and one must hope that it will be continued without polemics on the basis of verifiable facts and based on criteria for value judgements that can be as clearly validated when they are challenged as Riegl's criteria a century earlier.

Today, when global digitization tends to confront humanity with an increasing replacement of the experience of the real by that of the virtual or the manipulated, when tourism of unprecedented magnitude encourages the creation of stage sets like Disneyland wherever it arrives with its value system of the marketplace, insistence on authenticity as a precious ethical value remains a demand of the highest priority on those to whom, regardless of where they are, the stewardship of the cultural heritage is entrusted.

The author acknowledges with gratitude the assistance and advice he recveived from Professor Pramod Chandra; Dr. Rohit Ranjitkar; Sarah Whiting, PhD; Professor Michael Witzel, and his wife, Mary Patricia Sekler, PhD.

Eduard F. Sekler © 2003



The Sulima Pagoda

# ENDNOTES

**What Is a Pagoda? (3-9)**

1  Yule, Henry and Burnell, A.C. *Hobson-Jobson Glossary of Colloquial Anglo-Indian Words and Phrases, and of Kindred Terms, Etymological, Historical, Geographical, and Discursive.* First edition 1886. Delhi: Rupa Paperbacks. Rpt. 1986. pp. 652-657.

2  Slusser, Mary Sheperd. *Nepal Mandala. A Cultural Study of the Kathmandu Valley.* 2 vols. Princeton, New Jersey: Princeton University Press, 1982. Vol.1, p. 162.

3  Enders, Sigfried and Gutschow, Niels. *Hozon.* Stuttgart: Mengers, 1999. p. 123.

4  Kramrisch, Stella. *Exploring India's Sacred Art.* Philadelphia: University of Pennsylvania Press, 1983. p. 259: "This virtuosity of organization of symbolic structure in all its intricacies gives final exposition of the power held to be inherint in the temple walls."

**Conservation in Nepal: A Review of Practice (11-25)**

1  Oldfield, Henry Ambrose. *Sketches from Nepal.* London: 1880.Vol.II, p. 289.

2  Shamshera. Bramha. *Nepalako Mahabhukampa.* First edition, Calcutta: 1936.

3  For more details see Amatya, Saphalya. *Architectural Conservation in Nepal: A Retrospect.* In Parajuli, Yogeshwar K. (ed.) *Bhaktapur Development Project: Experiences in Preservation and Restoration in a Medieval Town (1974-1985).* Lalitpur: 1986.

4  Marshall, John. *Conservation Manual. A Handbook for the Use of Archeological Officers and Others Entrusted with the Care of Ancient Monuments.* Calcutta: 1923.

5  Marshall, p. 10.

6  Gutschow, Niels. *Die Restaurierung des Pujhari Math in Bhaktapur/Nepal,* in: Deutsche Kunst und Denkmalpflege. Munich: 1972. Vol. 30, 2, pp.103-118.

7  Sanday, John. *Building Conservation in Nepal. A Handbook of Principles and Technique.* UNESCO, Paris: 1978.

8  see Becker-Titterpach. Raimund. *Denkmalpflege im Rahmen des Stadtentwicklungsprojektes Bhaktapur (1974-86),* in: Deutsche Kunst und Denkmal-pflege. Munich: 1990.Vol. 49, 2, p. 134.

9  Gutschow, Niels. *The Restoration of the Cyasilin Mandap in Bhaktapur,* in: Kailash. Kathmandu: 1976. Vol. IV, 3, pp. 227-236.

10  Sekler Eduard. *Masterplan for the Conservation of the Cultural Heritage in the Kathmandu Valley.* UNESCO, Paris: 1977.

11  Gutschow, Niels and Hagmüller, Götz. *Die Rekonstruktion des achteckigen Pavillons (Cyasilin Mandap) auf dem Darbar Platz in Bhaktapur (1987-1990),* in: Deutsche Kunst und Denkmalpflege. Munich: 1990. Vol. 49, 2, pp. 137-155. *The Reconstruction of the Eight-Cornered Pavillion (Cyacilin Mandap) on Darbar Square in Bhaktapur-Nepal.* in: Ancient Nepal. Journal of the Department of Archaeology. Kathmandu: 1991. No. 123-125, pp. 1-15.

12  Watanabe, Katsuhiko (ed.). *The Buddhist Monastries of Nepal. A report on the I Baha Bahi Restoration Project,* Nippon Institute of Technology, Japan: 1998.

13  Hagmüller, Götz. *Das Patan Museum/The Patan Museum,* in: Architektur Aktuell. Vienna: 1997. No. 208, pp. 74-87.

14  Theophile, Erich and Ranjitkar, Rohit. *Timber Conservation: Nepalese Pagoda Temple,* in: Santosh (ed.) *Architectural and Urban Conservation.* Calcutta: 1996. p. 156.

15  Op. cit. p. 160.

16  Michelmore. David. *Training Workshop 20th September to 5th October 1994, Kathmandu 1994* (typescript).

**Iconography (47-49)**

1  Slusser, Mary Shepherd. *Nepal Mandala.* 2 vols. Princeton, New Jersey: Princeton University Press, 1982. Vol. 1, p. 142.

2  Pruscha, Carl. *Kathmandu Valley: The Preservation of Physical Environment and Cultural Heritage Protective Inventory.* Vienna: Anton Schroll & Co., 1975. Vol. 2, p. 202.

3  Wiesner, Ulrich. *Nepali Temple Architecture.* Leiden: E.J. Brill, 1978. Vol. 3, p. 100.

4  Ibid, p. 64.

5  Sakya, Hemraj. *Sivadeva Samskarita Unkuli Sri Rudravarna Mahavihara Samksipta Paricaya.* 1090 N.S.: Patan. p. 20.

6  Slusser, op.cit., photograph no. 162.

7  Ibid, Photograph no. 194.

8  Ibid, Photograph no. 207.

9  Locke, John K. *Buddhist. Monasteries of Nepal.* Kathmandu: Sahayogi Press, 1985. p. 92.10 Coomarswamy, Ananda K. *Yaksas.* Washington: 1928, 1931, Rept. 1971) p. 9.

11  Regmi, Dr. *Medieval Nepal, part III.* Patna:

1966. p. 1a33.

12  Pandeya, Rajavali. *Hindu Dharmakosa.* Lucknow: Uttar Pradesa Hindi Samsthan, 1988. 2nd edn., p. 530.

13  Ibid.

14  Stutley, Margaret and James. *A Dictionary of Hinduism.* New Delhi: Heritage Publishers, 1986. Pp. 345-346.

15  Sharma. Liladhara. Bharatiya Samskrtikosa. Delhi: Rajapala & Sons, 1995. P. 736.

**Ritual Life of Sulima Square (86-93)**

1  Bhattacharyya. Narendra Natha. *History of the Tantric Religion.* Reprint, Delhi: Manohara Publishers & Distributers, 1992. p. 470.

2  Personal communication with Sri Heramba Rajopadhyaya, January 14, 2000.

3  Regmi, Dilli Raman. *Medieval Nepal.* Calcutta: Firma K. L. Mukhopadhyay, 1966, Part III, p. 60.

4  Vajracarya, Devendra (ed.). *Japa tuṃ ek cinari.* Kathmandu: Japa Tum Sahayaoga Samiti, n.d. pp. 12-14

5  Rakesh, Ram Dayal. *Folk Tales from Mithila.* New Delhi: Nirala Publication. 1996. pp. 55-103.

6  Siddhivanta Josi was a famous ninth century Tantric astrologer. See Wright, Daniel (ed.). *History of Nepal.* reprinted, Delhi: Low Price Publications. 1990. pp. 110-112 and Deviprasada Lamsala (ed.). *Bhasa Vamsavali.* Kathmandu: Nepal Rastriya Pustakalaya. 1976. Part II, pp. 24-25.

7  For a summary of the story see: Josi. op. cit.

**The Artificial Life of Heritage (95-101)**

1  Report of UNESCO on the Kathmandu Valley World Heritage Site. 1998. p. 46.

2  See for instance Hobhouse, Hermione. *Lost London. A Century of Demolition and Decay.* London: Macmillan, 1971, and Paris Perdu. *Quarante Ans de Bouleversements de la Ville.* Paris: Carré, 1991.

3  Koolhaas, Rem. *Small, Medium, Large, Extra-Large.* Rotterdam: 010, 1995. pp. 1248 and 1263.

4  Sanday, John. *The Kathmandu Valley.* Odyssey Illustrated Guide. Hong Kong: The Guidebook Company, 1995. pp. 59 and 69.

5  Denslagen, Wim. *Restoration in Western Europe: Controversy and Continuity.* Amsterdam: Architectura & Natura, 1994.

6  Watkin, David. *Morality and Architecture. The Development of a Theme in Architectural History and Theory from the Gothic Revival to the Modern Movement.* Oxford: Clarendon Press, 1977.

7  Buruma, Ian. *The Missionary and the Libertine. Love and War in East and West.* London: Faber and Faber, 1996.

8  According to Niels Gutschow (during my visit to Nepal in November 1999).

9  An important study on this theme is: Hobsbawm, Eric and Ranger, Terence. *The Invention of Tradition.* Cambridge: Cambridge University Press, 1983.

10  Watanabe, Katsuhiko. *The Buddhist Monasteries of Nepal. A Report on the I Baha Bahi Restoration Project.* Nippon Institute of Technology, Japan. 1998.

11  Ranjitkar, Rohit and Theophile, Erich. *Sulima Ratnesvara Temple, Patan. Historic Structure Report.* Lalitpur: Kathmandu Valley Preservation Trust, 1998.

12  Gutschow, Niels und Hagmüller.. *Die Rekonstruktion des achteckigen Pavillons (Cyasilin Mandap) auf dem Darbar Platz in Bhaktapur (1987-1990),* Deutsche Kunst und Denkmalpflege. Munich: 1991. pp. 137-155, p. 50.

13  Wei, Chen and Aass, Andreas. *Heritage Conservation: East and West,* ICOMOS Information 3. 1989. pp. 3-8.

14  Said, Edward. *Orientalism.* Penguin Books, 1991. No. 38 (1978).

15  Mitter, Partha. *Much Maligned Monsters. History of European Reactions to Indian Art.* Oxford: Clarendon Press, 1977. p. 210.

16  Dumont, Louis. *La Civilisation Indienne et Nous. Esquisse de sociology comparée.* Paris: Armand Colin, 1964. p. 34.

17  Quoted by Naipaul, V.S. *India, A Wounded Civilization.* Penguin Books, 1977. p. 103.

18  Chakrabarty, Dipesh. *Postcoloniality and the Artifice of History: Who Speaks for "Indian" Pasts?* In: Representations 37, 1992. pp. 1-26.

19  Le Monde (8 August 1990) and Saint-Sernin de Toulouse. *Trésors et Métamorphoses. Deux siècles de restaurations 1802-1989.* Catalogue of the exhibition at the Hôtel de Sully in Paris, 1990.


**Techniques in the Architectural Preservation in Nepal (103-105)**

1  Gutschow, Niels and Hagmüller, Götz. *Die Rekonstruktion des achteckigen Pavillons (Cyasilin Mandap) auf dem Darbar Platz in Bhaktapur (1987-1990),* Deutsche Kunst und Denkmalpflege. Munich: 1991. Vol. 49, No. 2, pp. 137-155. Gutschow, Niels and Hagmüller, Götz. *The Reconstruction of the Eight-Cornered Pavilion (Cyasilin Mandap) on Darbar Square in Bhaktapur, Nepal,* Ancient Nepal. Journal of the Department of Archaeology. Kathmandu :1991. No. 123-125, pp. 1-15.

2  Watanabe, Katsuhiko (Ed.), *The Buddhist Monasteries of Nepal. A Report on the I Baha Bahi Restoration Project.* Nippon Institute of Technology, Japan. 1998.

3  Hagmüller, Götz. *The Patan Museum,* in: Architektur Aktuell. Vienna: 1997. No. 208. pp. 74-87.


**Postscript (124-130)**

1  Wayne Curtis, "belle epoxy," *Historic Preservation,* LII, Nr. 3, May/June 2000, p. 39

2  "Die Baukunst besteht nicht in Worten/ sondern in einer sichtbaren und handgreifflichen Demonstration," Georg A. Böckler, *Neues...Seulen Buch,* Frankfurt am Main, 1684, quoted in Ulrich Schütte, *"Ordnung" und "Verzierung": Untersuchungen zur deutschsprachigen Architekturtheorie.* (Dissertation, Ruprecht-Karl University, Heidelberg ), Bamberg, (M. Schadel), 1979, p. 5. (translation by the author)

3  *Shorter Oxford English Dictionary,* 2nd ed., Oxford, 1936, p. 125

4  Lionel Trilling, *Sincerity and Authenticity,* Cambridge, Mass., 1972, p. 99

5  *Operational Guidelines for the Implementation of the World Heritage Committee,* Paris, UNESCO, WHC-97/WS/1 Rev., Feb. 1998, p.7

6  Nabuo Ito, "'Authenticity' Inherent in Cultural Heritage in Asia and Japan," *Nara Conference on Authenticity, Proceedings,* Knut Einar Larsen edit., Trondheim, Norway, (Tapir) 1995, pp. 35, 36

7  ICOMOS UNITED STATES, Report for the 1996 Interamerican Symposium on Authenticity, p.3 http://www.icomos.org/usicomos/authenticity/useng.html

8  See note 6, pp. XXII - XXV

9  David Lowenthal, "Authenticity Rock of Faith or Quicks and Quagmire?" *Conservation, the Getty Institute Conservation Institute News Letter,* XIV, Nr. 3, 1999, p. 5

10  Alois Riegl, "The Modern Cult of Monuments: Its Character and Its Origin" translated by Kurt W. Forster and Diane Ghirardo, *Oppositions,* XXV, Fall 1982, pp. 21 ff.

11  Ernst Bacher edit., *Alois Riegl/Kunstwerk oder Denkmal?...,* Vienna, (Böhlau) 1995, pp. 20 ff.

12  See note 11, p. 105. Ernst Bacher *op. cit.* p. 28 has pointed out the significance of this passage (translation by the author)

13  Erica Avrami, Randall Mason, Marta de la Torre, *Values and Heritage Conservation,* Los Angeles (The Getty Conservation Institute), 2000

14  See note 6, p. 331

15  "Statement by Greece om Authenticity," Appendix VIII, Report of the 22nd Session of the World Heritage Committee, Tokyo 1998, p. 121 (translation by the author)

16  see note 6, p. 41

17  Bernhard Kölver, *Re-building a stupa: architectural drawings of the Swayambhunath,* Bonn, (VGH Wissenschaftsverlag), 1992

18  Kathmandu Valley Preservation Trust, "Historic Structure Report, Tum Baha Narayan Temple," unpublished MS, Patan, 2000, appendix

19  I am grateful to Professor Michael Witzel for having provided me with this information.

20  The Trust is a charitable organization incorporated in Massachusetts with the following purpose: "To develop, promote, coordinate, and assist activities and strategies for the wise use and conservation of the cultural heritage of the Kathmandu Valley... and surrounding areas for the benefit of future generations throughout the world." (Articles of Organization approved by the office of the Massachusetts Secretary of State, p. 1). It was founded in 1990 by Watson Dickerman, Michael Doyle, Erich Theophile, and Eduard Sekler, Chairman.

# BIBLIOGRAPHY


Amatya, Saphalya. *Nepal's Strategy on Heritage Conservation, Heritage of the Kathmandu Valley*-Proceedings of an International Conference in Lübeck, June 1985. Sankt Augustin: VHG Wissenschaftsverlag. 1987. pp. 95-103.

Becker-Ritterspach, Raimund. *Nepal—Urban Renewal. The Restoration of Bhaktapur, in:* Unasylva 30. Rome: 1978.

Bannerjee, Nil Ratan. *Nepalese Architecture.* Delhi: Agam Kala Prakashan. 1980.

Becker-Ritterpach, Raimund. *Denkmalpflege im Rahmen des Stadtentwicklungs-projektes Bhaktapur (1974-86),* Deutsche Kunst und Denkmalpflege. Munich: 1991. No. 49, pp. 124-136.

Bernier, Ronald. M. *The Nepalese Pagoda: Origins and Style.* New Delhi: S. Chand & Company Ltd. 1979.

Bernier, Ronald M. *The Temples of Nepal: An Inventory Survey.* New Delhi: S. Chand & Company Ltd. 1970.

Bjorness, Hans. *A Cultural Heritage Conservation Strategy in the Context of Urban Development—The Case of Kathmandu, Nepal,* ICOMOS International Wood Committee (IIWC), 8th International Symposium 1992. Oslo: Tapir Forlag, 1994. pp. 49-84.

Department of Archaeology. *Safeguarding and Development Initiatives for World Heritage in the Kathmandu Valley.* Kathmandu: UNESCO. 1996.

Denslagen, Wim. *Restoration in Western Europe: Controversy and Continuity.* Amsterdam: Architectura & Natura. 1994.

Enders, Siegfried and Gutschow, Niels *Hozon. Architectural and Urban Conservation in Japan,* Stuttgart: Edition Menges. 1998.

Graskamp, W. *Nepal: Ein Muster an Musealisierung,* Frankfurter Hefte. Frankfurt, 1975. No. 30, pp. 27-34.

Gutschow, Niels. *The Pujahari Math: a Survey of Newar Building Techniques and Restoration Methods in the Valley of Kathmandu,* in: East and West. 1976. No. 26, pp. 191-204.

Gutschow, Niels *The Restoration of the Cyasilim Mandap in Bhaktapur,* in: Kailash. Kathmandu: 1976. No. 4, pp. 227-236.

Gutschow, Niels. *Die Restaurierung des Pujahari Math in Bhaktapur/Nepal,* in: Deutsche Kunst und Denkmalpflege. Munich: 1972. No. 30, pp. 103-118.

Gutschow, Niels. *Architectural and Urban Preservation in Nepal,* in: Art and Archaeology Research Papers. London: 1980. pp. 90-96.

Gutschow, Niels. *Stadtraum und Ritual der newarischen Städte im Kathmandu-Tal. Eine architekturanthropologische Untersuchung.* Stuttgart: Kohlhammer. 1982.

Gutschow, Niels. *Restaurierung und Rekonstruktion. Gedanken zur Gültigkeit der Charta von Venedig im Kontext Südasiens,* Deutsche Kunst und Denkmalpflege. Munich: 1991. No. 49, pp. 156-160.

Gutschow, Niels and Hagmüller, Götz. *Die Rekonstruktion des achteckigen Pavillons (Cyasilin Mandap) auf dem Darbar Platz in Bhaktapur (1987-1990),* Deutsche Kunst und Denkmalpflege. Munich: 1991. No. 49, pp. 137-155.

Gutschow, Niels and Hagmüller, Götz. *The Reconstruction of the Eight-Cornered Pavilion (Cyasilin Mandap) on Darbar Square in Bhaktapur, Nepal,* in: Ancient Nepal. Journal of the Department of Archaeology. Kathmandu: 1991. 123-125: 8-14.

Hagmüller, Götz. *Das Patan Museum - The Patan Museum,* in: Architektur Aktuell. Vienna: 1997. No. 208, pp. 74-87.

Hutt, Michael. *Nepal. A Guide to the Art and Architecture of the Kathmandu Valley.* Kiscadale: Paul Strachan. 1994.

Kleinert, Christian. *Integrated Urban Renewal and Development in South Asia - The Bhaktapur Development Project,* in: Geo Journal. 1.1977

Kölver, Bernhard. *Re-building a Stupa.* Bonn: VGH Wissenschaftesverlag. 1992.

Korn, Wolfgang. *Traditional Architecture of the Kathmandu Valley,* Kathmandu: Ratna Pustak Bhandar. 1979.

Lowenthal. D. *Possessed by the Past. The Heritage Crusade and the Spoils of History,* New York: The Free Press. 1996.

Marshall, John. *Conservation Manual. A Handbook for the Use of Archaeological Officers and Others Entrusted with the Care of Ancient Monuments,* Calcutta: Superintendent Government Printing. 1923.

Menon, Krishna. *Conservation in India, A Search for Direction,* in: Architecture + Design. Delhi: 1989. Nov/Dec. pp. 22-27.

Menon, Krishna. *Rethinking the Venice Charter: The Indian Experience,* in: South Asian Studies. 1994. No. 10, pp. 37-44.

Oldfield, Henry Ambrose. *Sketches from Nepal.* London: W. H. Ellen. 1880.

Parajuli, Yogeshwor. *Experiences in Preservation and Restoration in a medieval Town (1974-1985).* Lalitpur: Bhaktapur Development Project. 1986.

Rau, Heino. *Workshops of Traditional Newar Woodcarving,* in: Journal of the Nepal Research Centre (JNRC). Kathmandu: 1985. Vol. VII, pp. 141-182.

Sanday, John. *The Hanuman Dhoka Royal Palace, Kathmandu: Building Conservation and Local Traditional Crafts,* in: Art and Archaeology Research Papers. London: 1976.

Sanday, John. *Building Conservation in Nepal. A Handbook of Principles and Techniques.* Paris: UNDP/UNESCO. 1978

Sekler, Eduard. *Nepal, Cultural Heritage. Master Plan for the Conservation of the Cultural Heritage in the Kathmandu Valley.* Paris: UNDP/UNESCO. 1977.

Samshera, Brahma. *Nepalako Mchabhukampa.* Calcutta: Ratnakar Press. 1936.

Slusser, Mary Sheperd. *Nepal Mandala, A Cultural Study of the Kathmandu Valley,* 2 Vols. Princeton: Princeton University Press. 1982.

Slusser, Mary Sheperd. *Indresvara Mahadeva, a Thirteenth Century Nepalese Shrine,* in: Artibus Asiae. 1979. Vol. XLI. 2/3.

Theophile, Erich and Ranjitkar, Rohit. *Timber Conservation: Nepalese Pagoda Temple,* Santosh Ghosh (ed.), Architectural and Urban Conservation. Calcutta: Center for Built Environment, 1996. pp. 153-161

Theophile, Erich. *Learning from Sulima: East Meets West in Nepal's Kathmandu Valley,* in: Orientations. Hongkong: Elizabeth Knight. 2000. pp. 66-67.

Watanabe, Katsuhiko. *The I-Baha-Bahi Restoration Project, Patan, Nepal, 1990-1993.* ICOMOS International Wood Committee (IIWC), 8th International Symposium 1992. Oslo: Tapir Forlag: 1994. pp. 125-132.

Watanabe, Katsuhiko (ed.). *The Buddhist Monasteries of Nepal. A Report on the I Baha Bahi Restoration Project.* Nippon Institute of Technology. 1998.

Wiesner, Ulrich. *Nepalese Temple Architecture.* Leiden: E.J. Brill. 1978.

Yule. H. 1886. *Hobson-Jobson, A Glossary of Colloquial Anglo-Indian Words and Phrases, and of Kindred Terms, Etymological, Historical, Geographical and Discursive.* Reprint Rupa Paperback 1986.

# INDEX

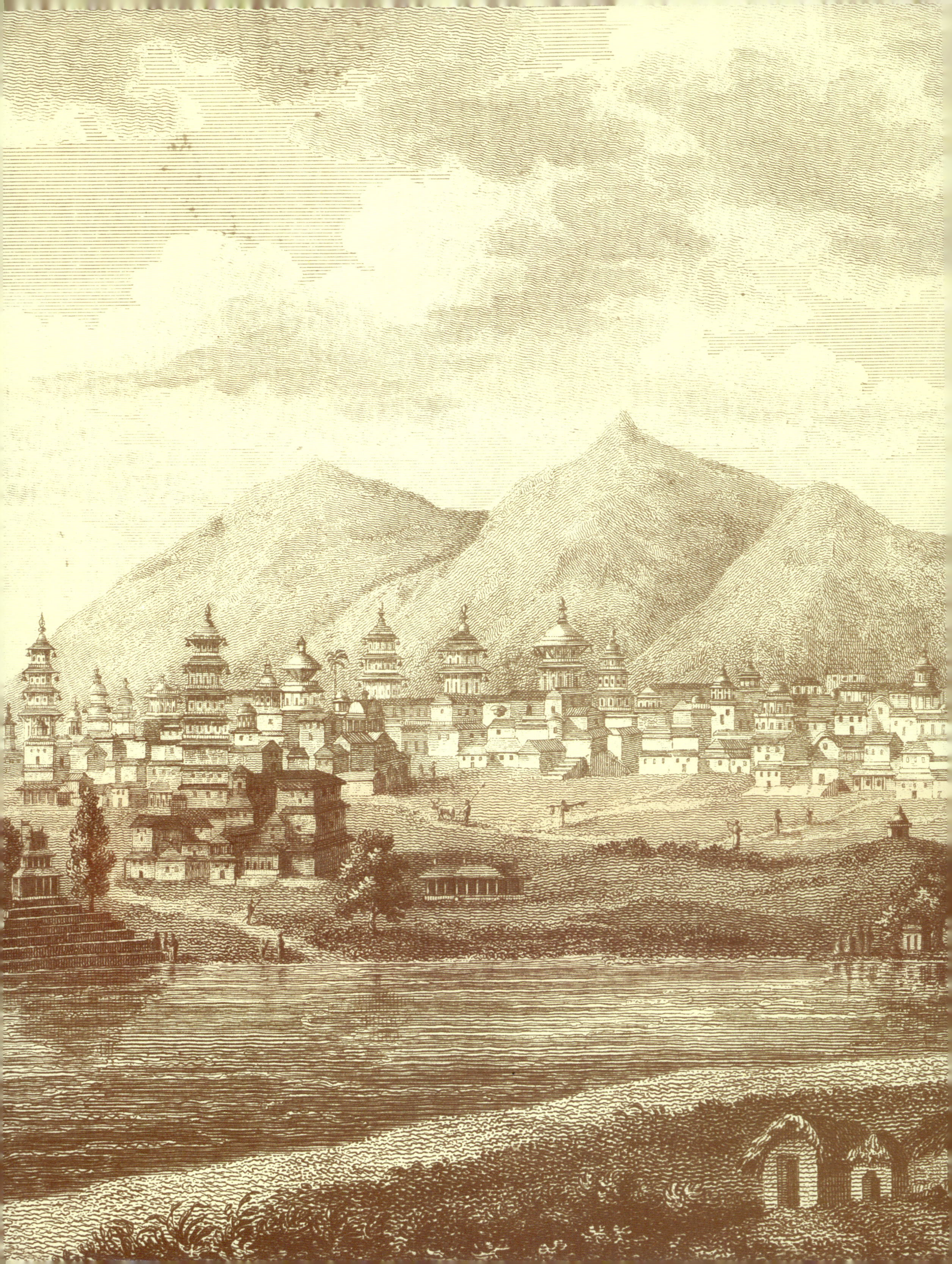